Multicultural Health Psychology

Multicultural Health Psychology

Special Topics Acknowledging Diversity

Michele K. Lewis

Northern Virginia Community College, Annandale

Allyn and Bacon

Boston • London • Toronto • Sydney • Tokyo • Singapore

Executive Editor: *Carolyn Merrill*
Series Editorial Assistant: *Lara Zeises*
Senior Marketing Manager: *Caroline Croley*
Production Editor: *Annette Pagliaro*
Editorial Production Service: *Walsh & Associates, Inc.*
Composition Buyer: *Linda Cox*
Manufacturing Buyer: *JoAnne Sweeney*
Cover Administrator: *Kristina Mose-Libon*
Electronic Composition: *Publishers' Design and Production Services, Inc.*

Library of Congress Cataloging-in-Publication Data

Lewis, Michele K.
    Multicultural health psychology : special topics acknowledging diversity / Michele K.
Lewis.
        p.   cm.
    Includes bibliographical references and index.
    ISBN 0-205-31855-X
    1. Clinical health psychology.   2. Ethnic groups—Health and hygiene.   3. Minorities—
Health and hygiene   4. Minorities—Medical care   5. Social medicine   6. Health—Cross-
cultural studies   I. Title.

R726.7 .L49 2001
616′.001′9—dc21

                                                                                    2001033678

Printed in the United States of America

10 9 8 7 6 5 4 3 2 1   05 04 03 02 01

This book is dedicated to Charles Lewis and Patsy Robertson, who have both passed on to the spiritual world due to chronic illness.

CONTENTS

Preface   xiii

1 Introduction   1

Health Psychology   1

Multicultural Health Psychology   1

Healthy People 2000   4

Health Statistics: Cultural Group Differences   5

Biopsychosocial Model   8

Recurring Themes in Multicultural Health Psychology   10

Research in Multicultural Health Psychology   13

Conclusion   14

Summary   14

Key Concepts   15

Study Questions   15

Student Activity   16

2 Diet and Health   17

Dietary Trends   17

Diet and Disease   18

Food Habits   22

Food Habits Across Ethnic Groups   23

The Psychology of Food Choice   29

Personal and Social Barriers   30

Cognitive Barriers   31

Disordered Eating   32

Cultural Sensitivity in Treatment   34

Conclusion   35

Summary   36

Key Concepts   37

Study Questions   38

Student Activity   38

3   Smoking and Health   41

Nicotine and the Committed Smoker   41

Smoking Incidence   42

Biopsychosocial Model and Smoking   43

Genetics and Smoking   44

Brain Activity and Smoking   45

Conditioning and Smoking   46

Cognition and Smoking   47

Social Learning   48

Smoking and Underrepresented Populations   49

Conclusion   52

Summary   52

Key Concepts   54

Study Questions   54

Student Activity   55

4   Substance Use and Sexual Behavior   57

Substance Abuse   57

Sexual Behavior   66

Personal Factors   72

Prevention/Intervention   73

Conclusion   76

Summary   76

Key Concepts   78

Study Questions   79

Student Activity   79

5   Exercise and Health   81

Health Benefits of Exercise   81

Personal Barriers   82

Social Factors as Barriers   85

Interventions   89

Conclusion   94

Summary   95

Key Concepts   97

Study Questions   97

Student Activity   98

6   Health Psychology and the Workplace   99

The Significance of Studying Health and the Workplace   99

Diversity in the Workforce   101

Variation in Decision Latitude and Job Demand   103

Job Strain and Shift Work   104

Sociocultural Factors and African Americans   105

Sociocultural Factors and Hispanic Americans   108

Sociocultural Factors and Asian Americans   110

Program Type   111

Conclusion   114

Summary   114

Key Concepts   116

Study Questions   116

Student Activity   116

7 Depression and Self-Injurious Behaviors   119

Statement of the Problem   119

Social Factors   121

Race/Ethnicity and Suicidal Behavior   123

Treatment Issues   128

Conclusion   130

Summary   130

Key Concepts   132

Study Questions   133

Student Activity   133

8 Personality and Health   135

Personality and Health Relationship   135

Five-Factor Theory   135

Generic Disease-Prone Personality Theory   138

Disease-Specific Personality Theory   139

Sense of Self/Identity   139

Stress   141

Sociocultural Factors, Personality, and Health   142

Emotion Expression   144

Conclusion   146

Summary   146

Key Concepts   148

Study Questions   149

Student Activity   149

9 Social Relations and Health   151

Social Support and Health   151

Relationships   153

Conclusion   162

Summary   162

Key Concepts   164

Study Questions   164

Student Activity   164

10   Spirituality, Music, and Laughter: Health Benefits   167

Spirituality and Health   167

Multicultural Health and Spirituality   170

Music and Health   174

Laughter and Health   176

Conclusion   178

Summary   178

Key Concepts   180

Study Questions   181

Student Activity   181

References   183

Index   197

PREFACE

Multicultural Health Psychology: Special Topics Acknowledging Diversity presents theories and research findings based on understudied groups. A multicultural approach to studying health is overdue. The significance of socioeconomic status, culture, race, ethnicity, and gender has not received sufficient discussion. These factors are critical to understanding health disparities for various groups.

The reason for a multicultural emphasis in this text stems from the ever-increasing diversity of the U.S. population. In the United States, one can find many ethnic groups and cultural practices. A multicultural perspective requires studying the diversity of people that make up a population, as opposed to focusing on only the majority culture within a society. There is much to be learned from a multicultural perspective. For example, recent arrivals in the United States often report that they engage in more health risky behaviors after they move to the United States. The increase in negative health behaviors for those adapting to a new culture is not a coincidence; it is often stress-related, which can influence their health and overall sense of well-being. This is particularly so if there is an extreme culture-clash between new experiences and traditional experiences. A multicultural perspective to health psychology addresses occurrences such as this.

A truly integrative approach to the study of illness and illness behavior should examine the cultural beliefs, values, and practices of the individual. For example, a health psychology researcher may develop a theory about illness behavior or about adherence to medical advice. If, however, the theories are not inclusive of cultural beliefs, values, and practices, then the researcher's theory may fail to adequately explain the behaviors of a diverse group of people.

Multiculturalism is a trend, specifically regarding health care, health education, and health research. A multicultural perspective must address a wide range of factors such as race, ethnicity, nationality, gender, religion, socioeconomic status, and sexual orientation. Specifically, a multicultural health perspective emphasizes the significance of each of these factors as it impacts the individual's health behaviors and his or her experience of illness. Educators should be aware of the need for students to learn about diverse cultures. Students must learn how an individual's cultural background can affect the choices that he or she makes when it comes to health behaviors such as exercising, eating healthy, or coping with job-related stress. Each of these issues is discussed in this text with regard to cultural context.

The features included in *Multicultural Health Psychology: Special Topics Acknowledging Diversity* will help students learn and appreciate multicultural significance. Students who plan to work in the health field should be knowledgeable about more than just their own cultures and lifestyles. If not, they will face quite a culture shock when they discover the differences in attitudes that affect the effectiveness of some treatment plans, research outcomes, and health programs. Students must not have a narrow focus regarding prevention and intervention. It is important that students understand that for clinicians, culture is very important in developing an effective treatment plan for a client. Even the clinician's own cultural background will affect how the clinician assesses, counsels, and relates to clients. Students planning to be clinicians will need to be aware that even what they consider to be normal or abnormal behavior in a client will be affected by cultural beliefs.

Features

The following features are contained in the text: (1) research findings pertaining to people of color, (2) bolded key terms that include many culture-specific terms for the groups being discussed, (3) candid health interviews with international and ethnic minority U.S. students, (4) student activity exercises that give students an opportunity to apply what they have learned about multiculturalism and health, and (5) common psychological theories such as conditioning, social learning, and personality theory that are presented with a special emphasis on race, ethnicity, gender, socioeconomic status, and sexual orientation.

Chapter Focus and Presentation

Each chapter—such as those on diet, smoking, exercise, and personality—includes information that leads students to think about the application of theories and treatments in psychology to persons who are less often represented in research studies. The examples given in the text generally refer to people of color, both males and females. Because I am aware that multiculturalism is broader than issues of race and ethnicity, the chapters also, where most relevant, highlight the significance of variables such as gender, sexual orientation, age, and socioeconomic status.

Another strong point of this text is that it is particularly flexible to suit any instructor's individual preference for order of chapter presentation. The text was written so that students will be equally comfortable with concepts and material across each of the chapters. The content is not presented in a hierarchical fashion in which each chapter builds upon the previous chapter. This gives the professor flexibility in utilizing this text to complement any course organization and/or primary text.

Chapter 1, however, does set the stage for the focus of the book by defining health psychology and the biopsychosocial model; it also highlights the need for increased attention to minority issues in health by presenting statistics relevant to Healthy People 2000. This follows a presentation of the meaning of culture and the multicultural health psychology approach. The opening chapter concludes with recurring themes/concepts that students will need to be familiar with in order to understand the health disparities across various groups.

Although instructors may present the chapters in any order, I have chosen to present the subjects of diet and smoking at the beginning of the text. Eating disorders, poor eating habits, and smoking addiction plague college students. These topics are presented early in the text so that students can become immediately engaged in material that may be of particular significance and relevance to them in their daily lives.

In several places, I also interchangeably use the pronouns "he" and "she" when making points; this is deliberately done to give students of both genders a more personalized presentation, rather than the standard use of "they" or "the individual."

Student Interviews

International students from various countries and ethnic minority U.S. students were interviewed for each chapter of the book (with the exception of Chapter 1). The students spoke candidly in response to questions that were posed to them in a one-on-one interview. Each interview is related to the chapter material in which the interview is contained. This gives students an opportunity to read vignettes of thoughts and experiences from a diverse group of students. The interviews help to shed light on the significance of cultural background in relationship to health beliefs and health behaviors.

"Spotlight on Biology" Boxes

Each chapter (with the exception of Chapter 1) contains a Spotlight on Biology. These boxes appear at the end of each chapter's material so that students are left with biologically based theory and research pertaining to the chapter material. Health prevention, health care, and health education are likely to be most effective when they stem from a multidisciplinary approach. Although health psychology includes more than biology in its emphasis, it is important that students understand that health psychologists remain aware of the significance of biological influences on health conditions and behaviors.

Key Concepts, Study Questions, and Student Activities

In order to assist students with the study and retention of text material, key concepts are bolded in the text of each chapter and also listed at the end of each chapter. Study questions relate to information presented in the chapter and will help students to determine if they grasped the key points from each chapter.

Finally, the student activities at the end of each chapter are intended to give students an opportunity to apply what they have learned by having them do an activity. The student activities include tasks such as conducting an interview, writing a research paper, writing an analysis of a book including consideration of cultural factors and health, watching a film that raises cultural awareness in the understanding of health, or listening to a particular music form. Each chapter has two options for student activity, which professors can use as course projects.

Acknowledgments

Acknowledgment to the Creator for the conception and completion of this work. Thank you to Danielle for the loving support (especially during that mishap with Chapter 7). Thank you to Erika Fitzpatrick for proofreading the early chapters. I would like to give special thanks to each of the students who gave of his or her time to be interviewed for the chapters. I would also like to thank the editors at Allyn & Bacon, Carolyn Merrill and Lara Zeises, as well as the weekend library staff at the National Library of Medicine. Finally, I would like to thank each of the reviewers of the manuscript: Barbara A. Bremer, Penn State University, Harrisburg; Sarah Erickson, University of New Mexico; Carmen Guanipa, San Diego State University; Regan A. R. Gurung, University of Wisconsin, Green Bay; Jan Hastrup, State University of New York at Buffalo; Marguerite Kermis, Canisius College; Anastasia Kitsantas, Florida State University; Theresa J. Martin, Eastern Washington University; Gabie E. Smith, Frostburg State University; William P. Wattles, Francis Marion University; A. Sandra Willis, Samford University; Patricia Wolskee, Capella University; and Maria Cecilia Zea, George Washington University. Your suggestions for improvements to this work are greatly appreciated.

1 Introduction

Health Psychology

It is a fact of life that at some point during his or her lifetime, the typical person succumbs to a sickness, disease, or simply feels "under the weather." Health psychology has evolved not only as a result of this fact, but also because of further evidence that when we compare the top 10 leading causes of death presently to the top 10 list in the year 1900, the change is astonishingly clear. Today in the United States, health complications, disease, and the use of medical practitioners are most often due to **chronic illnesses** such as heart disease, diabetes, and cerebrovascular diseases. Chronic illnesses are illnesses that develop gradually over time at a slow rate and can result in enduring a lifetime of complications. In the early 1900s this was not the case. The top 10 causes of death then were shorter-term medical illnesses resulting from viral or bacterial infections. These are categorized as **acute illnesses** and would include such illnesses as influenza, tuberculosis, and pneumonia. Today acute illnesses account for only 30 deaths per 100,000 citizens (Baum, Gatchel, & Krantz, 1997). **Health psychology** is concerned with understanding the healthy individual's practices, the behaviors related to the onset of illness in the unhealthy, and the methods that work best to promote healthy lifestyles. Because many of the chronic illnesses mentioned previously stem partly from the individual's behavior, psychology has come to play an integral role in health care. Health psychology shares its role with other disciplines such as medicine in the study of illnesses (many psychologists are now employed in medical settings such as hospitals); however, unlike medicine, health psychology deals with more than just the biological cause of and medical treatment of diseases. Health psychology's purpose is to disseminate knowledge through practice, research, and education that enlightens individuals as to the psychological, social, and biological factors affecting health outcomes, so that illnesses can be prevented.

Multicultural Health Psychology

Culture has been specifically defined as human designs for living that are based on the accumulated knowledge of a people, encoded in their language, and embodied in the physical artifacts, beliefs, values, customs, and activities that have been passed down from one generation to the next (Serafica, 1997). When considering social variables and health, culture is a significant factor. Unfortunately, however, it is still often the case that health psychology texts do not provide extensive coverage and sometimes no coverage at all of the relationship of culture to health practices, morbidity, and mortality (Baum et al., 1997; Brannon & Feist, 2000; Taylor, 1999). For example, racial and ethnic minorities suffer disproportionately from a number of psychosocial problems such as substance abuse, high unemployment rates, high dropout rates, and family disruption (Gil & Bob, 1999). Also, rates of some risky health behaviors can also increase as a result of immigration to a new culture for persons newly arriving in the United States (Vega, Alderete, Bohdan, & Aguilar, 1998).

Culture is a major factor in the structuring of human interaction, affect, and cognition. The culture of a patient can provide resources for coping with illness and hospitalization as well as affect the patient's acceptance of health interventions (Canino & Guarnaccia, 1997). Culture may also be a crucial factor in the explanation of why there are differences in compliance with certain medical advice. Generally, psychologists, sociologists, and anthropologists understand that culture is complex, creative, and dynamic. In addition, however, in acknowledging the significance of culture it is important for health professionals to distinguish **emic** versus **etic** cultural influences on health behavior. Emic describes categories of practices that are culture specific (i.e., Eastern vs. Western) or totally isolated from other cultures. Etic categories of behavior refer to cultural universals or general practices for all within a society. These would be behaviors that reflect the dominant cultural outlook of the society in general and are not unique to any one subgroup.

Quah and Bishop (1996) found that individuals high in Chinese cultural orientation were more likely to describe diseases using Chinese health concepts and less likely to describe diseases in terms of physical causality or chronicity. Individuals who were more likely to use Chinese health concepts were also more likely to state that they would seek treatment from a *sinseh*, or practitioner of Chinese medicine.

The practices of the *sinseh* differ substantially from the practices of Western medicine. Chinese medicine views disease as stemming from forces not necessarily connected to biological factors. The *sinseh* emphasizes disease resulting from internal disharmony and imbalance of body energies. In order to reestablish the balance and harmony of the energies in the body, an emic behavior of the *sinseh* might be to treat the illness by restoring the balance using foods and medicines believed to counteract the imbalance. Two Chinese health concepts are *yin* and *yang*; optimal health is maintained by keeping these in balance.

Similarly, in African American cultural studies, an **Afrocentric worldview** has been identified (Snowden & Hines, 1999). An Afrocentric worldview is defined as a basic set of beliefs and assumptions that reflect African values, including those related to health behaviors—one of which is the rate of use of health benefits and the display of formal health practices. There may be even less participation in standard traditional health care, particularly with respect to the elderly and those from specific regions. Alternative forms of treatment and coping with illness may be preferred. For example, elderly more traditional persons may want to use home remedies handed down through the generations of a family instead of traditional medicinal treatments. These may date back to specific practices of one's ancestors. Health practices are shaped by what the group adopts as its dominant cultural outlook. The use of any specific concepts and practices as a part of the Afrocentric worldview would be examples of emic behaviors.

The challenge for health practitioners is to refrain from allowing their experience with etic categories of behavior to prevent them from also recognizing relevant cultural practices of an emic nature. Emic factors, particularly for underrepresented ethnic and racial groups, have to be incorporated much more systematically into the techniques, treatment goals, and specific objectives in health promotion and treatment.

The term "culture" has been so widely used that its precise meaning varies from one situation to another. However, culture can be used broadly to refer to shared means of communication and social experiences of living in the world. The passage of time has not resulted in much consensus on the definition of culture; therefore, it is necessary to be specific about the meaning being used in this text for the term *multicultural health.*

Multicultural health refers to the complex interrelationship between one's cultural background and health. **Multicultural health psychology** considers a kaleidoscope of causes, experiences, expressions, and treatments for a plethora of human ailments among people of various backgrounds. Much of the variation in human health is not always necessarily related to genetic variation alone, but also to the different ways that we as people exist in the world, which includes our cultural background. The approach of multicultural health psychology:

- Considers the whole range of learned behaviors impacting health.
- Recognizes the interconnectedness of different aspects of life such as economics, religion, and gender as they impact health.
- Emphasizes the relationship between cultural groups and power distribution (i.e., prejudice and discrimination, racism).
- Highlights the coexistence of multiple cultures and subcultures in the same setting (MacLachlan, 1997).

Within a diverse society, educators, students, researchers, clinicians, and health care providers must recognize and show some progression toward a pluralistic approach to understanding health behavior. It is imperative to understand that any illness or health behavior occurs within a cultural context. The cultural context to some extent will influence the way in which suffering is caused, experienced, and expressed, as well as the consequences of such suffering. Any given factor—such as stress, for example—is likely to vary across cultural groups. The variation in stressors across cultural groups and socioeconomic classes is related to variations in physical disease processes for different groups.

It is common for some health professionals and students to fail to take the context of an individual's behavior into account. This causes a misattribution of the cause of the behavior to something within the individual. If there is a lack of understanding of the cultural context in which a behavior occurs, then the behavior may seem unwarranted or bizarre and pathological. Those involved in health promotion, prevention, treatment, research, and education must ascertain where they fit into the overall system and must not center the health care system or approach on themselves from their own biased cultural position.

Multicultural health psychology should include cultural sensitivity in education, client-clinician interaction, and prevention efforts. It should also consider (1) learning from one's clients; (2) using treatments that may or may not be fully understood in the clinician's own culture (i.e., consulting with a shaman or spiritual healer); (3) the cultural context of health behavior; and (4) that various cultures and subcultures exist in diverse societies, such that communities may differ from one another, for example, the African American community, the Deaf community, or the gay community.

Internationalization is producing more subcultures within traditionally recognized cultures. It is not likely that with the ever-diversifying social context in which we live that there will be a "melting pot" experience. Cultures are likely to remain somewhat different as people operate in ecologically different contexts; this makes a multicultural approach to understanding health necessary. The best approach for understanding health behavior is to consider culture, as well as the social, economic, and political context in which culturally different communities operate (MacLachlan, 1997).

As we begin the twenty-first century, increased diversity faces the scientific community of health researchers, educators, and clinicians. A continuing change in the United States has been the increased diversity of the population of its inhabitants, making it a nation with a variety of religions, ethnic groups, and culturally based attitudes and behaviors. As we acknowledge distinctions of a multicultural nature, we will also need to recognize the most effective means of addressing diverse needs. Variation across individuals exists for types of illness succumbed to, psychological variables that result in these differences, biological factors, and sociocultural factors that are highly related to the health-affecting choices that individuals make.

Particularly for new residents of the United States who have migrated from other countries, there is typically a period of adjustment that may take an emotional as well as a financial toll. This can result in stress that has implications for health; high consistent levels of stress can lead to physical complications. There is great disparity in health care availability and health behavior across social class (Carroll, Smith, & Bennett, 1996). Some residents are able to afford the highest quality care and others go without until gainful employment can be found that may provide health insurance. Also, depending on the occupation of the worker, even then the quality of the health care provided through the job may be minimal. It has been elsewhere reported that as of 1994, 37 million Americans have no health insurance, making preventive care and treatment for common illnesses impossible for them (Taylor, 1999). Those falling into this category are likely to be individuals lower in socioeconomic status and people of color living in the United States. The significance of this is indicated when percentages across ethnic and racial lines reveal marked differences in rates of both **morbidity**, numbers of individuals suffering from various types of illnesses, and **mortality**, number of deaths due to various causes. Members of ethnic and racial minority groups generally have higher rates of morbidity and mortality for the leading causes of death in the United States.

Healthy People 2000

On February 21, 1998, President Clinton announced a new initiative that set a national goal for the United States to eliminate long-standing disparities in health status that affect racial and ethnic minority groups. In order to reach this goal, the president outlined a five-step plan that would require the joint efforts of the federal government, the private sector, and local communities. The five steps of the plan are:

- Initiating a sweeping new outreach campaign led by the Surgeon General.
- $400 million to develop new approaches and to build on existing successes to address racial and ethnic health disparities.
- Announcing a major new foundation/public sector collaboration to address disparities.
- Developing more effective ways to target existing federal programs using researchers of the Centers for Disease Control, the National Institutes of Health, and other public health and science agencies to address health disparities.
- Issuing a national challenge to involve communities, foundations, advocacy organizations, and businesses to develop ways to target racial and ethnic health disparities.

These new goals are included as a part of **Healthy People 2000**, a program that sets the nation's health goals for the year 2010. Healthy People 2000 is a prevention agenda for the nation; it states national health objectives designed to identify the most significant preventable threats to health, and it establishes national goals to reduce these threats. Healthy People 2000 builds on initiatives pursued over the past two decades and it relies upon data from many sources (i.e., National Center for Health Statistics, FEDSTATS). The plans for meeting the goals for Healthy People 2000 were launched in January 2000 and includes plans for a mid-year review (2005), annual statistical reports, and progress reviews. Healthy People 2000 also calls for assistance from businesses, communities, national membership organizations, state and territorial health departments, national associations of state health officials, federal agencies, and nongovernmental organizations to assess progress towards meeting the objectives. The three overall goals of Healthy People 2000 are (1) to increase the quality and years of healthy life for all, (2) eliminate health disparities, and (3) to achieve access to preventive services for all people living in the United States.

Healthy People 2000 includes plans to eliminate the disparities in six areas of health status experienced by racial and ethnic minority populations. Healthy People 2010 (a report calling for public comment on the goals, priority areas, and objectives of Healthy People 2000) shifted emphasis from targeting special groups toward high standards of health improvement for all U. S. residents. The six target areas of the Healthy People 2000 initiative to eliminate racial and ethnic disparities in health are: Infant Mortality, Cancer Screening and Management, Cardiovascular Disease, Diabetes, HIV Infection, and Child and Adult Immunizations. Data are available to measure the progress in these target areas, thus making it easier to target them for study. Based on the statistics given for the six Healthy People 2000 targeted problems, the morbidity and mortality rates reflect the need for a culturally based discussion in health psychology and other related fields. The statistics on major health problems among minorities reveal the importance of meeting the needs of the underserved in the United States.

Health Statistics: Cultural Group Differences

Infant Mortality Rates

Infant mortality rates vary significantly among and within racial and ethnic groups. The infant mortality rate among blacks, Native Americans and Alaska Natives, and Hispanics in 1995 and 1996 were all above the national average of 7.2 deaths per 1,000 live births.

The greatest disparity exists for blacks, who had an infant mortality rate of 14.2 per 1,000 people in 1996. This is nearly two and one-half times that of white infants. The Healthy People 2010 project seeks to reduce infant mortality among blacks by at least 22 percent (U.S. Department of Health and Human Services, 1998a).

In addition, there are significant racial disparities in the receipt of timely prenatal care. In 1996, 84 percent of white women, compared with approximately 71 percent of black and Hispanic pregnant women, received early prenatal care. Among the leading causes of death in infants, the racial and ethnic disparity is greatest in the following:

1. Disorders relating to short gestation and unspecified low birthweight
2. Infections specific to the perinatal period and newborns affected by maternal complications of pregnancy
3. Sudden infant death syndrome.

There is a much higher incidence of preterm births among black mothers than among white mothers. Some underlying factors that play a role in preterm birth are chronic hypertension and bacterial vaginosis, which have higher incidence among blacks. Finally, minority populations are also at greater risk for sudden infant death syndrome (U.S. Department of Health and Human Services, 1998a).

Cancer Screening and Management

Cancer is the second leading cause of death in the United States, accounting for more than 544,000 deaths each year. About 1.4 million new cases were expected to be diagnosed in 1997, and approximately 7.4 million Americans have or have had cancer. For men and women combined, blacks have a cancer death rate about 35 percent higher than for whites. Specifically, the death rate for lung cancer is about 27 percent higher for blacks than for whites. The prostate cancer mortality rate for black men is more than twice that of white men. Vietnamese women in the United States have a cervical cancer incidence rate more than five times greater than white women. Hispanic women also suffer elevated rates of cervical cancer. The mortality rate from breast cancer for black women is greater than for white women. Hispanic, Native American and Alaska Native, and Asian and Pacific Islander women also have low rates of screening and treatment, limited access to health facilities and physicians, barriers to language, and negative provider attitudes, which negatively affect their health status (U.S. Department of Health and Human Services, 1998a).

Cardiovascular Disease

Cardiovascular disease, primarily coronary heart disease and stroke, kills almost as many Americans as all other diseases combined. It is among the leading causes of disability in the United States. Cardiovascular disease is the leading cause of death for all racial and ethnic groups. There is a major disparity that exists among groups. The disease disproportionately affects minority and low income populations. The age adjusted death rate for coronary heart disease for the total population declined by 20 percent from 1987 to 1995. For blacks the overall decrease was only 13 percent. Asian Americans have 40 percent lower coronary heart disease mortality than whites, but for blacks the rate compared to whites is 40 percent higher. However, stroke is the only leading cause of death for which mortality is higher for Asian American males than for white males. From 1988 to 1994, 35 percent of black males ages 20 to 74 had hypertension compared to 25 percent of all men. Mexican American men and women also have elevated blood pressure. Finally, black women (53 percent) and Mexican American women (52 percent) still have higher percentages of prevalence of obesity compared to white women (34 percent) (U.S. Department of Health and Human Services, 1998a).

Diabetes

Diabetes, the seventh leading cause of death in the United States, is a serious public health problem affecting approximately 16 million Americans. The prevalence of diabetes in blacks is approximately 70 percent higher than whites and the prevalence for Hispanics is nearly double that of whites. The prevalence rate of diabetes among Native Americans and Alaska Natives is more than twice that for the total population (U.S. Department of Health and Human Services, 1998a).

HIV Infection/AIDS

HIV infection/AIDS is a leading cause of death for all persons 25 to 44 years of age. Between 650,000 and 900,000 Americans are estimated to be living with HIV infection. Approximately 62 percent of the 604,200 adults and adolescents reported with AIDS in the United States have died from the disease. AIDS has disproportionately affected minority populations. Racial and ethnic minorities constitute approximately 25 percent of the total U.S. population, yet they account for nearly 54 percent of all AIDS cases. Although the epidemic has decreased in some populations, the number of new cases of AIDS among blacks is greater than new cases among whites. For white gay and bisexual males the number of AIDS diagnoses has decreased significantly since 1989. For black gay and bisexual males, however, the rate has increased. New HIV infection and AIDS due to injected drug use is also more concentrated in minority group populations (56% black, 20% Hispanic). Women and children account for more than 75 percent of cases among racial and ethnic minorities. During the years 1995 and 1996, AIDS death rates declined 23 percent for the total U.S. population, and decreased only 13 percent for blacks and 20 percent for Hispanics (U.S. Department of Health and Human Services, 1998a).

Child and Adult Immunization Rates

Immunization coverage for preschoolers is high in almost all states. The problem is that pockets exist in certain states and cities where there are still substantial numbers of under-immunized children. The concern is that for those in these underserved groups living in large urban areas, there is a potential for outbreak of disease. This is unfortunate since many diseases are preventable with vaccines.

In addition to children, older adults are at increased risk for many vaccine-preventable diseases. Nearly 90 percent of all influenza-associated deaths in the United States occur in people aged 65 and older. This is mostly due to older persons having a low vaccination rate. Approximately 45,000 adults die of infections related to influenza, pneumococcal infections, and hepatitis B despite available vaccines that will prevent these from occurring. There is a disproportionate prevalence of these diseases in minority and underserved populations (U.S. Department of Health and Human Services, 1998a).

Biopsychosocial Model

The most academically responsible way to educate the public and answer questions via health psychological theories and research is to use a biopsychosocial approach. The field of health psychology's premise is that mind and body together contribute to morbidity and mortality rates, thus a biopsychosocial model logically follows from this premise.

Upon encountering the term "biopsychosocial," students often look puzzled and ask, "Well, what does that mean?" When we break it down, you will see the simplicity of the word, and realize it is a concept that already makes sense to you. If you can understand the possibility that biological factors (cell aberration), psychological factors (belief that one will never have a life worth living with an illness), and social factors (estrangement from family) can affect prognoses, client health behavior, and treatment effectiveness, then you have a basic understanding of the biopsychosocial model. The **biopsychosocial model** necessitates the examination of biological influences, psychological influences, and social influences on behavior and treatment outcomes. The following is a description of a patient's behavior.

> For most patients afflicted with it, sickle cell disease is ceaselessly and interminably the dominating fact of each hour lived. No moment is free of the apprehension that an excruciating crisis may suddenly strike. Any illness, any hot summer's day, any overexertion can bring on a grueling agony of pain that lasts for days and requires astonishingly large amounts of narcotic to ease it, necessitating increases in dosage over the years as tolerance rises. Kip Penn has visited the emergency room of Yale New Haven Hospital literally hundreds of times for pain medication, and he has spent so many days as an inpatient that he long ago stopped counting the numbers of nightmarish hospitalizations he has endured. His admissions for pneumonia alone, a disease to which sicklers are particularly susceptible, number almost twenty.
>
> (Nuland, S. B., *The Wisdom of the Body*, 1997, (p. 112, Alfred A. Knopf, Inc., a Division of Random House. Reprinted with permission.)

Nuland's (1997) description of his patient's battle with sickle cell disease can be used to present an example of the biopsychosocial model of studying health. In the case of sickle cell anemia, physicians know the biological cause of this disease. There is a defective inherited gene that results in an abnormality of the production of hemoglobin, an iron-containing protein molecule found in red blood cells that carries oxygen to the tissues of the body. Persons with sickle cell anemia often endure excruciating pain as tissues normally supplied with oxygen from now blocked vessels experience a severe reduction in flow and receipt of oxygen throughout the body. The blood vessels have become obstructed because the abnormal red blood cells (due to the genetic defect) have an irregular shape (sickle shape) and an abnormal membrane; these abnormal red blood cells clump or jam together, thus blocking tiny blood vessels. Since there is a shortage in the flow of oxygen to the tissues, we say these individuals are anemic. This is the biological explanation for this pathology. For the practitioner whose only concern is with biology, then the biological facts of pathological conditions such as sickle cell would be the extent of that practitioner's focus. Those who support an emphasis on solely biological factors fail to consider the big picture and are not taking the more modern approach. The focus on strictly the biological is an old way of thinking that came out of the Renaissance and the advent of physical medicine. Focus on the mind was considered unscientific during that time, so biology was more highly regarded (Baum et al., 1997), although before the seventeenth century mind and body had once been considered connected. The focus on the biological when studying illness, referred to as the biomedical model (Taylor, 1999), has been the dominant approach for health practitioners for approximately the last 300 years. The **biomedical model** emphasizes that illness can be explained solely by abnormal biological processes such as neurotransmitter and hormonal imbalances and neurophysiological abnormalities. According to the biomedical model, abnormalities in systems of the brain or body alone account for illnesses.

Biomedical and epidemiological studies place the emphasis on the individual and the biological level when seeking to learn about an illness; the focus is on the individual in isolation from, or totally detached from the social environment (Spicer & Chamberlain, 1996). Regarding the previous example of the sickle cell patient, a biomedical model would only be sufficient for explaining the physiological cause of the illness.

However, health professionals advocating the biopsychosocial model are interested in the behaviors that the patient displays, whether in isolation or when among friends and family. They are also interested in knowing the psychological and social factors that are involved in something such as medical compliance or noncompliance.

A patient may follow doctor's orders precisely or she may ignore the advice and education that she has received about the illness. Health psychologists are concerned with understanding why these differences in compliance exist. The health psychologist looks for explanations of health outcomes that stem not only from biological factors, but the psychological and social factors as well. In health psychology, the belief is that the quality of health is determined by multiple causes and has multiple effects.

Let's take a look at some of the psychological and social factors that are relevant to Nuland's patient, Kip. Like the majority of persons diagnosed with sickle cell anemia, Kip is an African American. Kip comes from a stable working class family. Kip receives social support from his family, and this has been identified as a significant therapeutic factor, especially for members of minority groups (Canino & Guarnaccia, 1997; Tsutsumi, Tsutsumi, Kayaba, & Igarashi, 1998). Kip, however, was a self-described loner during his early developmental years. This is attributed to the fact that as a sickle cell anemic he had to refrain from overexerting himself, and thus could not play as long and as hard as the other children. Here we see the combination of social and psychological factors. Kip believed that he was different and he did not think that other children perceived him to be fun. His self-concept of a loner and his thoughts about his social acceptance resulted in a host of unhealthy behaviors. Like many "sicklers," Kip became a drug abuser (the excruciating pain that sicklers suffer from often causes a dependence on narcotics to escape the pain) because he continued to request opiate drugs from doctors and street dealers to alleviate the pain of his condition. On occasion, he was successful in getting excess medication from the doctors, but when this would not suffice he took to the streets and abused street drugs. In psychological terms, it was **negative reinforcement** that sustained Kip's drug behavior. Negative reinforcement is defined as the removal or escape from something undesirable that results in an increase in a response. Kip was able to escape or avoid pain when he took drugs; this escape from pain or removal of pain was what continued to motivate Kip's drug usage.

Kip supported his habit by becoming a drug dealer. Subsequently, he experienced one sickle crisis after another. The crises that Kip suffered from were due to his unhealthy lifestyle choices: overexerting himself in fights, aggressive outbursts, cocaine abuse, and assaults. Because Kip's life was spiraling downhill and his behavior was so deviant, Kip's family cut him off. This was a consequence that was sparked by his voluntary behaviors. These behaviors and consequences had deleterious effects on his physical condition. It is this type of information that biomedical models fail to consider when studying health and illness. In health psychology we do pay attention to these behaviors, particularly by trying to understand the thoughts and emotions underlying the decisions to engage in such behavior. The individual may even be aware that such behavior will negatively impact his or her health. Health psychologists also consider how social factors (estrangement from family) can affect an individual's coping with an illness and maintenance of healthy behavior.

Sadly, Nuland further reveals that Kip's father suffered from a massive heart attack and died. When Kip received the news, he was in the process of getting high. Kip's father's death changed his life forever. As a result of this and the assistance of an uncle, Kip gave up the drugs and the other risky health behavior that he had engaged in. The sickle cell crises ceased. Once a positive health action (quitting drugs) such as Kip's has been initiated, it has to be maintained. This may require restructuring the patient's thinking about his probability for continued success (Schwarzer, 1999).

Dr. Nuland is an M.D. and clinical professor of surgery. In his book, *The Wisdom of the Body,* he thoroughly explains the systems and various cells of the body. He provides several informative case studies such as Kip's, but he does not provide the reader with thorough additional explanations that relate to psychological and social factors. Thus we see the difference between a biomedical perspective and a focus that is biopsychosocial. This text, as overall in the field of health psychology, will highlight each of the biological, psychological, and social factors where appropriate.

Recurring Themes in Multicultural Health Psychology

In order to present topics in health psychology from a multicultural perspective, it is necessary to briefly define some significant concepts that are recurring in the literature. Throughout this text, the research studies that are referenced and the interviews presented will be based on research participants from a variety of cultural backgrounds. The recurring themes below are significant in isolation as well as in combination with socioeconomic status (SES). A multicultural discussion must highlight the relationship between socioeconomic status, stress, and health outcomes. The combination of these factors and SES largely explains group differences in health behavior and health statistics; these concepts will also be relevant to the information presented in the chapters to follow.

Acculturation

Acculturation is the process by which ethnic and racial minorities participate in the cultural traditions, values, beliefs, assumptions, and practices of the dominant society (Landrine & Klonoff, 1994; Nguyen, Messe, & Stollack, 1999; Snowden & Hines, 1999). For example, if a female from India never consumed alcohol in her country, but arrives in the United States and becomes a social drinker, this would likely be a result of increased acculturation; social drinking is a part of the cultural norm in the United States. The level of acculturation of an individual has been found to be related to the likelihood of engaging in various health behaviors (e.g., use of health services) and to symptom-related distress (Nguyen et al., 1999; Ramos Sanchez, Atkinson, & Fraga, 1999; Vega et al., 1998). Acculturative stress, which refers to discrepancies between the values and beliefs of a minority culture and those of the majority culture, can also exist. This should be acknowledged in therapeutic interventions (McNair, 1996).

Collectivism Versus Individualism

Cross-cultural psychologists, anthropologists, and sociologists use the terms collectivism and individualism to distinguish cultures along a continuum from being sociocentric to being individualistic. The **collectivist culture** is one in which the people in the culture define themselves in relation to others and see themselves as part of a network of interconnected people. The **individualist culture** is one in which the people see themselves as autonomous individuals, and distinguish themselves from others. Japan is an example of a collectivist culture (Tsutsumi et al., 1998); the United States is an example of an individualist culture. The type of culture has been found to play an important role in the mental and physical healing process and the resolution of crises (Canino & Guarnaccia, 1997).

Racial Identity

Racial identity refers to the significance and meaning that an individual places on race in defining themselves. Researchers may utilize research participants of a specific racial group, or compare racial or ethnic groups (Dressler, Bindon, & Neggers, 1998; Organista & Munoz, 1996; Rogers, Adamson, & McCarthy, 1997; Sellers, Smith, Shelton, Rowley, & Chavous, 1998; Serafica, 1997, 1999); however, knowing an individual's race should not be equated with knowing an individual's racial identity.

Sellers and colleagues (1998) describe a multidimensional model of racial identity. The dimensions include:

Salience: The extent to which one's race is a relevant part of one's self-concept at a particular moment or in a particular situation.

Centrality: The extent to which a person normatively defines himself or herself with regard to race.

Regard: The feelings of positivity and negativity toward being a member of a particular race.

Ideology: The viewpoint an individual may have on what it means to be a member of a group. Ideology affects how a member of any racial group thinks about his or her group's position relative to other groups. Using an African American example of differences in ideology, Louis Farrakhan, Martin Luther King Jr., and Colin Powell could be described as varying in ideology.

The different dimensions of racial identity are related to different behavioral and adaptational outcomes in a variety of contexts, including health.

Racial identity may be related to choice of clinician, belief in the quality of services and suggestions being offered by a health care provider, and belief in the uniqueness of one's circumstances as a member of a particular group. For example, a Mexican American male patient may feel that a Spanish-speaking physician would be more competent in meeting his needs, and a Mexican American female may not view being overweight as a rare condition for women of her race, but instead the norm. This could affect how she would react to suggestions by a doctor to diet or exercise for health purposes.

Cultural Sensitivity

Cultural sensitivity has been defined as the ability to balance a consideration of universal norms, specific group norms, and individual norms in (1) differentiating between normal and abnormal behavior, (2) considering etiological factors, and (3) implementing appropriate interventions (Gil & Bob, 1999). In order to incorporate cultural sensitivity, health professionals need to determine what the client views as the cultural norm. Health professionals must also implement treatments that can balance the different norms, as opposed to disregarding the client's cultural reference base. Psychologists and counselors of varying cultural backgrounds (Native American, African American, Latino, and Asian) have emphasized the importance of cultural sensitivity in human services (Diller, 1999). Issues that have been identified for some members of ethnic groups are the following:

- Asians—Value conflicts with parents and family, difficulties regarding identity issues, acculturation, extreme work ethics, and family obligations
- African Americans—Mistrust and avoidance of help seeking from established white agencies and institutions
- Native Americans—Loss of identity and disconnection from traditions due to systematic governmental actions and negative stereotyping
- Latinos/as—Collectivism, religiosity, culturally based expectations during meetings with health care providers (Diller, 1999).

Research in Multicultural Health Psychology

Health practitioners, educators, and researchers must avoid being ethnocentric when evaluating and attempting to treat and study the health behaviors of underrepresented minorities. Instead, **ethnoscience methods** should be used. Ethnoscience methods allow researchers to explore first hand the informant's own ideas and beliefs to discover the cultural themes and patterns that give meaning to the way people interpret their experiences and generate behavior (Bottorff et al., 1998). This requires conducting thorough qualitative interviews with clients.

Health researchers should address the specific concerns impacting ethnic minority groups. This can be achieved through university- and community-based research. Some concerns that impact minority groups have been identified as:

1) A failure to report information to minority research participants
2) A lack of diversity among those doing the research
3) Inappropriately studied and understudied minority groups
4) Culturally insensitive assessment instruments (Gil & Bob, 1999)

Research findings may lack validity if findings have been obtained from questionnaires that do not actually measure the true behavior, emotions, and thoughts of the research participants.

The American Psychological Association has recently established ethical guidelines for culturally competent research. The guidelines include but are not limited to:

a) Educate clients regarding the purposes of psychological intervention
b) Increase awareness of research and practice issues impacting ethnic minority populations
c) Incorporate ethnicity and culture in the understanding of psychological processes
d) Respect roles and beliefs within the client's culture
e) Consider the influence of negative environmental and other factors in problem assessment and intervention design
f) Attend to and work to eliminate biases, prejudices, and discriminatory practices (Gil & Bob, 1999).

The use of these guidelines, as well as the present work of some culturally sensitive practitioners and researchers, should contribute to the reduction in high morbidity and mortality rates for racial and ethnic minorities in the United States.

If each of the aforementioned guidelines and minority concerns are considered, the standard research methods in psychology are applicable when doing multicultural research in health psychology. Methods such as the case study, correlation, cross-sectional study, longitudinal study, and the experimental design or expost facto design have application in the discipline of health psychology. The method that a researcher chooses depends on the research question that the scientist is attempting to answer.

Conclusion

Health care in the United States is changing rapidly. This provides an even greater need for, and opportunities in the field of health psychology. Baum and colleagues (1997) have identified four major problems that presently face the U.S. health care system:

1. Rising health care costs.
2. Increased numbers of uninsured people.
3. Mediocre and non–cost-effective health care outcomes.
4. Barriers to effective health care for vulnerable or underserved groups in the society.

This chapter emphasized the importance of culture and the disparities in health statistics across racial and ethnic lines. The need for a multicultural perspective on health psychology is evident. As you continue reading this text, the cultural relevance to some common topics in health psychology will be further discussed. Primarily using research and examples that focus on racial and ethnic minorities, women, the elderly, gays and lesbians, and socioeconomic status, you will learn the salience of attending to sociocultural factors as well as biological and psychological factors when attempting to understand health behavior and illness.

Summary

Health psychology is a growing field of psychology that is concerned with understanding the healthy individual's practices, the factors related to the onset of illness in the unhealthy, and the methods that work best to promote healthy lifestyles. The purpose of the field is to disseminate knowledge through practice, research, and education that enlightens individuals as to the psychological, social, and biological factors together that affect health outcomes. Culture is a significant factor in understanding differences in health behavior, as well as it being significant to the effectiveness of research and treatment methods. Health psychology is based on a biopsychosocial model of studying health behavior. Multicultural health refers to the complex interrelationship between one's cultural background and health. Multicultural health psychology considers a kaleidoscope of causes, experiences, expressions, and treatments for a plethora of human ailments among people of various backgrounds. U.S. health statistics reveal disparities in the prevalence of leading causes of death for ethnic and racial minorities in comparison to whites. There are greater percentages of ethnic and racial minorities diagnosed with cancer, cardiovascular disease, diabetes, and HIV infection/AIDS. As a part of the Healthy People 2000 project, President Clinton issued a statement outlining a five-step plan to reduce the rates of ethnic and racial minorities affected by cardiovascular disease, cancer, diabetes, low immunization rates, HIV infection/AIDS, and infant mortality. Research from a multicultural perspective on health psychology should address the concerns that impact minorities and follow the APA ethical guidelines for culturally competent research. Using ethnoscience methods, all standard research methods are applicable with diverse groups. Finally, the multicultural perspective of health psychology highlights the significance of terms such as acculturation, collectivism versus individualism, racial identity, and cultural sensitivity.

Key Concepts

acculturation
acute illness
Afrocentric worldview
biomedical model
biopsychosocial model
chronic illness
collectivist culture
cultural sensitivity
culture
emic
ethnoscience methods
etic
health psychology
Healthy People 2000
individualist culture
morbidity
mortality
multicultural health psychology
negative reinforcement
racial identity

Study Questions

1. What is health psychology?
2. If you were to do a research paper on the history of major illnesses in the United States, what would be a major difference in the nineteenth century versus the present?
3. Define the biopsychosocial method of studying health and give an example.
4. How does the biopsychosocial method differ from the biomedical method?
5. What evidence is there for a need for an increased emphasis on culture in health psychology?
6. Why should health professionals pay attention to emic as well as etic categories of behavior?
7. For ethnic and racial minorities, what will be the focus of Healthy People 2000?
8. How might health behavior be affected by each of the following?
   Low acculturation
   Being from a collectivist culture
   Having a salient racial identity
   Receiving treatment from a culturally insensitive practitioner
9. What are the statistics for the percentages of morbidity for ethnic and racial minorities for the two leading causes of death in the United States?
10. What are the guidelines for culturally competent research?

Student Activity

Locate and interview a local health care professional (e.g., director of health facility, physician, therapist) who works with diverse clients. Ask questions to discover the unique aspects of treatment with the underserved in U.S. society.

OR

Interview someone from another culture and ask about health care and health care attitudes in their culture. How does this person believe their culture shaped their present health behavior?

2 Diet and Health

In Chapter 1 you learned that the leading causes of death in the United States have changed over the years from acute to chronic illnesses. Dietary trends are significant in consideration of this change, and an understanding of such trends is particularly relevant when it comes to dietary behaviors of U.S. residents at the beginning of the twenty-first century. Due to its linkage to several major health problems worldwide, a discussion of diet is crucial to any text on health psychology. Not only is there a relationship between food selection processes, dietary patterns, and the onset of various diseases, but these are also related to the onset of disordered eating. In attempting to understand dietary behavior, it is important to acknowledge the development of complex dietary patterns and to specifically highlight the need for diet counselors to be sensitive to sociocultural factors, including the ethnicity of their clients.

First, consideration will be given to the change in dietary patterns in general across the last two centuries. Second, the relationship between diet and disease will be presented. Finally, a discussion of the complexity of variables related to food selection in various groups as well as the individual will be covered.

Dietary Trends

The agricultural and industrial revolutions of the late eighteenth century had an impact on eating behavior (Rose, 1982). Subsequent to the population explosion and movement to towns away from farms, there was both a greater need for transportation and for food preservation. These factors influenced what was consumed as well as the methods for storing and transporting food for later consumption. As a food consumer of today, it may be difficult to imagine a time when meats and supplements such as margarine were not heavily consumed or produced. However, much of what we consume in our diet today represents a relatively recent trend. For example, a common ingredient of recipes today is margarine, which was first produced only about 100 years ago (Rose, 1982). The greatest dietary change, however, is attributed to the relatively recent change from poverty to affluence in the general population, leading to a trend from consumption of vegetable protein to animal protein. The increased consumption of animal protein results from the increase in consumption of meat, dairy, produce, and eggs, all of which may result in higher levels of saturated fat consumption.

Improper and excessive nutrition is related to many of the diseases characteristic of modern Western culture such as in the United States. In diet and nutrition literature, the diseases resulting from this trend in food consumption have been referred to as **Western diseases** (Rose, 1982). Western diseases include coronary heart disease (the leading cause of death in affluent Western societies), colon disease, large bowel cancer, gallstones, appendicitis, varicose veins, obesity, diabetes, hiatus hernia, atherosclerosis, hypertension, liver disease, dental caries, and obesity (Rose, 1982; Shur, 1982). These diseases are termed Western diseases because they have been related to diets that are characteristic of more economically developed countries. Western diets tend to be high in fat and sugar. The methods of preparation of foods also often include high levels of salt. Disease such as hypertension is epidemiologically related to salt intake.

Malnutrition from undernutrition is no longer a major health concern in Western cultures; instead, health professionals are dealing more with problems stemming from overnutrition and imbalance of nutrients, most often the fatty acids. Overnutrition and imbalance of nutrients is enhanced by the current trend of convenience and fast foods. Over half of our food today is synthetically processed. For example, for processing purposes, cereal and flour used for bread may be refined. The germ, bran, and other beneficial nutrients may be removed from these products and not replaced. Thus, the packaging and time needed for preparation of the food may result in an increased convenience for the consumer at the expense of important nutrients. As the public becomes more aware of this fact, consumers will hopefully take positive action to compensate for the deficiencies in prepackaged convenient foods.

Diet and Disease

In the United States, five of the ten leading causes of death are associated with dietary factors. Together coronary heart disease, cancer, stroke, diabetes, and coronary artery disease account for an estimated 65 percent of all deaths (Corwin, Sargent, Rheaume, & Saunders, 1999). The significance of a discussion of diet to the field of health psychology is particularly relevant because changing the way we eat is a behavior that is within the average person's power to control. The behavioral choices of people and how this affects health are of primary importance to health psychologists. The way that we eat has consequences for the onset of various diseases, as shown in Figure 2.1.

When discussing disease, it is possible to trace the epidemiology of the disease, which necessitates a biological description. For the previously mentioned Western diseases the etiology can often be traced to the biology of dietary composition. In addition to this, however, the what, why, and how of eating also involve psychological and social factors (recall the significance of the biopsychosocial model to health psychology).

Although there are several examples of Western disease related to diet, for purposes of highlighting the diet/disease relationship, we look specifically at three major diseases: cancer, diabetes, and cardiovascular disease.

Cancer

As a result of the collaboration of the American Institute for Cancer Research and the World Cancer Research Fund, a major international report entitled ***Food, Nutrition, and the Prevention of Cancer: A Global Perspective*** was written (American Institute for Can-

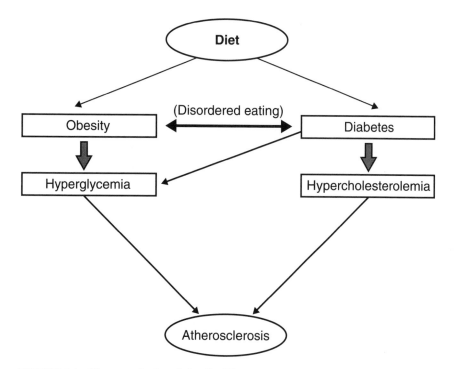

FIGURE 2.1   The complexity of the diet/disease relationship, including disordered eating.

cer Research, 1999). The report is the result of the review of more than 4,500 research studies and its production involved the participation of more then 120 contributors and peer reviewers. The report, which contains more than 600 pages, was published in September 1997 and examines the relationship between diet and eighteen specific cancers. The report provides new dietary guidelines for cancer prevention and offers public policy recommendations to help make cancer prevention an achievable goal (see Table 2.1 on page 20).

Two major statements underscored in the report are that (1) tragic numbers of cancer deaths can be lowered significantly and (2) cancer is a preventable disease. The report reiterates that our dietary choices play a central role in helping protect us against cancer. The foods we choose can also play a significant role in fighting cancer. It is known that the vitamins, minerals, fats, fiber, and phytochemicals associated with various foods can affect health and longevity.

Diet has been estimated to contribute to approximately 35 percent of all cancer incidences. Sorensen and colleagues (Sorensen, Stoddard, & Macario, 1998) cite that in more than 200 case control and cohort studies, persons consuming higher amounts of vegetables and fruits, or having higher blood levels of carotenoids, were less prone to develop various cancers. Included in this are cancers of the stomach, lung, and colon. For colorectal cancer, not all studies demonstrate a significant impact of increased dietary fiber on reducing the incidence of colorectal cancer (Fuchs et al. 1999). Studies have also indicated that increased

TABLE 2.1   Synopsis of Dietary Guidelines for Cancer Prevention from the International Report, *Food, Nutrition, and the Prevention of Cancer: A Global Perspective*

Choose predominantly plant-based diets

Avoid being underweight or overweight and limit weight gain during adulthood

Exercise

Eat 400 to 800 grams/day, or five or more portions/day, of a variety of vegetables and fruits all year

Eat 600 to 800 grams/day, or more than seven portions/day, of a variety of cereals, pulses, roots, tubers, and plaintains

Limit processed foods and limit consumption of refined sugar

Alcohol consumption is not recommended

Limit intake of red meat to less than 80 grams daily

Limit consumption of fatty foods

Limit consumption of salted foods

Avoid consumption of foods not stored at the proper temperature and prone to contamination

Do not eat charred food (avoid burning of meat juices)

consumption of vegetable and fruits is related to lower incidence of cancers of the oral cavity, larynx, pancreas, bladder, cervix, and breast.

Food, Nutrition, and the Prevention of Cancer: A Global Perspective is regarded as the best currently available advice on dietary actions to lower cancer risk. The report advises, among other statements, that consumers should choose predominantly plant–based diets rich in a variety of vegetables and fruits and minimally processed starchy **staple foods** to protect against diseases such as certain types of strokes and cancer. Staple foods are those that are at the center of an individual's or group's traditional diet and thus are a part of most meals. Staple foods are culturally derived, often supplemented with other foods to make a meal, and are difficult to replace in the typical person's diet. Staple foods have typically been a part of the individual's daily meals for so long that the average person would find it emotionally and physically dissatisfying to replace the staple food in the diet. Vegetables and fruits are sources of nutrients such as beta-carotene, vitamins C and E, folic acid, several minerals, and sources of other compounds such as fiber. All of these are believed to have a protective effect against cancer. Specifically, health sources recommend five or more portions a day of a variety of vegetables and fruits all year round. Unfortunately, though, it has been revealed that only 20 to 30 percent of U.S. residents consume the recommended five or more servings per day (Sorensen et al., 1998). This can likely be the case even when persons have knowledge of the recommended daily requirement and when they have knowledge of the diet and disease relationship (Laforge, Greene, & Prochaska, 1994). This is one behavioral phenomenon that health psychologists are particularly interested in addressing.

Diabetes

Diabetes mellitus is a complex chronic disorder of metabolism due either to a partial or a total lack of insulin secretion by the pancreas or an inability of insulin to function normally in the body. This produces abnormal levels of glucose in the blood. Treatment for diabetes depends on the severity of the disease; mild cases may be managed through diet alone, whereas more severe forms may require oral anti-diabetics or insulin injections. Not only is there a distinction between the insulin-dependent versus insulin-independent diabetic, but also some diabetics are overweight and others extremely lean. There is a difference in energy requirements for obese versus lean diabetics. For the overweight diabetic patient, dietary management's purpose is weight reduction. Weight reduction and maintenance at the new low weight leads to a reduction in elevated blood pressure levels, plasma cholesterol, and triglyceride (a compound consisting of a fatty acid and glycerol that is the principal lipid in the blood).

Hypercholesterolemia (elevated cholesterol levels in the blood) occurs more commonly in the diabetic than in the general population. The explanation for this has been linked to the low-carbohydrate, high-fat diet traditionally prescribed for diabetics (Chait & Bierman, 1982). Hypercholesterolemia, hypertension, and elevated triglyceride levels are all **atherosclerosis** (loss of elasticity in the wall of a blood vessel, leading to cardiovascular abnormality) risk factors. Atherosclerotic complications are the major cause of morbidity and mortality in diabetics of all types. When addressing the diabetic patient's condition, attention should be paid to the prevention of atherosclerotic complications through weight reduction and diet modification. Weight reduction and maintenance of a new steady state weight leads to a reduced likelihood of atherosclerosis. Also, in some cases it is particularly important for the lean diabetic to have appropriate caloric intake in his or her diet.

Although somewhat controversial and not completely recognized worldwide, some researchers advocate the use of a high-carbohydrate, low-fat diet for diabetics to reduce the onset of atherosclerosis (Chait & Bierman, 1982). This newer proposed diet has been advocated due to the complications from high-fat diabetic diets. It is believed that such a regimen can improve glucose tolerance and produce an increased insulin sensitivity. An increase in carbohydrate intake to recommended levels appears to be beneficial to blood glucose homeostasis. Chait and Bierman (1982) reported that plasma cholesterol levels were lower in diabetics on the low-fat, high-carbohydrate diet.

Hyperglycemia, elevated blood glucose found in diabetics, is commonly associated with coronary heart disease. Thus diabetics also have a high incidence of cardiovascular problems.

Cardiovascular Disease

Cardiovascular diseases typically involve the consideration of four behavioral areas: (1) the food and drink we consume, (2) the air we breathe, (3) how much exercise we get, and (4) how we cope with stress. Our food structure and eating habits, however, are fundamental to the development of epidemics such as coronary heart disease. Epidemiologists discuss the fact that a healthy habitual diet beneficially affects the incidence of coronary heart disease even under conditions of smoking, no exercise, stress, diabetes, and hypertension. It has been found that smoking combined with an unhealthy diet increases the risk of developing coronary heart disease (Rose, 1982).

When the diet consists of a high consumption of dairy products there is also associated coronary heart disease. Results of experimental studies have also suggested that dairy products are causal in the onset of coronary heart disease. These studies have used primate subjects and an experimental manipulation of their diets. High dairy diets in these studies resulted in elevated blood cholesterol and pathology of the coronary arteries (Rose, 1982). It is important to note, however, that provided the habitual high dairy diet has not produced advanced lesions, regression is possible through a change in diet.

Trans fatty acids (building blocks of lipids) are naturally present at low levels in meat and dairy products. This is a result of bacterial fermentation and ruminant animals. However, in addition to this, trans fatty acids are also formed during the process of **hydrogenation** of oil. This is a process used to transform oil from a liquid to a semisolid or solid state (i.e., the creation of stick margarine or butter). Currently, it is recommended that the public use vegetable oils in their natural state (liquid form) and after minimal hydrogenation. The reason for this is that soybean oil or semi-liquid margarine results in the most favorable total and low density lipoprotein cholesterol ("bad" cholesterol) levels and ratios of total cholesterol to high density lipoprotein cholesterol (Lichtenstein, Ausman, Jalbert, & Schaefer, 1999). It is recommended to the general public as well as to those with hypercholesterolemia to use liquid forms of vegetable oil and products made from this oil, as opposed to consuming the stick versions, which include sticks of butter and more solid forms of tub margarine. "Bad cholesterol" (low density lipoprotein) levels increase with consumption of hydrogenated oil. In addition to the previously mentioned dietary links to cardiovascular disease, there is also cogent reason for increasing dietary fiber due to its protective influence against coronary heart disease.

There is a great need for the dissemination of this dietary information on a wide scale. It is also important to begin such educational outreach early in life, since nutritional risk factors and dietary practices often develop early in childhood and adolescence (Corwin et al., 1999). Children and adolescents often consume diets high in saturated fat and cholesterol and exercise infrequently. These factors lead to health problems such as obesity, hypertension, coronary heart disease, elevated blood cholesterol, atherosclerosis, and diabetes.

Food Habits

In the previous section on diet and disease, it was necessary to discuss the link between diet and disease using a biomedical approach incorporating several medical terms. However, recall from Chapter 1 that this is not the sole focus of the field of health psychology. Thus we must consider psychological and sociocultural factors that impact the dietary behaviors of persons and groups that may lead to the development of disease. Specifically, in a multicultural discussion of diet and health, we can highlight the significance of psychological and sociocultural factors by studying the food habits of various ethnic groups.

The previous discussion of the link between diet and disease reveals that the consequences of food consumption are biological. Our individual biological functioning is in part affected by the foods we consume over the course of our lifetime. The big picture of food intake, however, includes studying what specifically people eat; how they eat; when, where, and how much they eat. When we study the big picture, we find that the what, how, when, where, and quantity of food consumption is influenced by psychological, socioeconomic, and cultural factors. A major sociocultural concept related to food consumption is **food habits**. Food habits refer to the way in which individuals or groups of individuals respond to both physical and sociocultural situations and select, consume, and utilize portions of the available food supply. Food habits are cultural. Food habits result from a combination of what nutrients people can get from their environment and foods people have learned to eat from their ancestors.

Ethnic groups can be defined as (1) members sharing fundamental cultural values and norms that differ from other groups, (2) members communicating and interacting together to reaffirm their ethnic identity, and (3) members and others commonly recognizing the group as distinguishable from other groups (Sanjur, 1995). The food habits of most ethnic groups, like many other cultural habits, are commonly resistant to significant change. In addition, food consumption often has interpersonal/social significance through its linkage to family functions. When changes in the food habits of ethnic groups do occur, it is often due to acculturation and/or assimilation. Let us now turn to a discussion of the origins and general dietary composition of various ethnic groups.

Food Habits Across Ethnic Groups

In Chapter 1 the term *ethnocentrism* was mentioned as an attitude to be avoided by health professionals when assessing and treating ethnic minorities. In addition to avoiding ethnocentrism, it is important to avoid stereotyping in a discussion of the food habits of ethnic groups. Therefore, the following sections are descriptions of **core foods** that generally are a part of the diets of many of a group's members. Core foods refer to foods that are universal, regular, staple, important, and rather consistently used. It should not be assumed that every member of the ethnic groups discussed in the following sections would consume all or any of the foods described. Just as all members of various ethnic groups do not all think, behave, and express emotions in the same manner, the same is true of the behavior of food intake. The information from the following sections on food habits of various ethnic groups was primarily developed from Sanjur (1995), Shur (1982), and Kiple and Himmelsteib (1982).

African Americans

Food habits are cultural and have historical significance. African Americans can predominantly trace their origin to West Africa. In studying the present diets of some African Americans, we see the influence of the precolonial days in West Africa, as well as the influence from the slavery period in the United States. Physicians and healers during precolonial West

Africa dealt with a heavily malnourished population. The diet was high in starches and low in protein. This is attributed to the fact that much of the cattle was diseased (insects contaminated them by biting them) and died. This made the likelihood of cattle farming slim and resulted in low-protein diets. There tended to be no supplements to the core of the starchy West African diet. This can be attributed to the customs. Few fruits and vegetables were eaten, eggs were not beaten, and there was virtually no consumption of dairy products.

Stimulation of dietary variety during precolonial West Africa was attributed to the consumption of cassava (manioc) and maize imported from America. This still reflected a high-carbohydrate, low-protein diet. The serious protein deficiency was exacerbated by the high acidic character of many of the soils of precolonial West Africa. This, along with the nitrogen deficiency of the soil, resulted in a reduced protein yield of the vegetable crop. Heavy rains also caused a low mineral content. The diets of West Africans were deficient in most of the B complex vitamins, vitamin C, calcium, and iron.

Further evidence for West African undernourishment is demonstrated by a comparison of the heights of slaves in the United States versus Creole-born slaves in the Caribbean. The newly arrived slaves from West Africa were significantly shorter than the slaves that were born on the islands. This was related to the poor diet of the slaves transported from West Africa.

One of the clearest residual influences of the precolonial West African diet is the high prevalence of lactose intolerance in modern-day African Americans. Seventy to 80 percent of the adult black population is lactose intolerant as opposed to 5 to 19 percent of whites (Kiple & Himmelsteib, 1982). How does this modern-day occurrence relate to the precolonial West African diet? Recall that in West Africa the diet was deficient not only in protein, but also in dairy products. When low levels of calcium were consumed in West Africa, the abundance of sunlight in the region allowed for the metabolism of the low levels of calcium consumed. However, when slaves were transported to America there was a reduction in exposure to year-round abundant sunshine, yet the diets were richer in calcium. Although the diet became richer in calcium, due to their past, the slaves had not developed the enzyme to break down the sugar known as lactose that is found in milk. This caused them to be unable to consume much milk. **Lactose intolerance** means there is an inability to digest milk and other dairy products. The level of the lactase enzyme that metabolizes lactose into absorbable sugars decreases. An individual with lactose intolerance who persists in drinking milk or consuming other dairy products experiences abdominal cramps, bloating, and diarrhea.

In summary then, slaves consumed very little milk, first because the South produced little of it, and second because they could not drink it. Ingestion of as little as one eight-ounce glass of milk will trigger symptoms in the lactose intolerant. So even where milk was available consumption was probably limited to a daily dollop in their coffee. For children, milk was sometimes available, but on a seasonal basis only. Thus, in the words of one student of southern foods, "although the food habits of whites and slaves were similar in many respects, one of the greatest differences was in the amount of dairy products consumed."

(Kiple & Himmelsteib, 1982, pp. 84–85. Reprinted with permission of Cambridge University Press.)

This example of lactose intolerance is a clear example of the way history and sociocultural factors relate to current diet. Without even knowing the food history, many African Americans may presently consume very few milk products to avoid the unpleasant biological manifestation of their dietary origins.

Whether presently residing in an urban or a rural area, many African Americans know the meaning of the term **"soul food."** Soul food is used to refer to the foods that blacks have enjoyed for years that are reminiscent of the big Sunday dinner of the former slave family. Where did this dietary pattern of eating stem from? There were two groups of slaves: field workers and house slaves. After working in the fields all day, field slaves wished to make a large quantity of food with little effort. This led to the combinations of big pots of stew, dried beans and peas, and greens of all types including collards, turnips, and kale. House slaves frequently cooked and ate the same foods that were served to Southern whites. A typical menu of that time would have been:

Southern fried chicken-Baked ham-Stewed beef
Steamed rice-Baked macaroni and cheese-Candied sweet potatoes
Fresh string beans-English (green) peas-Garden butter beans
Potato salad-Sliced tomatoes
Hot rolls-Light bread
Sweet potato pie-Fried pies-Pound cake (Shur, 1982)

Historically in the foods of slaves, and presently in modern-day soul food meals, spices, pepper, bay leaves, garlic, hot sauces, smoked bacon, salt pork, ham hocks, and neck bones are used to make ordinary foods more flavorful. For slaves this was done because they often cooked and ate what food was made available to them, and they often had to be ingenious to make the food tasty. Today this method of seasoning foods by some African Americans is a result of indirect social influence. In other words, as a result of the culinary rules of the culture handed down from generation to generation, this method of preparing foods exists and will likely remain for generations to come.

Pork is a common item in many soul food meals. The use of this particular meat also has historical relevance. Planters, large and small, across the pre–Civil War south consistently claimed that they issued an average of about three pounds of pork clear of bone per week per working slave. Slaves were not typically given beef. Slave owners believed that hog was the only proper meat for laborers. They also believed that fat bacon and pork were the most nourishing of all foods for the slaves. Pork, particularly if it is not lean meat, is high in fat. Slave owners believed that fatty articles of diet were appropriate because of their heat producing properties and contribution to more efficient labor. Today, pork high in fat is not a food of choice for many health-conscious persons. The belief of the slave owners that pork was the most appropriate food based on fat content is contrary to recommendations from health professionals to consume low-fat, low-salt foods.

Soul food with its regional variations is still considered economical, tasty, nourishing, rich, and filling food. However, the content and primary methods of preparation do not produce the healthiest of diets because soul food is relatively high in fat, salt, and sugar and can unfortunately be linked to a high incidence of hypertension, diabetes, and obesity in African Americans.

As mentioned previously, food habits are relatively stable and culturally learned, making change difficult. This is information that professionals attempting to influence dietary change should be aware of. For example, research studying African American women has revealed that black students indicate food preferences that are not significantly different from those of black mothers and grandmothers, although different from white students (Dacosta & Wilson, 1996). For many, the food preferences of young black women still reflect the preferences of their parents and grandparents.

Hispanics

Hispanic Americans come from many different backgrounds. Sanjur (1995) generally describes Hispanics as those who share a Spanish language heritage and trace their roots to the Spanish-speaking countries of Central and South America, Puerto Rico, the Dominican Republic, Cuba, and Mexico. Hispanic and Latino are the two most preferred descriptive terms by members of this group. Hispanic Americans of Mexican descent constitute the largest group living in the United States. For purposes of discussing food habits of Hispanic Americans, this section will discuss persons from Mexico, Puerto Rico, Dominican Republic, Panama, El Salvador, and Cuba. By virtue of the various nationalities listed above, it is apparent that Hispanic Americans refer to a large group of ethnically diverse persons. The precise point of entry into the United States for Hispanic migrants has a large and significant influence on present-day geographic location in the United States, as well as on some behavioral practices including diet.

Regarding Mexican Americans, the foods and methods of cooking vary. There are main ingredients, however, that seem to be found in all regions of the country. These ingredients are corn, beans, wheat, and different versions of chilies. Foods such as corn and beans have historically been a part of the Mexican diet; however, following the conquest of Mexico by the Spaniards, wheat was introduced into the country. People in the northern area of Mexico adopted the use of wheat. Other traditional components of the Mexican diet include foods such as squash, hot peppers, tomatoes, and onions. Sanjur (1995) cites a nationwide study of the Mexican diet that found that in general there were high levels of animal protein and low levels of vegetables and fruits in the northern region of the country. In southern Mexico, intakes of animal protein have been low throughout history. In the south, vegetarian diets were more common, and there was a greater consumption of corn, beans, and some vegetables such as squash, *nopales*, *quelites*, and potatoes. The southern diets were deficient in vitamins and minerals as well as protein. The diet of Mexico is often discussed based on rural diet versus urban diet and northern region versus southern region. Some persons may display a transitional diet, which is a rural diet transitioning to urban. The diets of residents of northern Mexico tend to be more urban. Urban diets substitute wheat for corn and animal products for beans. The modernization or urbanization (social factors) of diet in Mexican migrants results in an increased level of being overweight. Particularly, when studies have been done of dietary patterns in northern Mexico, the most important dietary change of the region has been an increased consumption of processed foods due to modernization and urbanization. Mexican Americans may retain traditional food habits of either the north or south of Mexico; however, with increased time in a different culture such as urban versus rural, there is often a change in diet due to acculturative factors. There is a high prevalence of being overweight and of diabetes in Mexican Americans and Puerto Ricans. Dietary factors are often linked to this prevalence.

Sanjur (1995) reports that the Puerto Rican Nutrition Committee found several decades ago that the basic dietary pattern of Puerto Ricans included rice, beans, starchy tubers, dried codfish, sugar, lard, and coffee across all economic levels. Historically, Puerto Rican food habits are largely a result of the influence of three major ethnic groups who resided on the island of Puerto Rico before and after the "discovery of America." These groups were the Taino Indians, the Spaniards, and the Africans. These groups also naturally influenced the methods of preparation of foods by Puerto Ricans.

Puerto Ricans and Mexican Americans prefer high-fat meats, and frying is a popular method of cooking. It has been shown that the mean fat intake from thirteen food items was higher in Puerto Rican respondents versus Central and South American respondents (Polednak, 1997). Whole milk has been identified as a major contributor to higher fat intake among Hispanic adults in the northeastern United States. There are strengths to the traditional basic Puerto Rican diet (high complex carbohydrates); however, the food habits generally are lacking in consumption of leafy green vegetables. The combination of rice and beans is a complementary staple of the Puerto Rican diet and is a good source of quality protein. To implement change for the better in this diet, there would need to be a focus on supplementing the high complex carbohydrate consumption with additional nutrients.

Dominicans and Puerto Ricans in the United States migrated from islands only 60 miles apart. Therefore, there are commonalities in the diets, but also differences. This once again shows the historical and geographic influence on present dietary behavior. Sanjur (1995) cites a study of Dominican women in the United States done in the mid 1980s that revealed the following daily food intake percentages: 80 percent milk, 83 percent rice, 60 percent juices, 53 percent plantains, 36 percent beef or chicken, and 80 percent beans. The high percentages of rice, milk, and beans indicate the stability in traditional food habits even following migration.

The Panamanian diet includes rice, oil, sugar, bread (replacing traditional tortillas), evaporated milk, beef, and eggs. It has been reported that with the exception of oranges, fruits and vegetables are significantly lacking in the list of foods consumed. Considering the recommendations for increased fruit and vegetable consumption to lower cancer risk, this is an area to be addressed with this population.

Malnutrition has been cited as significant in Salvadoran diets (Sanjur, 1995). This is due to a lack of protein, general calories, iron, and vitamin A. The basic Salvadorian diet is composed of corn (tortillas) and beans as staple foods. The rural diet typically consists of corn, beans, and sugar; urban diets are more likely to consist of meat and *pupusas* (tortillas stuffed with cheese or meat and cheese). As mentioned earlier regarding Mexican diets, Salvadoran cooking conditions and foods vary greatly from rural to urban environments; this is typically a social factor that affects food intake for all people.

Cubans have the highest socioeconomic ranking among U.S. Hispanics. As is frequently mentioned in the social science literature, economics is a major factor related to lifestyle. Cubans, due to their higher socioeconomic standing relative to other Hispanics, have been able to migrate to the United States and establish successful businesses. In southern Florida (Miami), for example, Cubans own more than 400 restaurants, which helps to preserve their traditional Cuban food habits. Compared with other Hispanics, Cubans in the

United States have maintained their culture extremely well and have held onto their traditional dietary patterns (Sanjur, 1995; Shorris, 1992). Foods largely consumed by Cubans have been reported as the following: eggs, bread, rice, chickpeas, sugar, lard, oil, and crackers. Eggs and fish are the main sources of protein. Seafood, fruit juices, canned fruit, and corn are rarely eaten.

Asians

Asians in the United States, just as Hispanics, represent individuals of various countries of origin. Food habits of the Chinese, Japanese, Vietnamese, and Filipinos will be discussed.

Cuisine refers to specific dishes and how they are prepared, as well as the culinary rules about the ordering of dishes within a meal (Rozin, 1996). The cuisine of the traditional Chinese diet consists of a brief cooking time, boiled foods, and foods stir-fried in a small amount of hot fat. The style of cooking may be Szechuan, Mandarin, Shanghai, or Cantonese. As with other groups, acculturation plays a role in food choice with some traditional items such as rice, *dim sum*, tofu, and Chinese tea remaining in the diet. It is interesting to note the strong influence of acculturation that results in a dietary change even when the traditional foods are available. Particularly for the Chinese in the United States, this is evident since U.S. major cities possess several to many Chinese restaurants and groceries so that maintenance of traditional food habits is possible if desired.

Rose (1982) describes the Japanese as a modern, industrialized, stressed, heavily smoking, and exceptionally hypertensive society. Although this may be true, the Japanese are well nourished and have an attractive diet that relates to low levels of coronary heart disease. Typically, the Japanese have low (normal) blood cholesterol concentrations. This has been associated with a diet that is abundant in a variety of seafood, little meat or dairy produce, high consumption of cereals (rice mainly), legumes, and other vegetables. The diet is also low in fat with the exception of polyunsaturated soya bean oil. Studies of the diets of Japanese Americans, however, reveal the negative consequences of acculturation. Specifically, Shur (1982) cites dietary differences for Japanese in the United States versus in Japan, and studies have also shown a significant difference in weight for those in Japan versus the United States. Japanese Americans tend to weigh 15 lbs. more than their counterparts who reside in Japan. The acculturative process across generations may also produce a change in attitude toward food and other traditions.

The acculturative process is also an issue when observing Vietnamese and Filipinos in the United States. The nutrient intake for the Vietnamese in the United States is affected by age, which often reflects generational differences attributed to acculturation (Shur, 1982). Generally, the Vietnamese diet is high in carbohydrates. The Vietnamese diet in the United States typically consists of traditional food patterns mixed with American foods.

Studies of the Filipino diet have primarily revealed frying, sautéing, and boiling as the most common cooking methods. Acculturative effects are evident in studies that found that the daily caloric intake was higher for Filipinos in Los Angeles compared to those in the Philippines. The Filipino Americans' diets contain twice as many calories that come from protein and three times as many calories from fat. Further exacerbating this acculturative effect, studies have revealed that traditional Filipino beliefs value fatness and "just eating" without regard for being thin. Filipino women in Canada mentioned maximizing disease resistance, but they did not necessarily possess a desire for thinness or for avoiding high consumption of fat, rice, and junk food (Farrales & Chapman, 1999). Instead, the study found that the traditional culture of Filipino women associates a thin body/person with sickness and an unappealing appearance.

The Psychology of Food Choice

Rozin (1996) states that humans are biologically able to ingest a wide variety of potential foods. We also have biological predispositions to avoid or be suspicious of new foods and potentially toxic foods. In addition, there is a somewhat innate tendency to prefer sweet and fatty tasting foods, yet dislike bitter and irritating foods. Biology, however, is not the sole influence on food choice. As the previous discussion of various ethnic groups revealed, our social experiences also determine food choice. Most of our beliefs and attitudes derive from socially transmitted information that includes the ethnic group we belong to as well as the geographic location in which we live. The social influence deeply ingrained in one's life course may make changing unhealthy eating particularly challenging.

Furst and colleagues (Furst, Connors, Bisogni, Sobal, & Falk, 1996) define the **life course** as the personal roles and the social, cultural and physical environments to which a person has been and is exposed. The life course provides an orientation for food choices through past, present, and future roles and experiences. It is the underlying source of many factors that shape food choice. For example, if a Puerto Rican female is presently in her mid 50s, single, a mother of four, working two jobs making minimum wage, from a working class family of eight, and from a rural area, the life course of this woman includes all of this information. The life course involves how all of this in combination relates to her past, present, and future dietary behavior. For any individual, it is possible to obtain facts about the person's life, and begin the process of assessing (1) why the present food habits exist, (2) what barriers to change may exist, and (3) the best intervention for change.

Regarding diet, you read how the life course impacts food choice for various ethnic groups. However, food choice involves not only the life course but also a series of influences that are a part of the life course. This includes the various personal systems such as how food is sensed and perceived by the individual, how much one can spend on food, and what is convenient to prepare (Furst et al., 1996). Figure 2.2 shows some likely considerations that are a part of making a typical food selection.

Consider for a moment that the daily food choices you make (meals, snacks, and junk food) are affected by a multitude of factors. How and what you eat would be significantly different if you lived during a different century, originated from a different nation, were of a different ethnicity, and were reared around persons very different from your present family.

It has been mentioned that changing poor eating habits is not an easy task. This has been demonstrated by studies that have identified the multitude of barriers to change. The difficulty of changing eating habits may be of a personal and social nature, or it may be of a more cognitive nature.

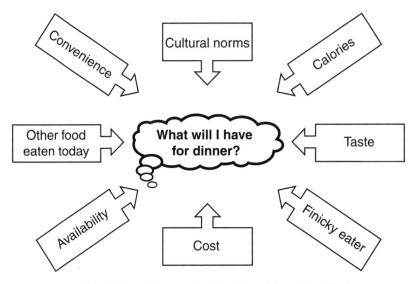

FIGURE 2.2   Complexity of factors involved in making a food choice.

Personal and Social Barriers

Often when persons do not consume the recommended levels of fruits and vegetables, there are a number of factors preventing this from occurring (Uetrecht & Greenberg, 1999). Barriers specific to fruit and vegetable use may include factors such as time, taste, ability to choose nutritious foods, family influence, difficulty changing habits, and low income (Ahluwalia, Dodds, & Baligh, 1998). The availability of foods in the physical environment is also important. Particularly for low income persons in the urban United States (still a disproportionate number of whom are ethnic minorities), access to quality produce may be limited. Supermarkets and grocery chains in higher socioeconomic areas may sell produce that is of substantially better quality than in less affluent communities. Unfortunately, this reflects the still-pervasive existence of discriminatory behavior. Those of power and influence in the retail sector need to take additional responsibility or be held accountable for the quality of goods sold in the stores. It has been found that low income and less educated persons have significantly more barriers to fruit and vegetable consumption. However, low income and less educated persons may still have high nutritional concerns. They are more likely to report that they do not make dietary changes due to the higher cost of foods perceived to be healthy (Dittus, Hiller, & Beerman, 1995).

When family influence is identified as a barrier to making dietary changes, this necessitates a discussion of social support. Social support has gained prominence due to its potentially protective influence on physical and psychological well being. Social support has been linked to a number of healthy behaviors, and it has been found to be significant for readiness to make dietary changes in a group of Hispanic and African American workers (Sorensen et al., 1998). Coworker support and household support were strongly related to readiness for dietary change. Programs for dietary change in minority individuals should especially emphasize social support. Recall from Chapter 1 that collectivism is common in minority groups such as Asians, African Americans, and Hispanics. Thus, individuals from these group are likely to benefit from having social support for dietary change. Individuals are less likely to eat healthy if their families consume a high quantity of unhealthy food during family get-togethers (typical of collectivist cultures). It is harder to adhere to a recommended healthy diet if the family uses social pressure to persuade another family member to eat unhealthy foods during a family reunion or a holiday dinner. Barriers to dietary change such as income, poor quality of produce, and lack of support are all examples of social barriers.

Cognitive Barriers

Cognitive barriers are also significant. Models such as the health belief model, the transtheoretical model, and also the food ideology system address the cognitive barriers to dietary change. The **health belief model** considers the attitude that an individual may have about the relationship between diet and disease, as well as the belief that the person has about his or her present dietary behavior (Strecher, Champion, & Rosenstock, 1997). The health belief model includes four beliefs or perceptions that, when combined, predict health-related behaviors. These are (1) the perceived susceptibility to disease, (2) the perceived severity of disease, (3) the perceived benefits of making the behavior change, and (4) the perceived barriers or costs associated with the behavioral change. Specifically, the individual's health beliefs can be a barrier to his or her dietary change if, for example, she or he does not believe that diet has a significant effect on the development of health complications. It has been found that some persons still report disbelief that fruits and vegetables have cancer-preventing attributes (Dittus et al., 1995). In this same study, subjects reported that they enjoyed their current diet, thought their current diet was good, and believed that there are too many dietary recommendations to reasonably expect compliance.

Self-efficacy, or the confidence in one's ability to change the behaviors, will also play a role. Self-efficacy has been found to be significant in a number of studies of dietary change (Corwin et al., 1999; Humphries & Krummel, 1999; Hyman & Ho, 1998). Self-efficacy affects the success of the dietary behavioral intervention, as well as the decision to engage in the behavior to change. Self-efficacy is what is being addressed in the **theory of planned behavior** (Ajzen, 1985). The theory of planned behavior considers the perception of how much control people feel that they have over their behavior. The more resources and opportunities people feel they have, the stronger is their belief that they can control their behavior. Factors that may affect perceived behavioral control regarding dietary change are low income (unable to afford healthier foods), difficulty in obtaining social support, and dependence on someone else who prepares the main meals (Furst et al., 1996).

The **transtheoretical model** addresses the cognitive barriers that affect a person's stage of readiness for changing his or her health damaging behaviors (Prochaska, DiClemente, Norcross, 1992). This model has been utilized when explaining dietary behavior (Glanz et al., 1994). It has been shown that persons in the stage called *precontemplation* (no intention of changing in the next six months) are highly resistant to change, and traditional health messages and action-oriented programs may be counterproductive for such

TABLE 2.2   **Stages of the Transtheoretical Model of Readiness for Change**

Stage 1 (Precontemplator):	One who has no intention of changing unhealthy behavior and may not even see that he or she has a problem.
Stage 2 (Contemplator):	One who has awareness of a problem and thoughts about changing behavior within the next six months, but the person has not yet made an effort to change.
Stage 3 (Preparation):	One who makes specific plans about change and is ready for action.
Stage 4 (Action):	One who has made overt changes in his or her behavior; behavior is modified during this stage.
Stage 5 (Maintenance):	One who is trying to sustain the changes made and trying to resist temptation to relapse.

persons (Laforge et al., 1994). Precontemplators are not likely to be positively affected by campaigns designed to prompt immediate compliance to the five-per-day health recommendations for fruit and vegetable consumption. For these individuals it would be more effective to discuss their experiences, hear their views, and educate them about the health benefits of dietary change. If you are presently an unhealthy eater, what stage of readiness are you in regarding making a change (see Table 2.2)?

The **food ideology system** is generally used to refer to the attitudes of an individual regarding general food consumption and attitudes regarding specific foods. An example of this would be if an individual regarded food as mainly for enjoyment (taste) and not nutrition or health. Someone who has this ideology (e.g., taste is most important) would not be attentive to healthy eating campaigns. Most people would agree that although fattening foods are the least healthy, they are also often the most tasty. For the person with a food ideology that centers on taste, it will not matter if a food is unhealthy if it tastes good. Sometimes, unfortunately, the individual's food ideology system may actually lead to disordered eating and subsequent health complications.

Disordered Eating

Eating disorders are relevant to the present discussion of diet because the onset of disease as well as food ideology may result in the development of attitudes that lead to disordered eating patterns. For example, the dieting and the weight gain associated with diabetes treatments precipitates a deterioration in eating attitudes that leads to the development of disordered eating (Khan & Montgomery, 1996). Disordered eating may be caused by a combination of genetic, neurochemical, psychodevelopmental, sociocultural, and cognitive factors (Akan & Grilo, 1995; Becker, Grinspoon, Klibanski, & Herzog, 1999; Hirsch, 1997).

Eating disorders are more prevalent in industrialized societies than in nonindustrialized societies and occur in all socioeconomic classes and major ethnic groups in the United

States (Becker et al., 1999). This was not always believed to be true. Recent studies reveal that eating pathology occurs across a broader race distribution than was once believed (Ko & Cohen, 1998; le Grange, Stone, & Brownell, 1998). For members of ethnic groups in comparison to whites, it may be that the specific type of eating disorders may differ, and individual members of various ethnic groups may be differentially affected by factors such as acculturation. African American and Hispanic women have been found to show significantly lower incidence of the specific eating disorder known as anorexia nervosa, although they may have higher levels of **purging**, which is self-induced vomiting and laxative or diuretic abuse (le Grange et al., 1998). This could be due to guilt from excess eating rather than a desire to be thin. In the aforementioned study in which black and Hispanic women had the highest incidences of purging in comparison to whites and Asians, the data was based on survey responses from subscribers to *Consumer Reports* magazine. It is important to note that the subscribers to *Consumer Reports* may not have been a representative sample of women, and any racial and cultural differences may have been masked. The *Consumer Reports* women may have all been quite similar (all were experienced dieters); the women of color may have been more acculturated than what would be found in other populations of minority women.

The lower incidence of anorexia nervosa among black and Hispanic women is likely due to differences in cultural attitudes pertaining to ideal body weight for physical attractiveness. The differences in cultural attitudes about weight and dieting are significant for explaining the differences in motivation to be slender cross racially. It has been found that black women's self-esteem is least affected when their weight is at its highest compared to Asian and white women's self-esteem during their excessive weight periods (le Grange et al., 1998). This suggests that there may indeed be differences in attitudes about body size and self-concept for women of different racial backgrounds. It is positive that overweight black and Hispanic women do not allow their body size to lead to depression; however, it is not healthy for them to reach extremes in weight with no motivation to reduce their weight through healthier eating and exercising. Thus, while their mental hygiene may be healthy, their physical condition may be poor. The acceptance within their culture of the larger body weight can be detrimental to health.

For Asian women on the other hand, a cultural tradition exists that is health affirming. Asian women feel more strongly than others that exercise helps control stress in their lives and that they are less likely to overeat when they exercise regularly (le Grange et al., 1998). This is consistent with the Asian communities' history of emphasizing martial arts as a part of a daily ritual to enhance productivity and health.

When most people hear the words "eating disorder" they immediately think of disorders such as anorexia nervosa and bulimia. Often what many people fail to recognize is binge eating disorder (Halmi, 1995). Excessive eating, which is related to binge eating, is the most prevalent eating disorder in our society. Women of color, in particular, may show high levels of compulsive eating disorder or **binge eating disorder** (Davison, 1999). Binge eating disorder is defined as binging more than twice per week with loss of control during such episodes and no purging involved (Ford, 1999). Due to the highly stressful life circumstances of poverty, poor health, sexism, racial discrimination, and domestic violence for many women of color in America, food provides solace. Women of color often wear many hats and meet the needs of many others in their family, yet they may not receive true intimacy and affection from their significant others. A person who is deprived of physical intimacy and affection may turn to food as a source of gratification. Compulsive overeating may be a displacement behavior in which the motivation for affection and sexual gratification is achieved through the pleasure of eating. Without even being aware of it, many women are seeking companionship, comfort, reassurance, warmth, and well-being from food. This occurs because these can be hard to find in other areas of their lives, particularly for many women of color.

The problem is that the eating is unconscious, and the immediate gratification is only temporary. The eating is so repetitive that this can lead to health problems such as obesity. African American, Hispanic, and Native American women have high levels of obesity; the specific explanations for this are multiple (Kumanyika, 1995). An often-cited explanation is the cultural acceptance of larger body size among women of these groups who may be less westernized in their attitudes (Zerbe, 1993). When women of color are less westernized in their attitudes they seem to have protection against eating disorders such as anorexia and bulimia, but they may also have attitudes about being overweight that are less healthy. The accepting attitude about excess weight should not be reversed in these women to one of obsession about being thin; however, clients should be educated about the health benefits of losing weight. This has to be done in a way that is sensitive to the client's esteem. It should also include educating the client about realistic expectations for weight loss due to certain biological factors. A woman who presently overeats and is obese can be educated about improving her health and reducing her weight; however, she should also understand her present weight in relation to biology and **set point theory**.

Set point theory suggests that each person has an established body weight based on genetics and early feeding experiences. According to this theory, each person has a set point weight that is either high (heavy person), low (thin person), or average (Keesey, 1995; Leibowitz, 1995). Any extreme deviation from the set point weight by losing or gaining many pounds will cause the motivation for food intake and the whole body metabolism to change in favor of restoring the set point weight (Keesey, 1995). It is important for an obese person to understand this so that he or she can understand that his or her weight loss may be limited to a certain pound range based on an elevated regulatory set point weight. With knowledge and acceptance of this, the person who wants to lose weight may be less likely to resume disordered compulsive eating due to depression and frustration over their inability to lose extreme amounts of weight. There is a vast amount of literature available on disordered eating. Overall, measures of acculturation, self-esteem, societal influences, and cultural differences in acceptance of larger body size may be increasingly significant to the future study of eating disorders in diverse populations (Ogden & Thomas, 1999; Wilfley & Rodin, 1995).

Cultural Sensitivity in Treatment

Several issues arise in consideration of culture and dietary change. One such factor is the use of bilingual and bicultural professionals and recruiters when working with diverse groups of clients. Diet counselors who are familiar with the food habits of diverse groups or who are members of ethnic groups themselves may be particularly sensitive to customs, the need for social support, and the significance placed on maintaining certain customs. The

Spotlight on Biology: The Biology of Eating

Although there are psychological and sociocultural factors involved in our motivation to eat, the types of foods that we select and the quantity of foods that we eat also have biological influences. Researchers in the field of neurobiology have used integrative interdisciplinary approaches to obtain information about the various determinants of eating behavior, energy balance, and body weight. There are diverse signals involved in eating behavior, energy balance, and body weight. These signals include simple nutrients in the blood such as glucose, neurotransmitter molecules, neuropeptides, and hormones.

Common eating disorders such as anorexia nervosa and bulimia nervosa may have neurochemical links. Systems in the body and several areas of the brain are involved. The drugs most commonly used in the management of obesity, anorexia nervosa, and bulimia nervosa have their primary effect by modulating the balance between neurotransmitters such as serotonin, norepinephrine, and dopamine. Patients with anorexia, bulimia, stress-related eating, food cravings, and seasonal appetite disturbances may have altered levels of these neurotransmitters in their cerebrospinal fluid. An inability to gain weight or a loss of motivation to eat, as well excessive weight gain and overeating, can be linked to neurochemical activity as well as psychological and sociocultural factors.

Source: Leibowitz, 1995, pp. 3–7.

---

key would be to maintain a balance in being sensitive to cultural issues yet refraining from being tolerant of health-risky eating patterns. Most counselors dealing with multicultural populations will find it necessary to acknowledge their own personal beliefs, practices, and values that may conflict with their clients'. Cultural empathy is beneficial in working with multicultural populations. Researchers have revealed that members of ethnic minority groups negotiate among conflicting cultural beliefs about body size, food, and health (Farrales & Chapman, 1999). In working with diverse groups, it is important to set goals as in any dietary change program. The key is to do this in such a way that trust, rapport, and respect are a part of the process. Particularly when ethnic minority group members report large numbers of barriers, clients will need a specialized intervention that is more intense and one that acknowledges the cultural information received from the client in the interview. For example, if a client reports a general lack of support from family, some interventions may require training or role playing to assist the individual in managing high risk situations, such as holidays and other traditional celebrations (Vasquez, Millen, Bissett, Levenson, & Chipkin, 1998). Overall, learning, understanding, respecting, and acknowledging the cultural ways of ethnic minority clients is imperative if professionals are to successfully affect change in these groups.

Conclusion

Diet and eating patterns are a part of the field of health psychology because poor dietary habits are linked to major disease. It is important to understand that the onset of disease as a result of diet is preventable. In some instances, individuals need to be educated on the diet and disease relationship. In other cases, the knowledge of the relationship between diet and disease may already exist, but other social and cognitive factors within the individual may need to be addressed in order to change present behavior. There is a multitude of factors related to the food choice process. This necessitates that those working to change poor eating habits understand the significance of these factors in isolation and combined. Health professionals need to educate themselves on the backgrounds of ethnic minority clients so that they can better understand not just the biological effects of food intake, but also psychological and social factors that are involved.

Summary

A change in dietary trends over the last century has resulted in negative consequences for health. Presently, there is a greater prevalence of diseases know as Western diseases, which are diseases characteristic of economically developed countries. There is a significant diet and disease linkage. Leading causes of death such as cancer, diabetes, and cardiovascular diseases are often linked to diet. Diet is associated with five of the ten leading causes of death. Diet is regarded as being so significant to disease such as cancer that a major international report has been published that examines the relationship between diet and eighteen specific cancers. A discussion of food habits requires studying the origin of core foods in the diets of various ethnic groups. This also highlights major sociocultural factors in food intake. It is important to dissect the major contributing factors to the maintenance of poor eating habits. Often there are personal, social, or cognitive barriers preventing individuals from changing their eating habits. It is not uncommon for aspects of diet and disease to sometimes lead to disordered eating. Particularly, it has been revealed that eating pathology occurs across a broader race distribution than was once believed. This has implications for health professionals who work with diverse populations. Overall, learning, understanding, respecting, and acknowledging the cultural ways of ethnic minority clients are imperative if health professionals intend to successfully effect change in dietary behavior.

Student Interview

Age: 39
Gender: Female
Country of Origin: Dominican Republic
Years in the United States: 18

1. **What, if any, is the most significant change for you in your eating habits since living in the United States?**
   When I first came here, I suffered because I would not eat with my hands (i.e., no hamburgers (or french fries). I would have to wait until I could cook a meal; therefore, I would go a long time before eating. Slowly I began buying pastas and fruits from the supermarket. I was also a student then.

2. To what do you attribute this?

I was just accustomed to eating healthy and not fast foods. Fortunately, I did not pick up bad habits like eating junk food. Now I have my kids to think of and their eating. I guess a person's situation, such as having a family, has a large effect.

3. Do you have friendships here with others from your country? If you were to have a dinner with them what might the meal consist of?

Yes, I have friendships here with women from my country, but we are each married to Americans. We usually do not have Dominican food when we get together; we eat like tourists who visit this country.

4. What, if any, are poor eating habits of people of your region of your country?

Eating too much fat. The people there eat excessive food with oils, and they eat pork. However, people there do also eat rice, beans, and pasta, which is healthy. The fat that I prefer in my foods is olive oil, I won't touch anything else. People there also eat fish, grain, and fruits and vegetables, which is very healthy.

5. Are you often conscious of body image and what you are eating? In other words are you concerned about unhealthy eating that may lead to excess weight?

I am conscious of weight and body image, and what I'm eating. I'm fifteen pounds over my weight due to a sedentary life. I'm too busy to exercise right now.

6. How much do people (both men and women) in your country focus on body size, weight, and healthy food choices?

People are aware of body image, but they do not make dieting a part of their lives. In the Dominican Republic people live for dancing! That is a good form of exercise. They love music; taking away music is like taking away their souls.

7. Are desserts (sweets) a popular food choice in your country?

Yes, they love sweets, especially cake. Lots of rich cakes!

8. How often do you "eat out" versus stay home and cook?

I cook five days a week, not on the weekends. I put healthy food on the table during the week, and we go out and do family dining on the weekends.

9. Have you ever dieted to achieve a goal weight?

Once I did diet. My best friend in Italy was getting married (I was the maid of honor). I dieted to lose five pounds to fit a beautiful dress (designer) for the wedding. Overall, though, Dominicans are not into dieting.

10. What are the standards for physical beauty where you grew up?

Men don't like skinny women because they think that they look sickly. They like to feel a little flesh and not just bones. Many Dominican women are fashionable and beauty conscious, they must do their nails, hair, etc.

Key Concepts

atherosclerosis
binge eating disorder
core foods
cuisine
ethnic groups
food habits
food ideology system

Food, Nutrition, and the Prevention of Cancer: A Global Perspective
health belief model
hydrogenation
hypercholesterolemia
hyperglycemia
lactose intolerance
life course
purging
self-efficacy
set point theory
soul food
staple foods
theory of planned behavior
transtheoretical model
Western diseases

Study Questions

1. We live in an age of convenience. How has this negatively affected diet?
2. Dietary factors are associated with five of the ten leading causes of death. What have studies revealed about the link between diet and cancer, diabetes, and cardiovascular disease?
3. Why is the report from the American Cancer Institute and the World Cancer Research Fund regarded as such a significant publication?
4. Why is it said that unhealthy staple foods may be highly resistant to elimination from most people's diets?
5. Which of the following should you choose for general cooking purposes: (a) a stick of butter, (b) a tub of margarine, or (c) a bottle of soybean oil. Why?
6. What are food habits and how do food habits develop?
7. Why is the prevalence of lactose intolerance in African Americans a good example of historical, social, and biological factors combined?
8. What is meant by the life course influence on food consumption?
9. What is the difference between social and cognitive barriers to changing diet?
10. What are some issues to consider to ensure cultural sensitivity in treating health-risky eating habits in ethnic minority populations?

Student Activity

Visit at least two different grocery stores or markets that are located in different socioeconomic areas (e.g., suburban grocery vs. barrio market) of any metropolitan area. Write a short comparative essay presenting any differences you see in quantity, quality, and type of products offered.

OR

Rent from any local video store the movie "Soul Food" (20th Century Fox, 1997), which depicts the story of an African American family and shows interpersonal conflict within the family. How does the film demonstrate that conflict resolution and family bonding center around food preparation and consumption? (This film gives an accurate representation of the food content of large soul food meals discussed in this chapter.)

CHAPTER

3

Smoking and Health

Nicotine and the Committed Smoker

In the previous chapter you learned how the food choices that we make have a significant impact on health. This chapter will present the behavior of smoking and its deleterious effects on health. The previous chapter highlighted the multitude of factors that culminate in a final food choice; many of these factors stem from deeply ingrained food habits of the individual's culture. Smoking, as with diet, may also be influenced by a multitude of biological, psychological, and sociocultural factors. In many ways, however, smoking seems to impact behavior and subsequently health in a uniquely sinister manner. **Nicotine**, the poisonous alkaloid found in tobacco, does not have clean isolated effects that can be reliably found in all smokers, but instead it may produce varying effects depending on the dosage and the smoker. Nicotine provides pleasure to the addicted smoker, while simultaneously gradually impairing respiratory and cardiovascular systems. Also, the time of day that nicotine is administered may affect the stimulation of the release of stress-related hormones (Thakore, Berti, & Dinan, 1999).

Following repeated use, nicotine can cause the smoker to crave and obsess over it, even though the smoker may be aware of smoking's harmful effects. The **committed smoker** (a current smoker who has been smoking for at least ten years) craves over and obsesses about a cigarette. This places smoking for the committed smoker in the category of **addictive behavior**. Addictive behaviors are repetitive, often pleasurable behaviors associated with a loss of control and unpleasant effects when ceased. Those in favor of policy-led interventions have stated that addictive behaviors are the result of a complex interplay of processes, few of which may be under the sole control of the individual smoker (Marks, 1998). For typical addicted smokers who have experienced several unsuccessful attempts to quit, it is perhaps easy for these individuals to agree with the notion of having little control over the powerful effects of nicotine.

In some cases the onset of smoking may be attributed to a lack of education about the damage that can occur, but given the widespread public information pertaining to the harmful effects of smoking, lack of knowledge as an explanation may not be as probable as other explanations. The field of health psychology is concerned with the prevalence of smoking in society. Health psychologists are interested in discovering ways to prevent the numbers of new smokers and increasing the cessation rates for current smokers. Given the numbers of smokers old and new, this objective is not an easy one to meet.

Smoking Incidence

Smoking related diseases claim an estimated 430,700 lives each year. Included in this number are those indirectly affected by **environmental tobacco smoke (ETS)** and premature babies affected by prenatal maternal smoking. ETS is defined as secondhand smoke involuntarily inhaled by nonsmokers from other people's cigarettes. ETS has been linked to approximately 3,000 lung cancer deaths annually in U.S. nonsmokers. In addition to the relationship to lung cancer, high current and lifetime ETS in healthy nonsmoking young males has been found to be associated with significantly elevated blood pressure and heart rate relative to similar young men with minimal to no current or lifetime ETS exposure (Stoney, Lentino, & Emmons, 1998). These differences were shown at rest as well as during stress episodes.

The American Lung Association reports that direct smoking or first-hand smoking costs the United States approximately $97.2 billion each year in health care costs and lost productivity (American Lung Association, 1998). This is due to the fact that direct and indirect smoking exposure can be associated with physiologic changes that facilitate the progression of processes that result in increased atherosclerosis and illness behavior.

The link between smoking and cancer as well as the link between smoking and heart disease is commonly discussed. Specifically, there is information available that cigarettes contain at least 43 distinct cancer-causing chemicals and that smoking is directly responsible for 87 percent of lung cancer cases. Smoking has also been linked to most cases of emphysema and chronic bronchitis, and it is also a major culprit in coronary heart disease (CHD) and stroke (see Figure 3.1).

In particular, when stress is substantial for the smoker, there are increases in lipid levels and **fibrinogen** (Davis, 1999). Fibrinogen is protein that is found in the blood plasma; it is essential to the process of blood clotting. Increased lipid levels and fibrinogen can contribute to **thrombi** (blood clots attached to the interior wall of an artery or vein) development and increased CHD. In addition to cancer and CHD, nicotine may be causally related to malignancies in other parts of the body such as slow healing wounds, infertility, exacerbation of asthma, increased frequency of colds and ear infections, sudden infant death syndrome, and peptic ulcer disease.

Social psychologists, health psychologists, and physicians should be concerned not only about the numbers of current adult smokers, but also the prevalence of teens that begin smoking each year. It is estimated that at least 4 million U.S. teenagers smoke cigarettes, and 24.6 percent of high school seniors smoke daily. Cigarette manufacturers have successfully campaigned to target adolescent and teen smokers as evidenced by the fact that approximately 90 percent of smokers began smoking before the age of 21. Unfortunately, it has been shown that even low intensity smoking during younger years can have negative consequences, as this can lead to smoking at higher levels rather than returning to nonsmoking (Janson, 1999). It is important to acknowledge, however, that age of initiation to tobacco is not so important in and of itself as is the context in which early smoking takes place (Mott, Crowe, Richardson, & Flay, 1999).

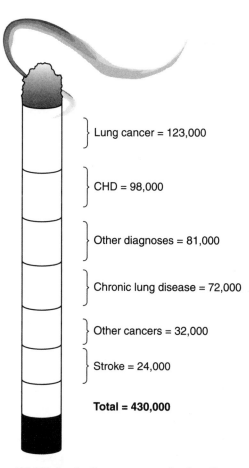

Lung cancer = 123,000

CHD = 98,000

Other diagnoses = 81,000

Chronic lung disease = 72,000

Other cancers = 32,000

Stroke = 24,000

Total = 430,000

FIGURE 3.1   Annually, 430,000 deaths from cancer and other diseases are attributable to cigarette smoking.

Source: Centers for Disease Control

Biopsychosocial Model and Smoking

As with all topics presented in this text, it is important to examine the biological, psychological, and sociocultural factors that contribute to the onset and maintenance of smoking. These factors can be specifically examined by focusing on issues such as genetics, brain activity, conditioning, cognition, social learning, and studies of smoking in underrepresented populations. Each of these issues should be considered in prevention and intervention efforts. Specifically with respect to studies of smoking in underrepresented populations, an increase in these studies and prevention efforts is greatly needed.

The American Lung Association (1998) reports that although smoking has declined among the white non-Hispanic population, tobacco companies have increased efforts to target both African Americans and Hispanics through intense merchandising. This is being done through billboards, the media of ethnic minority groups (i.e., magazines), and sponsorship of civic groups, athletic, cultural and entertainment events. The American Lung Association reports that the prevalence rates of smoking are highest among Native Americans/Alaskan Natives (36.2 percent), followed by African Americans (25.8 percent) and whites (25.6 percent), and lowest among Asians and Pacific Islanders (16.6 percent). It is not surprising that tobacco companies may wish to increase targeting efforts of Hispanic groups or Asian groups, since the smoking prevalence in these populations is less common than in non-Hispanic African Americans and whites. Differences across ethnic minority groups in smoking effects, smoking behavior, and even the brand of cigarette smoked can be attributed to a myriad of factors that can be genetic, psychological, or social (Kilbey, 1999; Klonoff & Landrine, 1999; Lafferty, Heaney, & Chen, 1999; Lerman et al., 1999).

Genetics and Smoking

The issue of genetics and smoking may well be an area where the general public has a lack of knowledge. Psychobiologists have studied the significance of neurotransmitter levels to the onset of various disorders such as schizophrenia and Parkinson's disease. A major excitatory neurotransmitter related to these disorders and other behaviors is **dopamine**. This chemical has also been discussed as a possible explanation for the genetic effects contributing to smoking.

Dopamine has been implicated in brain-stimulation reward research. The activity of dopamine within the **nucleus accumbens**, the brain's pleasure and reward center, seems to have the greatest influence on the rewarding properties of stimulation of the medial forebrain bundle of the brain. The pleasurable feeling from stimulation of this area results in repeated behaviors that are motivated by a desire to reexperience the satisfying release.

Previously, it was mentioned that nicotine is a powerful substance that produces a craving and obsession in the addicted smoker. The reinforcing properties of nicotine have been attributed to nicotine's effects on dopamine transmission. Nicotine has been shown to stimulate dopamine release and to inhibit dopamine from being reuptaken, resulting in an increase in the levels of available dopamine, and thus an increase in its pleasurable effects. **Reuptake** refers to the reabsorption of an excessive amount of a neurochemical. When there is an excessive amount of a neurochemical released into the junction between neurons, sometimes the excess is reabsorbed into the cell from which it was released. Since nicotine interferes with the reuptake of dopamine, dopamine is able to linger in the system longer and produce pleasurable effects in the committed smoker.

Lerman and colleagues (1999) report that genetic variation in the dopamine receptor gene (DRD2) and the dopamine transporter gene (SLC6A3) may influence concentrations of and responses to synaptic dopamine. This study also found that persons with a certain type of dopamine receptor gene were found to be more likely to exhibit compulsive and addictive behavior. The genotype related to compulsive and addictive behavior—DRD2-A1—is more common in African Americans (Lerman et al., 1999). This finding is significant when one considers the prevalence of committed smokers who are African American.

In contrast, the Lerman and colleagues (1999) study indicates that those with a genotype of SLC6A3-9 and higher levels of endogenous synaptic dopamine should have less need to use exogenous substances such as nicotine to stimulate dopamine transmission. These studies have revealed that those with SLC6A3-9 have a sufficient availability of dopamine and sufficient receptors for normal dopamine transmission that prevent the need for nicotine (Sabol et al., 1999).

Nicotinic acetylcholine receptors are the point of entry for nicotine into the central nervous system. These receptors moderate the kind and magnitude of nicotine's effects, which includes the pleasurable nicotinic dopaminergic effects (Pomerleau & Kardia, 1999). What all of this means is that for some smokers, their genotype will lead them to have a more difficult time quitting smoking. Research has also shown that having a variant of a particular gene may reduce the likelihood of developing nicotine addiction (U.S. Department of Health and Human Services, 1999).

For some smokers there is a genetically determined increased likelihood of addictiveness that is driven by the insufficient supply of dopamine naturally existing in their brain. This type of smoker will have less resistance to nicotine due to the increased biological need for dopamine. It is this type of smoker that would benefit most from smoking interventions such as pharmacologic therapy.

Brain Activity and Smoking

As highlighted in the previous section, brain stimulation reward effects can be related to genetics when discussing nicotine's effects. Another separate and fascinating aspect of nicotine's effects is that drug-related cues can act as incentives to promote drug use. This happens as a result of brain reward systems being activated or primed, leading to increased arousal and activity, pleasure, and a heightened tendency to pursue reinforcing stimuli such as addictive drugs. What does this mean for the smoker attempting to abstain? Smokers who are in the process of abstaining from smoking are experiencing greater asymmetry (differences in hemispheric activity) of the left and right sides of the brain. Research results have revealed that smoking—and even preparing to smoke, being around smokers, or exposure to other smoke related cues—will have reliable effects on EEG asymmetry (Zinser, Fiore, & Davidson, 1999). Asymmetry in the brain is related to approach versus withdrawal motivational states. Asymmetry (greater left hemisphere activity) in the brain is increased when smokers are craving a cigarette or exposed to smoking cues. The onset of smoking results in a reduction in the asymmetry in the brain. Smoking, or exposure to smoke, results in more balanced hemispheric activity for those who are addicted but have been newly abstaining.

The arousal of the brain as reflected by the EEG suggests that nicotine produces arousal that is similar to normal sensory stimulation (Krogh, 1991). The arousal effects of nicotine, which mimic normal sensory arousal, are different from the arousal effects produced by other substances such as caffeine or amphetamines. In addition, Krogh (1991) reports that nicotine is achieving much of its alerting effect on the brain because of its action on the **reticular system (RTS)**, which are cells affecting arousal found in the brainstem.

Cells in the RTS respond to nicotine via nicotinic receptors. These cells respond to nicotine as well as they would to the body's own neurotransmitter, **acetylcholine.** So, in fact, nicotine arouses the smoker in ways that are similar to the methods and effects of naturally produced chemicals.

Although you have been presented with much about nicotine's arousing effects, it is important to remember that nicotine is a kind of transient stimulant that has a breadth of effects varying across individuals. For example, do you know of anyone (perhaps yourself) who smokes a cigarette in order to relax, as opposed to stimulate?

Conditioning and Smoking

Classical conditioning involves learning to associate two stimuli in the environment, eventually leading to a learned response to a stimulus. Classical conditioning can occur under numerous conditions with numerous stimuli. To say that a person or animal has been classically conditioned is to say that the person has learned the meaning of a stimulus and gives a response to that stimulus that indicates previous experience with the stimulus. The pleasurable effects of nicotine in the brain act as a naturally reinforcing stimulus for smokers. When cues become associated with cigarette smoking, these cues may later be able to produce a motivation to smoke. There are certain cues that are related to smoking that in isolation may eventually produce the same cravings for a cigarette, as does nicotine. Environmental cues related to smoking can elicit increased smoking for smokers, or lead to relapse in smokers who have quit.

Classical conditioning effects have been evidenced in smokers via observed increases in pulse, urge to smoke, and positive mood when smokers are exposed to smoking-related cues (Lazev, Herzog, & Brandon, 1999). One smoking-related cue may be the smell of cigarette smoke, such as when there is exposure to other smokers in a smoking environment. Cues related to smoking may affect whether a smoker resists a temptation to smoke or has a relapse.

Paradoxical smoking has been identified as smoking under stress, smoking with coffee, or smoking after a meal (Snel & Lorist, 1998). Paradoxical smoking involves conditioning because a cup of coffee, if consumed with a cigarette repeatedly, will eventually in isolation make the smoker have the craving for nicotine. If the smoker is educated about the process of and powerful effects of classically conditioned stimuli, then the smoker can be better prepared to avoid smoking related cues that might lead to relapse or increased frequency of smoking.

The effects of rapid smoking demonstrate further evidence of learning factors in the experience of cigarette craving. **Rapid smoking** is an aversive conditioning technique based upon the principles of classical conditioning in which the subjects smoke enough to produce significant aversive experiences. During rapid smoking, the smoker puffs frequently until he or she feels ill, repeating the process several times. Rapid smoking studies provide evidence that when the desirable behavior (smoking) is associated with a negative consequence (feeling ill), there can be a decreased desire to smoke (Houtsmuller & Stitzer, 1999).

Operant conditioning, the learning of the association between a response and a consequence, has also been found to be effective as a means of promoting smoking abstinence (Gilbert, Crauthers, Mooney, McClernon, & Jensen, 1999). Specifically, money can act as a learned reinforcer, also known as a **secondary reinforcer**. Although money may not be immediately thought of in relationship to the promotion of smoking abstinence, it has been found that substantial monetary reward can be highly effective as a means of promoting smoking abstinence. In the Gilbert and colleagues (1999) study, a financial incentive for not smoking motivated a majority of smokers to maintain abstinence for at least 31 days.

Negative withdrawal occurs in the newly abstinent smoker and in the smoker who is not abstaining but merely overdue for a cigarette. Negative withdrawal maintains smoking through negative reinforcement, a type of operant conditioning. Smokers may continue to smoke in order to avoid or escape the negative withdrawal effects. **Negative withdrawal** in part consists of cigarette craving, negative mood, and hypoarousal (Bolin, Antonuccio, Follette, & Krumpe, 1999). Overall the withdrawal effects of smoking are the sum of all the negative things that happen, and negative feelings that occur when the smoker quits smoking.

Cognition and Smoking

Mental processing is affected by nicotine (Krogh, 1991). Many smokers acknowledge that smoking produces an undeniable improvement in their mental efficiency. Specifically, the effects of nicotine can help smokers to function better and keep their performance steady (Mancuso, Andres, Ansseau, & Tirelli, 1999). Smoking enhances the thoughts that the smoker has regarding the competency or ability to master a task, and this reinforces the smoking behavior. Nicotine helps the smoker to maintain concentration over time by enabling the smoker to block out distractions (Kassel & Shiffman, 1997). This is highly relevant in the workplace, for example, which is one of the major contexts in which the smoker frequently needs to take a break and smoke. Although the workplace is a primary environment in which smoking occurs, smoking acts as a general aid that helps people to function in various contexts. In essence, many smokers turn to cigarettes as a coping mechanism.

There are three ways that stress occurs: major life events, minor life events, and long-term chronic difficulties (Dugan, Lloyd, & Lucas, 1999). There may be differences in the ways that individuals choose to deal with these stressors that reflect the individuals' coping strategies. Not surprisingly, individuals do not always utilize productive coping strategies when stress occurs. Smoking is an example of a nonproductive coping strategy. It has been found that there are situations in which adolescents, specifically, are more likely to choose smoking as a resource for coping with stress. These situations are (1) perception of more stress in one's life, (2) using fewer problem-focused coping strategies and more cathartic strategies, (3) greater feelings of negative affect, and (4) feelings of being in an uncontrollable predicament (Dugan et al., 1999). There is no clear-cut explanation for why some individuals may choose smoking or other substance use over other coping strategies. It is also perhaps the case that when an individual chooses smoking as a resource for coping with stress, it prevents that person from later trying other coping strategies that might be healthier such as prayer, exercise, or social support.

Cognition should also be considered in smoking studies when it comes to the thoughts and images individuals use to resist temptations to smoke. It has been found that whether an abstaining smoker has a relapse is related to the use or nonuse of cognitive coping strategies (Bliss, Garvey, & Ward, 1999). A cognitive coping strategy may be a thought to oneself such as "I can beat this habit, it's not impossible, and today I am choosing a healthier lifestyle."

When relapse occurs in abstaining smokers, it may not be due to a lack of knowledge of coping strategies, but a lack of perseverance when there are repeated strong temptations to smoke. Relapse and continued smoking can also occur if the abstaining smoker is lacking in confidence or self-efficacy regarding his or her ability to remain abstinent, or if the smoker is not in a stage of readiness to quit smoking. The smoker may also ignore and deny smoking-related symptoms in addition to not being in a stage of readiness to quit (Clark, Hogan, Kviz, & Prohaska, 1999; Lafferty et al., 1999). If intervention efforts focus on enhancing the smoker's self-efficacy as well as training the smoker in the use of cognitive and behavioral coping strategies, then perhaps there will be more positive outcomes to cessation attempts. The significance of social and cognitive factors to smoking behavior is evident by examining the five major types of smoking relapse situations. The five situations that smokers should be cognitively prepared for as situations likely to lead to relapse are social gatherings, home relaxation, smoking restrictions at work, high arousal work situations, and domestic boredom (Christen & Christen, 1990).

Social Learning

Social learning refers to learning through observation or learning from exposure to immediate others and society. Why both immediate others and society? Here are two examples: (1) Since the early 1900s there has been a significant increase in the numbers of female smokers, and (2) Most committed smokers began smoking prior to the age of 15 (Janson, 1999). In the first example, societal acceptance of smoking by women has changed over the decades such that women have been socially supported in their decision to smoke, compared to in earlier times when smoking for women was not socially acceptable. An increase in cigarette advertisements and movies displaying female smokers teaches that this is an acceptable behavior. This teaches that a woman who smokes is not only displaying acceptable behavior, but also in many cases the female smoker is portrayed as more confident and sexy when holding a cigarette.

In the second example, smoking in the teen years is often a result of peer influence. Adolescents desire to be accepted and well liked by their peers. This statement has been supported by research that revealed that African American youth may refrain from smoking in order not to be perceived as different from peers, whereas Latino youth may smoke in order to be accepted as similar to peers (Griesler & Kandel, 1998). Psychosocial factors such as social conformity and rebelliousness may in some cases override the positive effects of coping and personal resources (Koval & Pederson, 1999). Koval and Pederson (1999) found that for adolescent males, rebelliousness was a powerful predictor of smoking. It is likely that these males used smoking as an attempt to assert independence and take risks. It is also likely that smoking in order to accomplish these goals is socially learned. It is interesting to note that in this same study, further evidence of social learning was evidenced by the fact that for female adolescents, the most important factor related to smoking was whether the girls' mothers smoked.

Smoking and Underrepresented Populations

The discussion up until this point in the chapter has been a standard biopsychosocial presentation, excluding a discussion of cultural factors. However, no chapter on smoking would be complete without a discussion of such factors. One relevant factor in discussing health issues in ethnic minority populations is socioeconomic status. There are substantial numbers of ethnic minority groups living at or below poverty in the United States. Low socioeconomic status combined with smoking presents a major problem. This is particularly a problem when the government implements pricing policies that result in an increase in the price of tobacco. The economically deprived may be experiencing financial difficulties, but they are not reducing their consumption of tobacco (Marks, 1998). So, in fact what is happening is that due to their addiction to nicotine, the economically deprived person may still spend money on cigarettes. The money that they allocate to purchasing cigarettes subtracts from money to be used for food, savings, clothing, or rent. If the economically deprived smoker sacrifices money for food, clothing, and shelter, then this worsens his or her health chances. Therefore, what is needed are economic policies to reduce inequalities, and cognitively focused counseling to address the irrationality underlying decisions to purchase cigarettes even when money is scarce. Since it has been found that money can act as a reinforcer that motivates smokers to abstain (Gilbert et al., 1999), this approach may work particularly well for ethnic minority groups of addicted smokers who are of lower socioeconomic status.

Intervention efforts with ethnic minority groups should also specifically consider neighborhood effects on smoking. It has been found that measures of neighborhood deprivation continue to have an independent effect on individual smoking status (Duncan, Jones, & Moon, 1999). We often read of problems occurring in communities. We do not hear as much about the effects of living in a particular neighborhood that is a part of a larger community. A consideration of neighborhood effects is particularly salient to the present discussion for ethnic minority groups. Ethnic minority groups are more likely to have a collectivist versus an individualist orientation. This means that they may often show concern for extended family living in the neighborhood as well as neighbors and their children. In ethnic minority neighborhoods where residents are encouraged to work together on neighborhood committees, much could be done to decrease the quantity of smoking and drinking advertisements that contribute to the blight, deprivation, and poor health of some residents. Also if ethnic minority residents of a neighborhood are encouraged to collectively take on civic responsibility, this activism could help to decrease the numbers of local merchants who sell cigarettes to minors, which is a common occurrence in urban neighborhood settings (Voorhees et al., 1998). Before professionals can intervene in this manner, it is necessary to first obtain information on both the health attitudes of the community and the specific neighborhood.

In populations of ethnic minorities of lower socioeconomic status, there are great numbers of stressors in their lives. Often this may be related to high-demand, low-paying, and low decisional control employment. The workplace is crucial to the present discussion on smoking because smoking occurs more often in the workplace than during other times (Krogh, 1991). Due to the magnitude of stressors for ethnic minorities in America, smoking is very likely to be used as a coping mechanism. As the ethnic minority smoker acknowledges the magnitude of stressors in his or her life, he or she may start to lose feelings of self-efficacy as well as lose feelings of internal locus of control regarding the power to quit smoking. This highlights how stress effects cognition and subsequently the efforts to cope. Intervention efforts with this population should use a culturally sensitive approach to cognitively restructure attitudes towards smoking. Also, it is important to inform smokers of the relationship between stress and vascular reactivity, which in many cases may be exacerbated by smoking. Llabre and colleagues (Llabre, Klein, Saab, McCalla, & Schneiderman, 1998) found specifically that when African Americans were exposed to stressors in an experimental study, they were more likely be of the vascular reactor type (a change in normal functioning of the blood vessels) as opposed to myocardial (a change in normal function of the heart muscle). This has implications for development of cerebrovascular disease for African Americans who are smokers, employed in stressful occupations, and dealing with other stressful life events.

Earlier in the chapter, it was mentioned that African American smokers are more likely to possess the genotype that leads to a nicotine addiction (Lerman et al., 1999). It has also been stated that racial differences in brand of cigarette preferred may have underlying biological explanations; specifically, there may be differences in lung construction and the action of cilia in the lungs (Kilbey, 1999). Supporting the findings of other research in this area, Klonoff and Landrine (1999) found that 63.4 percent of black smokers smoked menthol cigarettes. Menthol cigarettes are easier on the lungs for African Americans (Kilbey, 1999). In African Americans, menthol cigarettes reduce (not eliminate) the severe coughing and other negative respiratory effects associated with smoking nonmenthol cigarettes. However, in addition to this explanation for racial differences in brand of cigarette preferred, there are conditioning and social learning explanations. The manufacturers of various brands of cigarettes target certain populations of smokers through their advertisements, which differentially affects what type of smoker prefers what brand.

In Chapter 1 it was mentioned that acculturation is relevant to many issues in health psychology for ethnic minority populations. Here, for the behavior of smoking we must once again consider this variable. The level of acculturation of ethnic minorities in the U.S. influences smoking behavior, but not in the same manner for varying groups. For example, it has been found that when African Americans are more traditional versus acculturated, they are more likely to be smokers (Klonoff & Landrine, 1999). However, the opposite appears to be the case with Asian groups and Latino populations. For Asian and Latino groups, smoking is less likely to occur if these groups are more traditional versus acculturated (Lafferty et al., 1999; Thridandam, Louie, Fong, Forst, & Jang, 1998). Once again, it is important to remember to avoid making broad sweeping generalizations about entire groups. Even within a racial group there can be differences for specific ethnic groups. Lafferty and colleagues (1999) found that in a study of Cambodian, Laotian, and Vietnamese males, there were differences across these ethnic groups for stage of readiness to quit smoking and the pros and cons the men mentioned for continuation or cessation of smoking. When studying ethnic minority groups, it is important to study the level of acculturation, the relevance of a collectivist culture versus individualist culture, and gender issues. Each of these can be significant regarding the attitudes toward smoking and can affect smoking behavior. Any intervention used with ethnic minority populations should consider the cultural attitudes towards smoking in the community, neighborhood, and family. For individual smokers who may be one of several persons in the family who have smoked for many years, it will be important to treat smoking as an issue for the entire family.

Spotlight on Biology: Nicotine Dependence

The pharmacological and behavioral processes that determine tobacco addiction are similar to those that determine addiction to drugs such as heroine and cocaine. Tobacco dependence was first included in the *Diagnostic and Statistical Manual of Psychiatric Disorders* in 1980. There is remarkable consistency in the signs and symptoms reported from various parts of the world when cigarette smokers stop smoking. These signs include craving for tobacco (nicotine), irritability, impatience, frustration or anger, anxiety, difficulty concentrating, restlessness, decreased heart rate, increased appetite, weight gain, depression, disturbed sleep, constipation, difficulty in socializing, decreased levels of adrenaline and noradrenaline in urine, altered electroencephalographic (EEG) patterns while awake (increased slow waves) and while asleep (increased dream sleep), and decrements in performance on a variety of cognitive tasks.

The variability in the actual nicotine that smokers intake provides part of the answer to the question of variability in symptom severity among smokers. Smokers can vary not only in frequency of each cigarette, but also puff frequency, puff volume, depth of inhalation, duration of inhalation, degree of dilution of smoke, and how close to the tip each cigarette is smoked. There can be wide variation in nicotine intake among smokers who smoke a comparable number of cigarettes of the same brand. When tobacco smoke is inhaled, a small mass of nicotine is rapidly absorbed from the alveoli (tiny sac like structures in the lungs) and may pass quickly into the brain. For many smokers, dependence on tobacco is in large measure a result of the reinforcing effects of these masses of nicotine transported to the brain. This may be experienced thousands of times in the course of a year in the form of a pleasurable stimulating sensation, often described as a rush. For this reason and other psychosocial reasons, tobacco dependence can be exceedingly resistant to change, despite real threats to health and to life.

Source: Jaffee, 1990.

Interventions with ethnic minority populations should also utilize culturally appropriate health education and prevention strategies. Even the phrasing and nature of exercises used in smoking cessation programs developed for the general population may need to be changed. For example, in the study of Southeast Asian males (Lafferty et al., 1999) it was found to be inappropriate to question the subjects about the individual benefits of smoking without talking about the cultural community and the family. As with other health-damaging behaviors, for ethnic minorities it is necessary with smoking to garner some social support from family for the smoker to rely upon during times of possible relapse. It is important for health professionals to acknowledge that the programs developed for the general population may be less effective for ethnic groups, who may have deeply ingrained culturally determined health risky behaviors. This is likely the case with Native American smokers. The high percentage of smoking in the Native American population may very well reflect cultural tradition and attitudes toward smoking.

In any addicted smoker, interventions should logically address the negative withdrawal that occurs during abstinence. This can be addressed via various forms of nicotine replacement procedures. However, specifically in ethnic minority populations, the biology of the addiction needs to be treated along with specialized interventions that utilize cultural information conducive to achieving more success in quitting. One such example of how this could be done would be to incorporate elements of spirituality from cultural practices into the interventions (Christen & Christen, 1990).

Conclusion

Smoking has deleterious effects on health, and for this reason serious and innovative preventive and cessation methods are needed. Advocates of the tobacco industry and those who work in the tobacco industry feel that policy-led interventions are excessive. Their opinion is that no matter the negative health effects of smoking, it is still a voluntary act. Tobacco advocates feel that the smoker is not being forced to initiate the habit, so smokers need no government protection. This sort of reasoning, however, does not recognize the powerful influences of psychological and social factors in the environment that make resisting the behavior difficult for many adult consumers and impressionable teens. These factors in the environment motivate the onset of smoking, a behavior that becomes a pervasive part of the smoker's life. Once the behavior is initiated there are multitudes of factors that maintain the behavior. In addition, the behavior for the smoker becomes difficult to stop as a result of a definite chemical addiction. During intervention efforts to help smokers to quit, the focus should be on breaking the associations of smoking with pleasure, restructuring the negative cognitive processes that maintain the behavior, and acknowledging the social and cultural influences. The efforts to intervene in this area are particularly crucial for ethnic minority smokers, who continue to show high percentages of smoking.

Summary

Nicotine may be described as a sinister substance because of what it does to the smoker. It is a substance that provides pleasure in several ways, among which are feelings of calm during stress, stimulation during boredom, and a sense of mastery during tasks. However, the cost for all of this is the gradual destruction of the cerebrovascular and respiratory systems of the smoker's body, along with other malignancies related to smoking. One area of smoking research that the general public may not be as familiar with is the genetic basis of some smokers' addiction. Dopamine, an excitatory neurotransmitter, has been implicated in genetically related smoking addictions. Specifically, the type of dopamine receptor and dopamine transport genes that a smoker possesses may affect the smoker's responsiveness to nicotine and the likelihood of developing a nicotine addiction. The reinforcing effects of dopamine are related to the brain stimulation reward center of the brain (nucleus accumbens) and also the reticular system. Also biologically, cravings for a cigarette may be associated with an increase in asymmetry of the hemispheric activity of the brain. Beyond focusing on biological factors such as genetics and brain activity, a complete understanding of smoking requires a consideration of conditioning factors, cognition, social learning, and cultural influences. Particularly as a result of noting the percentages of smoking for Native Americans, African Americans, and Hispanic groups, the prevention and cessation efforts of professionals should be sensitive to the special needs of ethnic minority groups.

Student Interview

Age: 23
Gender: Male
Country of Origin: Greece
Years in United States: 2

1. **Are you a regular smoker? If yes, how did this habit start? If no, to what do you attribute never becoming a smoker?**

   Yes, I am a regular smoker. I was 17 when I started with my friends. I would have two on Saturdays only at first, then every day alone. Now I have a pack a day. My smoking has increased since living in the United States, I think because I live alone now. My parents are not here so this increases my smoking. I can't smoke in front of my Mom because I respect her and she hates it.

2. **How prevalent was smoking in your community, family, or school?**

   My Mom doesn't smoke. My Dad stopped two years ago. I have uncles who smoke but my sisters don't smoke.

3. **Tell me something that you know about smoking and health.**

   Smoking may cause cancer if the lungs are affected. It also affects your brain. I get nervous and irritable when I don't smoke for a few hours. Cigarettes damage the whole body. I exercised from a young age. When I exercise, I don't feel as tired and I smoke less also. But now I have actually stopped exercising because of the cigarettes. I just can't do as much exercise now because of the smoking.

4. **What do you think are strong explanations for why people begin smoking?**

   Well, I know for myself that I started just for fun with my friends.

5. **The people whom you know who are smokers, how are they similar or different from yourself?**

   All of my friends smoke and we are all students. Also, my girlfriend smokes. When we go out and drink we smoke. I must have a drink now with my cigarettes. I also smoked and drank when I was in the army with my army buddies.

6. **What do you believe would be an effective means of preventing teen smoking?**

   I believe that friends are a major influence, so maybe some major kind of peer intervention.

7. **Describe the community setting in which you now live. Do you pay attention to ads for cigarettes in the magazines or community?**

   Well, smoking for me now is such a habit at this point that the ads in the community and in the media don't really matter to me.

8. **Are there restrictions on smoking in your country? Is there a certain age requirement for example, or place where it can be done?**

   In Greece there are no age restrictions on getting cigarettes or where it can be done. Because it's not illegal, kids don't care about doing it.

9. **Have you ever attempted to quit smoking?**

   Yes, when I'm sick I don't smoke. I also stopped for a while when I was in the army, but I must have something else to keep me busy.

10. **What are your attitudes about females who smoke versus men who smoke?**

    I'm okay with women smoking. Years ago (fifteen to twenty years) in Greece women were hiding their smoking.

This is especially necessary subsequent to the revelation that many treatment techniques for the general/mainstream population may be inappropriate and thus ineffective for ethnic minority smokers.

Key Concepts

acetylcholine
addictive behavior
classical conditioning
committed smoker
dopamine
environmental tobacco smoke (ETS)
fibrinogen
negative withdrawal
nicotine
nucleus accumbens
operant conditioning
paradoxical smoking
rapid smoking
reticular system (RTS)
reuptake
secondary reinforcer
social learning
thrombus/thrombi

Study Questions

1. Name three reasons that nicotine can be described as a sinister substance.
2. If your roommate is a smoker, can this affect you?
3. Other than lung cancer, are there other ailments that have been significantly related to smoking? What are some of these?
4. In the chapter, what were some reasons presented as likely explanations for why teen smoking is so prevalent?
5. After reading the chapter, what information could you offer others about genetics and smoking addiction?
6. If a smoker has endured several hours without a cigarette and is badly craving, what would an EEG reveal about his brain?
7. Some smokers must have a cigarette with their cup of morning coffee. What is the explanation for this?
8. Explain from a classical conditioning standpoint how rapid smoking may work in smoking cessation programs.
9. In situations when an abstaining smoker has a relapse, what are some social and cognitive explanations?
10. How does the specific neighborhood of groups of ethnic minority urban residents relate to the display of healthy behaviors or risky health behaviors?

Student Activity

Obtain various magazines and newspapers for which the target audience is people of color (African Americans, Latinos, and Asians). Write a descriptive report of the frequency of cigarette ads observed and the details of the characteristics of the advertisement that are meant to entice the desired population.

OR

Have your instructor approve your questions, and then interview three different people of color of varying ages who are current smokers. The three people should come from each of the following three age groups: (a) teen/young adult, (b) mature adult, 30s and 40s, and (c) elderly smoker, 60s. What patterns seem consistent across groups and what differences did you find for how each became a smoker?

CHAPTER

4 Substance Use and Sexual Behavior

In the previous chapter on smoking it was emphasized that smoking is best understood by examining biological factors, the psychology of conditioning, and social factors related to learning such as from family, peers, cultural influences, and the community. The present chapter on substance use and sexual behavior also necessitates the consideration of many factors. Particularly in ethnic minority populations, more studies are needed, although some studies have focused on these groups (Estrada, 1998; Myers et al., 1997). Health professionals have much to accomplish in addressing these issues with ethnic minority populations. The intervention must begin at an early age because drug experimentation, for example, often begins in the early adolescent and early teenage years (see Table 4.1 on page 58).

Whether youth use drugs is also relevant to the likelihood of their engaging in other risky behaviors as well, such as sexual risk taking (see Table 4.2 on page 59).

When considering sexual behavior and drug experimentation for all age groups, it should be acknowledged that the behaviors will be regulated by important social factors such as:

- Gender
- Ethno-racial group
- Occupation
- Income/wealth
- Regional and cultural expectations
- Norms of social acceptance (Alaniz, Treno, & Saltz, 1999; Caetano & Clark, 1998)

Risky behaviors such as sexual risk taking and substance abuse are complex behaviors with multiple causes. There are successive layers of societal influence on such behaviors. This chapter presents the layers of social influence as related to substance abuse, sexual behavior, and interventions designed for those people who are addicted, infected, and at risk.

Substance Abuse

In the previous chapter you were presented with a brief discussion of the biology of addiction to nicotine and the brain stimulation reward center, the nucleus accumbens. For other substances we can also discuss the biology of addiction; however, substances vary in whether they lead to psychological dependence or physical dependence. In this section, the

TABLE 4.1   Prevalence of Past-Month Drug Use in the United States, by Age, Sex, and Race/Ethnicity, Represented in Percentages: 1996

Type of drug	Age group				Sex		All ages, both sexes
	12–17	18–25	26–34	35+	Male	Female	
Any illicit drug use							
White	9.2	17.0	8.8	2.9	8.1	4.1	6.1
Black	8.6	15.7	8.8	3.8	9.9	5.7	7.6
Hispanic	9.2	10.9	5.7	1.5	6.7	3.8	5.3
American Indian/Alaskan Native	18.4	25.4	18.9	3.7	15.1	8.0	11.3
Asian/Pacific Islander	5.5	7.1	2.0	2.9	5.1	2.5	3.7
Marijuana							
White	7.3	14.4	6.6	1.9	6.4	2.9	4.6
Black	7.3	13.9	9.2	3.3	9.1	4.5	6.6
Hispanic	6.9	8.3	3.6	1.0	4.7	2.7	3.7
American Indian/Alaskan Native	18.4	25.4	12.6	3.7	14.3	6.4	10.0
Asian/Pacific Islander	*	6.1	*	*	*	1.6	2.7
Cocaine							
White	0.5	2.3	1.3	0.4	1.1	0.5	0.8
Black	*	1.1	3.1	0.6	1.4	0.8	1.1
Hispanic	1.1	2.1	1.4	0.6	1.6	0.6	1.1
American Indian/Alaskan Native	*	*	*	*	*	*	*
Asian/Pacific Islander	*	*	*	*	*	*	*
Alcohol							
White	20.4	65.6	66.0	54.3	61.2	47.7	54.2
Black	14.7	49.6	55.7	42.0	52.3	33.5	41.9
Hispanic	19.9	49.8	50.6	44.0	54.8	31.1	43.2
American Indian/Alaskan Native	8.1	67.0	49.4	13.2	40.2	18.2	28.2
Asian/Pacific Islander	5.2	39.5	41.9	42.1	44.7	29.8	36.9
Heavy alcohol							
White	3.2	14.9	7.9	3.6	9.4	2.0	5.5
Black	1.7	7.4	5.8	5.5	9.1	2.3	5.3
Hispanic	3.4	10.6	5.8	5.4	10.2	2.1	6.2
American Indian/Alaskan Native	*	*	7.1	0.0	12.2	*	6.4
Asian/Pacific Islander	*	*	0.9	1.0	*	*	1.3
Cigarettes							
White	20.8	42.9	37.5	26.8	30.8	28.9	29.8
Black	11.9	28.5	33.5	34.7	36.1	25.7	30.4
Hispanic	14.8	30.1	26.3	24.7	31.0	28.2	24.7
American Indian/Alaskan Native	44.2	62.4	51.2	35.0	64.7	25.1	43.2
Asian/Pacific Islander	6.7	17.9	20.0	10.0	19.5	6.6	12.8

Source: National Household Survey on Drug Abuse, Substance Abuse and Mental Health Services Administration, Office of Applied Studies, 1998.

*Low precision, no estimate reported.

TABLE 4.2   Percentage of Youth Engaging in Risky Behavior, by Drug Users and Nonusers and Race/Ethnicity: 1995

Drug, type of use, and race/ethnicity	Fight in last 12 months	Carried weapon in last 30 days	Rarely wears a seat belt	Multiple sex partners during last 3 months	Ridden in car while driver was drinking	Used drugs or alcohol before last sexual encounter	Used no condom during last sexual encounter
Marijuana							
Lifetime use							
White	48.2	26.8	31.4	14.8	55.7	25.0	33.6
Black	51.4	32.7	42.0	30.9	52.7	22.3	28.5
Hispanic	61.4	37.3	24.7	18.3	63.6	23.3	37.8
Other	57.5	37.3	26.8	18.2	56.6	25.2	33.7
No lifetime use							
White	27.4	13.2	13.1	2.2	25.5	3.7	11.2
Black	30.5	11.3	22.6	9.5	23.7	1.8	16.9
Hispanic	32.3	12.1	12.5	4.1	36.2	2.3	17.6
Other	32.5	8.0	14.1	4.8	22.9	1.9	11.3
Used last 30 days							
White	51.9	32.4	36.0	19.2	65.3	33.3	36.1
Black	56.0	39.1	46.9	38.4	64.5	33.5	27.2
Hispanic	67.7	46.4	31.3	24.4	74.5	31.5	43.0
Other	63.2	46.1	36.6	22.0	71.0	33.8	41.4
No Use last 30 days							
White	30.6	14.2	15.5	3.4	28.7	5.5	15.1
Black	34.0	14.2	25.6	12.0	26.4	2.7	20.3
Hispanic	38.6	16.2	13.6	6.1	40.3	5.4	21.6
Other	36.8	12.4	14.3	6.9	26.7	4.9	14.3

Source: U.S. Dept. of Health and Human Services, National Institute on Drug Abuse, Drug use among racial/ethnic minorities (1998)

psychosocial explanations for drug use will be presented as they pertain to studies of ethnic minorities.

Adolescent substance use has been given much attention through extensive research (Brooks, Stuewig, & LeCroy, 1998; Sullivan & Farrell, 1999). There is good reason for this given the susceptibility of many teens to drug experimentation pressures. Research has identified that when teens experiment with **gateway drugs,** they are at increased risk for subsequent usage of illicit or hard drugs (Ellickson, Collins, & Bell, 1999; Sullivan & Farrell, 1999). Gateway drugs are alcohol, tobacco, and marijuana. Many of the studies focus on trying to identify the protective factors and risk factors related to teens' likelihood of drug experimentation. In trying to identify these factors, the layers of societal influence become apparent for various ethnic groups studied. In studying drug behavior, ethnicity and the family combined play a significant role.

Family and Ethnic Identity

In a study of Mexican American early adolescents, a family-based model was used to understand adolescent substance use (Brooks et al., 1998). It was found in this study that for both males and females, the family was a significant factor. Other research has also highlighted the need to acknowledge gender differences within the family (Alaniz et al., 1999). Whether drugs are used in the family, as well as the overall functioning of the family, can be a very important factor in teen substance use. Family functioning may influence the overall family's use of substances, as well as affect the teen's school and peer attachments.

Familism, which emphasizes strong family ties, is the cultural norm within Hispanic populations. The family is a source of support even during assimilation into U.S. culture. Familism represents a view of the family as the central organizing focus of Hispanic life, and the emphasis on the family extends far beyond the nuclear family.

Not only Hispanic youth benefit from the protective factor of family when it comes to substance use. Both African American and Hispanic youth have been found to have relatively low risks of alcohol use and abusive drinking patterns related to family influences (Johnson & Johnson, 1999). Researchers state that the structure and dynamics of African American and Hispanic families create negative beliefs regarding alcohol that buffer the young person from becoming involved with drinking. It is especially heartening to obtain such a finding for a substance such as alcohol. Often because of alcohol's status as a legal substance, the harmful effects of it are downplayed in comparison to illicit drugs. Anti-drug television public service announcements contain highly dramatic and intense anti-drug messages that implicate illegal substances, but they often neglect alcohol to the same degree. It is worth noting by parents of European descent that Hispanic and African American parents influence the attitudes of their children in ways that they may lead them to resist alcohol consumption even when they are around drinkers later in their lives. This is particularly relevant for the college years when drinking on campus may be viewed as the norm. Mainstream parents can learn from parents of color about how to positively influence teens to abstain from alcohol use. For example, African American and Hispanic families build a protective constellation of alcohol-related beliefs, expectancies, norms, motives, and attitudes that discourage drinking (Johnson & Johnson, 1999). The children learn from the parents that their families are of the utmost importance. This accords the parents potentially greater and more lasting influence over their offspring (Brooks et al., 1998; Johnson & Johnson, 1999). The parents attach negative connotations to behaviors such as drinking and they emphasize that such behavior would disrupt family relations.

Although the family has been shown to be a protective factor in ethnic minority youth, bear in mind that there are layers of influence on risky behavior. Thus, research has also focused on ethnic identity as an influence on substance use; particularly, this is another protective factor to be considered along with family (Brook, Balka, Brook, Win, & Gursen, 1998). **Ethnic identity** refers to the degree of identification with people of similar heritage and the admiration that one has for people of one's heritage; it is a subjective sense of ethnic group membership (Brook et al., 1998). When doing research to understand differences in health behavior, this is an important construct. Ethnic identity includes the dimensions of **ethnic attachment** and **ethnic affiliation** and it is ever changing as opposed to stable (Phinney, 1996). Ethnic attachment is the individual's expression of psychological attachment to the group on the basis of cultural origin or heritage. Ethnic affiliation refers to the heritage of those selected as friends. Ethnicity, however, is not simple. It is highly complex and should not be thought of as a factor that in isolation plays a substantial role. There are at least three aspects of ethnicity that may account for psychological importance (Phinney, 1996):

- The cultural values, attitudes, and behaviors that distinguish ethnic groups
- The subjective sense of ethnic group membership (ethnic identity)
- The experiences associated with minority status such as powerlessness, discrimination, and prejudice

Each of the three aspects of ethnicity may have consequences for the individual's health decisions. The three aspects of ethnicity can be further explained using the example of Native Americans.

The values and attitudes present in an individual's culture may dictate how they behave regarding alcohol and other substances (Gutmann, 1999). In some cultures, such as the Native American Incas, historically the use of psychoactive substances was ingrained in the culture of the people during formal ceremonies or rituals (French, 2000). The Incas during the pre-Columbian era used alcohol as an integral part of rites, and aboriginal Indians also used dozens of mushrooms, plants, and tree barks in association with sacred rituals. There is little evidence that these psychoactive substances were abused during pre-Columbian times, but instead substances were regarded as necessary for spiritual activities. Thus the present attitudes and values held by some Native Americans about psychoactive substances may relate to the cultural and historical significance of substance use.

French (2000) explains how variation in the ethnic identity of Native Americans is related to differences in their susceptibility to alcoholism. He describes the contemporary Native Americans in a spectrum that consists of three categories: traditional, middle class, and marginal Native Americans. Traditional persons make up about 20 percent of the 1.2 million enrolled Native Americans. Their blood degree and physical appearance is close to Native Americans of the pre-Columbian era and they are often described as full bloods, real Indians, or conservative Indians. Their attitudes toward alcohol are less likely to lead to alcohol abuse.

The middle class category makes up a smaller percentage than the traditional category. They are described as the affluent Native Americans regardless of their blood degree or physical appearance. Regarding their ethnic identification, they are similar to the mainstream, and they are most favored by members of the larger dominant society. Due to their ethnic attachment and ethnic affiliation with whites, they do not generally enjoy the respect of their Native American peers as evident by the derogatory labels given to them by other Native Americans such as "white Indians" and "Uncle Tomahawks." Their drinking patterns are similar to those of whites.

Marginal persons make up the majority of Native Americans. This group includes those who identify with and are often enrolled as tribal members but do not share the traditional physical appearance (they may appear white or African American). This group also includes those who may have a Native American physical appearance yet they do not know the language or the traditional customs. They are described as marginal because they are caught between two worlds (the U.S. dominant society and their Native American heritage) without belonging to either. They are faced with a dilemma because they may have the physical appearance of a traditional Native American and the desire to be Native American, but they do not know their traditional cultural ways or how to learn about their heritage. Marginal Native Americans, due to the stress and strain of their identity crises, are the ones most likely to be arrested for public drunkenness and alcohol related offenses (French, 2000). They also suffer more from alcohol-related mental and physical health problems such as fetal alcohol syndrome (French, 2000). From the previous descriptions of the differences in Native American ethnic identity and drinking patterns, it is revealed how identity and attachment relate to the likelihood of indulging in a health risky behavior such as excessive drinking.

Ethnicity also includes the experiences that are a part of minority status such as powerlessness, violence, and prejudice. This is also evident in a discussion of the treatment of Native Americans. French (2000) presents information about three inebriated Navajo men who in 1974 were found in separate locations, severely beaten, tortured, and burned in Farmington, New Mexico. The perpetrators of the crime were three Anglo teens from Farmington who were carrying out a tradition among white teenagers. The hate crime was tolerated as a sort of father-to-son rite of passage, and it produced an environment for increased violence toward Native Americans. Ongoing exposure to such treatment, and the isolation, poverty, and dilapidation of life on some reservations have been associated with depression and boredom that may be relieved by using alcohol (French, 2000). Using the examples from Native American culture, we see how each of the three aspects of ethnicity has relevance to behavior such as drinking.

Differences in ethnic identity may also cause differences in how members of the same ethnic group think about their gender roles and expectations for their behavior. This has been demonstrated in a study of Mexican American Latina adolescents who differ from their family members in identity. In this study, it was found that when the family was traditionally Latino and the girl was a feminist, the Latina adolescent exhibited increased frequency of cigarette use, alcohol use, and increased quantity of alcohol use (Felix-Ortiz, Fernandez, & Newcomb, 1998). "Feminist" in this study was defined as being more American-oriented in terms of language, familiarity with U.S. culture, behavior, and attitudes about traditional sex roles. Differences in "feminist" attitudes are especially likely to occur when there are substantial age differences in the family members. This is referred to as *intergenerational discrepancy* and can lead to a negatively charged family environment that is correlated with adolescent problem behavior. Although some may equate the results of this study to the typical rebellious behavior of adolescents, it actually goes beyond this, and researchers attribute the finding to the differences in cultural identity of the youth versus the parents. The differences in cultural identity are related to different values and motivations.

Ethnic identity is also significant for African American youth. Strong African American ethnic identity has been found to enhance the beneficial effects of protective factors stemming from the personality, the family, and peers (Brook et al., 1998). For example, if there are two adolescent African American males, both from supportive positive families, the adolescent who has positive family characteristics combined with strong feelings of ethnic belonging and pride will be less susceptible to drug use than the other teen who has low black ethnic identity. The pride factor of ethnic identity allows the adolescent to resist drug offerings from strangers and enhances the positive personality characteristics of the adolescent. The conclusion to be drawn from this is that if the African American adolescent has high self-esteem, positive family structure, and strong ethnic identity, she will be less likely to allow an outsider (stranger) to entice her into taking a harmful substance into her body. This could negatively affect all the aspirations that she has.

Although a discussion of the psychological benefits of a strong ethnic identity may seem a given, it is not a given that ethnic minority youth will develop positive ethnic identity, affiliation, or attachment. The impressions that ethnic minority youth may have about themselves and others of their heritage may be negative because of the media and the general society's attitudes (Wyatt, 1994). Thus something such as **African centrality** may be critical. African centrality is a viewpoint that allows African Americans to define who they are by their own criteria, and it results in a change in irrational negative beliefs that the individual has about his or her heritage/race (Fudge, 1996). African centrality and the development of a positive ethnic identity are negatively correlated with the likelihood of substance abuse. The benefit of this is evident with adolescents and also with adults who may be in behavioral therapy to enhance their ethnic identity (Fudge, 1996).

Since there are varying research results for studies on alcohol versus illicit drugs, studies often specify what type of substance abuse is being investigated. For alcohol as well as illicit drugs, factors such as the family and ethnic identity remain relevant. In a study of African American, Mexican American, and Asian American adolescents, the bonds with the family were inversely related to any use of illicit drugs other than marijuana, which was not studied (Ellickson et al., 1999). This study also found some differences across the ethnic groups. Mexican Americans were most affected by family factors. These adolescents tended to come from a context of strong family ties, and thus they tended to be highly affected by divorce or other family disruption. Such family factors were more likely to lead to drug use in the Mexican American adolescents.

Asian Americans were most affected by school failure: Adolescents who were outside of their culture's social norms of placing a high value on education were more likely to act out in deviant ways such as drug use. African American adolescents were less likely to use illicit drugs; this has also been demonstrated in other research (see Figure 4.1 on page 64).

Social Forces

Ellickson and colleagues (1999) refer to **social control theory**, which states that the ties with social institutions such as the family, school, and religious institutions inhibit drug use by promoting conformity to group norms. Ellickson and colleagues (1999) offered explanations of outcomes for Mexican American and Asian American adolescents' drug behavior. Recall that familism was believed to be related to the Mexican American students' behavior, and since Asian American culture places a high value on education, this was thought to be related to the Asian American students' drug use. The same authors, however,

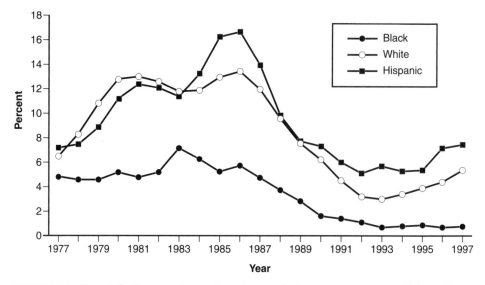

FIGURE 4.1   Trends in the prevalence of cocaine use in the past year among 12th graders, by race/ethnicity: 1977–1997.

Source: Monitoring the Future Study, University of Michigan, 1997

were unable to offer an explanation for why African American adolescents show low usage of hard illicit drugs. In attempting to explain this low illicit drug usage, it is necessary to consider the large and complex influence of society, politics, economics, culture, and personality factors and the broad social organization that often affects many African American adolescents. The social organization reflects the allocation of social resources, monetary resources, and values and norms of the ethnic group. Consider the following example:

> Andre has had a disruptive family life. His parents are separated, and instead of living with either parent, he lives with an aging grandparent. The grandmother is the court-appointed guardian. The biological father plays no major role, although he is present. Andre is impressionable, as many teens are, and he has deviant peer relationships with boys who smoke cigarettes, drink beer, and are apathetic regarding school. Andre has no siblings, although he wishes he had a big brother. He tries to obtain work in his community in order to have spending money, but this proves to be unsuccessful. Due to the influence of his peers, Andre has adopted some rebellious behavior. Because of some negative stereotyping and peer associates, some local neighborhood employers do not want to "risk" giving Andre a job. There is an older drug dealer in Andre's neighborhood. The dealer has an expensive car, nice clothes, and plenty of cash. Andre sees no real punishment of the dealer's behavior. The dealer approaches Andre and makes him an offer to work for him doing a little dealing. Among Andre's associates and family members he does not know of anyone who has as much money as the dealer. Andre has feelings of low self-efficacy about his ability to get money by other means. Andre does not refuse the offer. He sees this as an opportunity to make some money, if only temporarily.

The previous example is fictitious and is presented only to give an example of some important events outside of a teenager's family that could lead to deviant behavior. The above example cannot be generalized to all young black urban men. The percentage of young black males who are engaged in such described illegal activity represent only a minority of individuals. Instead, the above example is used only to demonstrate how some adolescents develop deviant behavior. Notice that at no point during the example does it say that Andre becomes a heroin or crack addict. Nor does it say that Andre has been exposed to illicit drug users in his peer group or family. An adolescent like Andre may see models of illicit drug use in his community but not directly among his friends or family. The values and norms that he may learn from family and friends may be a desire for money and material goods, influence, and power. His esteem level may be raised once he is making money. The influences on such behavior are multiple factors. Let's examine this further according to an often studied social theory, structural strain.

Structural Strain

The previous example using Andre represents **structural strain.** Structural strain is a theory that states that drug-related and other undesirable behaviors are seen as symptoms of a broader underlying isolation from mainstream opportunities and rewards (Brunswick, 1999). Tension can exist between socially desirable goals and the inability to achieve these goals through socially accepted means. Structural strain may be particularly relevant for ethnic minority adolescents when they are from lower socioeconomic areas and are seeking some means of escape from their situation. Structural strain is important to trying to understand differences in substance use patterns for white versus ethnic minority groups. Structural strain, as stated above, results in tension. The tension may be dealt with in different ways, such as illicit drug use and distribution, drinking, smoking marijuana, or even depression. The information presented earlier on the minority status of marginal Native Americans and their subsequent drinking patterns also supports the structural strain theory of behavior. Therefore, in trying to understand the substance use behaviors of the ethnic minority adolescent, it is necessary to look beyond a focus on just the individual. The individual must be studied in relationship to the larger social context.

Heavy drug use is typically a marker of those outside traditional norms and institutional bonds; the stress of this may exacerbate substance use effects on health (Brunswick & Messeri, 1999). The stress of this creates different types of involvement with substances and also the type of substance used. Thus, understanding the African American adolescent's lower involvement with illicit substances requires acknowledgement of many structural strain factors.

Another reason to focus on social theories such as structural strain is the evidence that biological factors may be less important to racial differences in drug dependence (Gelernter, Kranzler, & Satel, 1999). Research has shown, for example, that for cocaine dependence, and specifically the severity of cocaine dependence, there is no link to the D2 dopamine receptor alleles or haplotypes in either whites or African Americans (Gelernter et al., 1999). This type of finding should encourage researchers to attempt a greater understanding of the relevant social explanations for differences.

Primary Socialization Theory

Studies of substance abuse often focus on the family, school, and peer influences, which are defined as primary socialization sources (Younoszai, Lohrmann, Seefeldt, & Greene, 1999). **Primary socialization theory** is a social learning theory that proposes that both prosocial and deviant behaviors are learned predominantly through the three socialization sources of family, school, and peer clusters (Leukefeld & Leukefeld, 1999). For both adolescents and adults it is believed that much drug use is learned and reinforced through social interactions rather than primarily the result of emotional distress. Complex interactions actually determine the outcomes for substance abuse. Earlier it was mentioned that ethnic identification can have a strong effect on substance use. In dealing with ethnic minorities, it is important to remember that all members of an ethnic group will not be at the same level when it comes to their ethnic/cultural identification. This means that they may be operating, as a result of this, in different subcultures of their larger ethnic group. Different subcultures will often have different norms for substance use.

An adult or an adolescent may have strong positive ethnic/cultural identification that is influenced by the family as a source of primary socialization. However, the person may also belong to a subculture of peers (another source of primary socialization) that has more lax attitudes and norms for drug use. Culture and primary socialization show reciprocal influence. Consider the following example:

> Yoshi, who is Asian American, may have a cultural identity that has been shaped by traditional parents. Elements of this may be passed on to her children and their children. In this example, the primary socialization source of family will shape the culture of the offspring.

Reciprocation occurs, however, because culture also determines the socialization sources. Culture (and also subcultures) determines the norms that are transmitted within the family, religious institutions, and schools. Cultural norms may determine behaviors such as parenting style or appropriate gender roles. Culture specifically determines who has the primary influence on social behaviors and attitudes. In some cultures the parents are most influential in preventing deviant behavior, and in some other cultures it may be other relatives or neighbors (Oetting, Donnermeyer, Trimble, & Beauvais, 1998). The key to intervention for substance abuse in ethnic minority populations is to acknowledge the complex nature of its causes, which may include broken prosocial links with family, general society, peers, the school system, or the workforce.

Sexual Behavior

Sexual risk taking can be discussed in isolation or as combined with substance abuse. Specifically, sexual risk taking is discussed in health psychology as a result of the sexually risky behaviors that lead to the diagnosis of HIV/AIDS. Ethnic minorities have disproportionately high percentages of HIV/AIDS (see Chapter 1). The rates are growing at an alarming rate for adolescents, due to their attitudes and social factors (Kotchick, Dorsey, Miller, & Forehand, 1999; Miller, Forehand, & Kotchick, 1999). The rates are also high for ethnic minority women who are primarily contracting the virus through heterosexual contact and through sex with intravenous drug users (Schneiderman, 1999). In discussing sexual behavior in ethnic minority populations, some specific areas for consideration are the following: psychosocial factors and adolescent sexual behavior, psychosocial factors related to differences in HIV/AIDS survival rates, the cultural influence on condom use and sexual identity, and the victimization experiences of women. In order to meet the goal of maximizing the sexual health of diverse populations, it has been suggested that researchers also increasingly consider income, gender, sexual orientation, religious beliefs and cultural values as specific study variables (Wyatt, 1994). These should all be considered as variables for examining sexual knowledge, sexual socialization, and the process and context of learned sex-related information.

Family Factors

The previous discussion on substance abuse in adolescents addressed the significance of the family. The family has also been shown to play a significant role in the degree of sexual risk taking among teens. In a study of single-parent ethnic minority families, higher levels of maternal sexual risk-taking behavior were associated with higher levels of adolescent sexual risk-taking behavior (Kotchick et al., 1999). Mothers, whether single or living with fathers, were critical to whether adolescents demonstrated responsible sexual behavior. This should not be surprising for ethnic minority adolescents, who due to their culture may be very family oriented. Therefore, it should be understandable that a family member can have a major influence on the sexual attitudes and behavior of ethnic minority adolescents. Family influence may be significant for frequency of sexual intercourse and number of sexual partners (Miller et al., 1999). It is particularly noteworthy that ethnic minority women can have a powerful influence on shaping their children's sexual behavior. This fact is one that can be capitalized on in health promotion interventions. Many women may not be aware of the powerful influence that they alone have, even when another adult is in the home other than the mother. Mothers should be made aware of the power of their influence. Sexual behaviors that the mother displays can be targeted for change or enhanced if positive.

Another finding from research is that the mother's quality of communication about sex is more important than actually discussing many different sexual topics (Miller et al., 1999). This is a particularly useful finding for parents who may be low in sexual comfort, which makes them avoid discussing sex at all with their adolescents. Also, some parents believe that talking of sex with adolescents will lead to an increase in sexual experimentation. This is not necessarily true—the research suggests that a quality parent/child discussion about sex might actually be beneficial for youth.

For Latinos, familism, as mentioned earlier in this chapter, is also significant to discussions of sexual behavior. Because the traditional Latino adolescent respects the parent's position, the parent's attitude about sexual behavior will be key. Familism is important in isolation, and also when it is considered in conjunction with the level of acculturation. For example, parental attitudes have been shown to be more likely to influence Latino adolescent sexual behavior in San Juan, Puerto Rico, than Latino youth in New York City and Alabama (Kotchick et al., 1999). This can likely be attributed to differences in degree of acculturation across the groups. Those adolescents in San Juan were more traditional and more influenced by their parents' sexual attitudes.

Research has also shown that parental awareness of children's activity is also significant to sexual behaviors. Miller and colleagues (1999) was unable to offer an explanation for why **monitoring** of adolescents by parents was related to more consistent condom use by the adolescent. Monitoring here specifically refers to knowing where the adolescent is and what they are doing the majority of the day. The sample in Miller and colleagues (1999) consisted of African American, Puerto Rican, and Dominican youth. With this ethnic minority sample, Miller (1999) found a significant positive relationship between monitoring and more consistent condom use. It is likely that these adolescents had a great deal of respect for their parents' attitudes and values (more likely in more traditional ethnic minority families, i.e., Kotchick et al., 1999). These adolescents may have been more concerned about disappointing their parents. If parents are high in monitoring, then their children who are engaging in sex may not want any mishaps to occur that may announce their sexually active status. Therefore, consistent condom use may be more likely to occur in order to prevent pregnancy or other behavior that the monitoring parents would be upset about. Overall, the research suggests that parental monitoring of teen behavior should be high and consistent.

Social interactional theory considers the role of interactions with family members and peers in the development of behavioral problems among adolescents. In a study comparing African American adolescents and white adolescents, African Americans were most likely to use condoms if they reported low family conflict, parental support, and involvement in family decision making; white adolescents were more likely to use condoms if they had parental support and friends who did not engage in problem behaviors (Doljanac & Zimmerman, 1998). For the African Americans, note that all of the significant factors for condom use pertain to the family. This finding once again highlights the importance of family for more traditional ethnic minority individuals.

Problem behavior theory suggests that the presence of one problem behavior in an individual potentiates the occurrence of other similar behaviors. Doljanac and Zimmerman (1998) found that both African American and white adolescents had self- reported high levels of risky sexual behavior that were related to antisocial behaviors, cigarette use, alcohol use, substance use, and academic difficulties. Only for African American adolescents, however, was it found that high levels of family conflict were associated with low levels of condom use. While most intervention efforts with teens may logically conclude that the parents should play a role, recent studies seem to be repeatedly finding that for ethnic minority youth there needs to be specialized intensive development of family-oriented programs.

Ethnicity and HIV/AIDS

African Americans and Hispanics are disproportionately affected by HIV infection and death from AIDS. Understanding more about the underlying explanations for this is important. Although the issue has been raised, research has not shown that there is a race-related difference in HIV/AIDS disease progression (Murrain, 1996). This finding averts the focus from biological explanations for the disproportionately high rates of HIV/AIDS deaths in African Americans and Hispanics. Instead, the focus turns to psychosocial factors. No matter the race, the infection and progression of the disease is relatively the same.

Murrain (1996) obtained findings that suggested that the difference in HIV/AIDS survival rates for whites versus African Americans and Hispanics is due primarily to African

Americans' and Hispanics' being diagnosed later with the virus. Psychologists should consider the role of socioeconomic factors in this racial disparity. It is still the case that many ethnic minorities are living close to, at, or below the poverty level and are not able to afford quality health care. HIV/AIDS efforts need to focus on ways to include the economically disadvantaged minority in responsible high-quality treatment and research programs. These programs should have outreach workers who can make contact with the persons least likely to voluntarily walk into a health facility for testing or volunteer to participate in research. Outreach efforts need to be planned such that they increase the likelihood of earlier diagnosis.

Another related issue here is the relationship of poverty, social isolation, and social conflict to physical stress and mental health. Poverty is stressful and leads to lower likelihood of receiving quality health care. In addition to poverty, however, African Americans and Hispanics may be experiencing strong feelings of isolation and social conflict in their neighborhoods, communities, or work environments as a result of their HIV/AIDS status. This could lead to social withdrawal and demotivation to have regular checkups, let alone specific testing for HIV/AIDS.

For ethnic minority women living with AIDS, social conflict may amplify the negative effects of HIV/AIDS-related physical symptomatology (Shrimshaw, Siegal, & Karus, 1999). Even moderate levels of social conflict may magnify the negative effects of the physical symptoms of HIV/AIDS (Shrimshaw et al., 1999). Findings such as this indicate that negative social factors can exacerbate physical symptoms of HIV/AIDS. African Americans and Hispanics in comparison to whites may differ in the levels and types of social conflict they experience, thereby affecting their rate of progression of the illness.

Researchers have also written about stages of racial identity and how this may relate to health behavior (Fudge, 1996). Specifically, during the progression toward development of a positive self-image that is consistent with the ethnic minority's heritage (but not anti-other races), an African American may go through a stage of being so immersed in "blackness" that there is intense suspicion and anger toward mainstream traditional health professionals. There may also be a rejection of anything related to the mainstream. This has been defined as the **immersion** stage of racial identity. Racial identity is believed to be related to health behaviors (Fudge, 1996). This is significant to discussions on HIV/AIDS in ethnic minorities. The following is an example:

> Fernando is in the immersion stage of racial identity. He knows that the AIDS virus is real, however, he doesn't trust the researchers who study the disease, nor does he trust the theories of the disease's origin. He is not only suspicious of facts being reported about the virus's prevalence in ethnic minorities, but specifically he doesn't have any interest in reading mainstream health material, or seeking health care from most traditional doctors. If he were in the early stages of disease, he might not take the necessary medication due to a lack of overall belief in its effectiveness.

For many who read the previous example, it probably will sound like just another paranoid personality type or someone demonstrating prejudice. The way of thinking described in the example develops, however, due to a complex layer of social factors pertaining to prejudice, racism, and discrimination that the ethnic minority has experienced in society. This is what the immersion individual expresses and thinks. Someone in this stage would likely refrain from going to a mainstream health care facility to be screened for HIV/AIDS or participating in needle exchange programs. This could result in a person receiving a late diagnosis with the disease that leads to poorer survival rates with the illness. Health professionals at all levels should consider the client's stage of racial identity in addition to socioeconomic status.

In general, when speaking of human sexual behavior as opposed to animal mating behavior, we must consider that psychological and sociocultural factors are germane. Sex for humans is distinct from sex in animals because of the many complex underlying social, cultural, and cognitive influences on human sexual behavior. Culture and all that it entails is significant and has long-term consequences.

Gender, Sexual Orientation, and Sexual Behavior

The relationship of culture to condom usage and risky sexual behavior is relevant to discussions of Latino and African American men and women. For both groups, traditions may be highly important. Specifically for Latinos, **machismo** and **marianismo** are concepts that reflect proscribed expressions of what is acceptable sexual behavior between men and women (Wood & Price, 1997). *Machismo* is a sociocultural behavior of highly traditional Latino males (not all Latino men) in which the Latin male exhibits an overbearing attitude toward persons in inferior positions, and he demands complete subservence. This attitude dictates the relationship between the man and woman in sexual relationships. Wood and Price (1997) describe this as an attitude that includes the more traditional male seeing the woman as something to be sexually conquered and taken for his own pleasure.

They describe *marianismo* as a sociocultural behavioral pattern of the highly traditional Latina (not all Latinas) in which she relates to Mary (the mother of Christ) by believing that she is morally superior and spiritually stronger than the man. She accepts that her partner is unfaithful with multiple partners because her suffering helps her identify more with Mary, the mother of Christ. She is expected to resemble the Virgin Mary in attitude and demeanor. If the husband cheats, it allows the woman to become the *mater dolorosa* or the suffering mother. She, however, remains faithful and may only want to have sex for her husband's pleasure or for procreation (Wood & Price, 1997).

The manner in which these attitudes translate into risky sexual behavior is significant. There are different gender-based standards when it comes to respect for sexual conquests. Traditional Latino males, through *machismo* behaviors, show their dominance and virility by sexual aggressiveness. This may include numerous sexual conquests even if the male is married.

Acculturation once again needs to be considered when working with Latino populations, because less acculturated males are more likely to have more sexual partners. Less acculturated women are more likely to abide by *marianismo* and accept their partner's infidelity. The woman may not request that her primary partner wear a condom during their sexual intercourse even if she desires to make such a request. This has been found in Latino populations as well as with more traditional African Americans (Marin & Gomez, 1997; Polacsek, Celentano, O'Campo, & Santelli, 1999). This suggests that these women must be empowered. They often fear that their partners will think that they themselves are being promiscuous if they request that a condom be used.

The *machismo* male is more likely to use a condom with secondary partners, but not with his primary partner, thereby putting his primary partner at risk for STDs (Marin & Gomez, 1997). More acculturated females are less likely to demonstrate *marianismo* and are more likely to have multiple sex partners and also engage in IV drug use (Marin & Gomez, 1997). Interventions should be gender based and specifically assess level of acculturation in the male and the female.

Proscribed expressions such as *marianismo* and *machismo* are related to other issues as well. For example, sexual comfort and sexual coercion are relevant to this discussion. Marin and Gomez (1997) suggest that highly traditional Latino men and women may believe that a man shows less respect for a woman if he talks to her about sex, or believe it is dangerous for a woman to know as much or more about sex as a man. These attitudes reflect low levels of sexual comfort that lead to a failure to even talk of condoms within the relationship. It has also been found that more traditional gender role beliefs were associated with more coercive sexual behavior and lower levels of sexual comfort (Marin, Gomez, Tschann, & Gregorich, 1997). Wood and Price (1997) refer to the *machismo* attitude as a working class sexual ethic and suggest that this attitude may be related to class across race or ethnicity.

For more traditional African Americans and Latinos, homophobia and a lack of acceptance of sexual orientation may also be significant for gay Latino and African American males because they have to endure the triple threat of prejudicial treatment due to their race, sexual orientation, and possibly HIV/AIDS status (Myers et al., 1997). They are likely to experience significantly greater psychosocial distress than white gay males, non-gays, and those at a lower risk for HIV infection (Myers et al., 1997).

Among Latinos, groups being highly affected by HIV/AIDS are homosexual males and intravenous drug users. Internalized homophobia presents a problem for substantial populations of African American and Latino males (Myers et al., 1997). Males who are less acculturated and perhaps of lower socioeconomic levels may be less likely to report having same-sex experiences. It is also the case that even if they acknowledge same sex activity, it does not result in their labeling themselves as gay or bisexual. They are likely to feel that the same sex behavior is insignificant compared to their primary relations with women.

Just as the attitudes of *machismo* lead to sexual aggression and multiple sexual conquests in a heterosexual context, the same can apply for same sex encounters. Males who have sex with males may also achieve feelings of dominance and sexual virility by acquiring multiple sexual conquests. However, Marin and Gomez (1997) cite that there have been strong biases in the reporting of same sex behavior among Latino males. Those more likely to report same sex activity are more likely to be over 25 and highly acculturated. Thus, there are very powerful homophobic components in more traditional African American and Latino populations.

Often in homosexual relations among Latino males and African American males, the male who does the penetrating does not adopt the label of homosexual or bisexual (Myers et al., 1997). They perceive themselves as strictly heterosexual and may engage in ongoing sexual behavior with other men while having wives or girlfriends who have no knowledge of this. Relevant to what was mentioned earlier regarding traditional ethnic minority women who feel powerless to request condom usage, this puts some women at great risk of infection.

In many instances with ethnic minority males of more traditional status, the male may drink more and feel it is his duty as a man to have many sexual conquests. For many traditional Latino and African American males the attitudes related to *machismo* dictate how they behave in general, and specifically how they behave sexually with the same or opposite sex. Although changing these attitudes is not easy, it is necessary to attempt to bring the males to an understanding of the negative health consequence of their attitudes and behaviors.

As mentioned elsewhere in this text, minority populations constitute the fastest growing HIV infected population in the United States. Minority women, in particular, are most vulnerable. HIV infection is the second leading cause of death for African American women aged 25 to 44, and the third leading cause of death among Latina women of the same age group; it is the sixth leading cause of death for white women (Centers for Disease Control, 1996). There are several underlying explanations for this. The attitudes of *marianismo* and *machismo*, risky sex with intravenous drug users, the women themselves being intravenous drug users, and sex with men who may be "in the closet" or in denial about their bisexuality are all factors. However, research has also considered the victimization experiences of women and HIV infection. **Victimization experiences** are defined as mugging/robbery, physical assault, or completed rape (Kimerling, Armistead, & Forehand, 1999). The environments of many ethnic minority women, particularly urban women, are crime ridden. Unfortunately, in many of the urban areas where lower socioeconomic status women reside, there are structural strain and victimization experiences. Inner city low-income African American women who report traumatic exposure such as victimization experiences have almost three times the risk for HIV infection than similar women who do not report any traumatic events (Kimerling et al., 1999). The relative risk of criminal victimization in the Kimerling and colleagues (1999) study was approximately two to five times higher in the HIV-infected group than in the comparison group. The prevalence rates for all types of victimization were significantly greater in the HIV-infected group than in the comparison group. This finding is particularly important for treatment efforts. The trauma of victimization leads to accelerated progression of the disease of AIDS. Researchers related this to the experience of traumatic stress and immune system function.

Personal Factors

Individual cognitive factors such as self-efficacy, esteem, problems coping with stress, and perceived vulnerability will also partly determine whether a person uses drugs or engages in sexually risky behavior. Personal factors such as these are often not investigated sufficiently. For this reason many programs may be unsuccessful in changing risky behaviors. There is often a lack of understanding of the real issues affecting the health risky behaviors. This may be particularly the case for ethnic minority populations. In fact, it has been suggested that several of the popular conceptual frameworks used to examine risky behavior may have limited applicability to U.S. ethnic minority populations (Wyatt, 1994). The common theories are based on mostly mainstream persons with little variation in age, sexual history, sexual orientations, and lifestyles. Wyatt (1994) makes the point that, in many cases, these theories focus on reducing the intent to engage in risky sex, without considering whether the person even intends to engage in sex at all. Also as previously discussed, the victimization experiences of women can result in a lack of free will regarding sexual activity. For ethnic minority women who are susceptible to many structural strain experiences, it may not be appropriate to study their behavior using a focus only on intent. Their intent to engage in healthy practices may be strong, yet this may not occur due to other interfering factors such as financial dependence on a partner, unhealthy relationship issues, or other expectations from significant others (Wyatt, 1994). Each of these could cause the individual to feel that he or she has little influence and control over his or her sex life or opportunity to negotiate healthy decisions.

During intervention efforts, program planners must also expect that personal factors may be important as barriers to change. Personal factors proved to be significant in The Strengthening Families Program (USDHHS, 1997). The Strengthening Families Program was a three-year prevention research project funded by the National Institute on Drug Abuse for parents who wanted to improve their parenting skills to help their children avoid substance abuse. Although the program was highly successful with diverse groups of participants, some likely common personal barriers to attendance of the fourteen sessions were identified as the following:

- Lack of transportation
- Lack of child care
- Required time commitment
- Lack of interest in parent training
- Lack of feelings of program ownership
- Cultural differences between providers and parents
- Lack of trust in or fear of the program staff

Therefore, personal factors are significant to the study and treatment of health risky behavior.

Prevention/Intervention

Research with ethnic minority populations in this area has supported having culturally appropriate interventions that include the family and seek change within discrete community units such as schools, hospitals, churches, and recreation centers (Wood & Price, 1997). An example of this is the Family and Schools Together Program that empowers parents to be their child's prevention agent. It empowers the parents to run their own empowerment prevention programs. This sort of program works well because the family and school operate as a unit; it also includes using peer groups of parents. This is beneficial for minorities who may relate more to peers who are racially and experientially similar (McDonald & Sayger, 1998).

Ethnic minority individuals may not benefit from interventions that are not culturally congruent. **Cultural congruence** refers to delivering an intervention in ways that affirm the heritage, rights, and responsibilities of the ethnic group, using interactional styles, symbols, and values shared by members of that group. It has been found that ensuring cultural congruence in substance abuse intervention with African Americans produced all of the following: more involvement by clients in the experience, more self-disclosing about substance-abuse behaviors, more active participation, more favorable change in motivation to seek help, and higher counselor ratings for client preparation for change (Longshore, Grills, & Annon, 1999). Cultural congruence in interventions with African Americans has also shown increased effectiveness using culturally congruent AIDS educational videos (Herek et al., 1998).

It is important to incorporate cultural congruence into treatments while also avoiding making generalizations about entire groups (Zea, Quezada, & Belgrave, 1997). Specifically, ethnic differences have been observed regarding substance abuse. For example, it has been revealed that Puerto Ricans tend to inject more common drugs like heroin, cocaine, and speedballs in comparison to Mexican Americans and African Americans. Mexican Americans are more likely to share (receive and give) injection equipment prior to or after its use. African American drug injectors more consistently report fewer other risky behaviors than either of the Latino groups (Estrada, 1998).

Similar to the differences in behaviors of subgroups of Latinos, Asian American youth may also show differences in risk factors. Certain groups (Southeast Asian refugees, Koreans, and Filipinos) have higher risk factors for alcohol and other drug abuse (Zane, Aoki, Ho, Huang, & Jange, 1998). Specific types of prevention strategies may be more effective in different Asian American groups (Zane et al., 1998). It is very important for health professionals to support culturally appropriate interventions that target the specific behaviors and characteristics of each different racial/ethnic group (Castro & Tafoya-Barraza, 1997).

Health professionals must also consider that inner-city lower socioeconomic individuals who abuse substances and are isolated in the community will not readily walk into facilities for treatment for substance abuse or HIV screening. Effort must be directed toward accessing these persons (Klein, Eber, Crosby, Welka, & Hoffman, 1999). For example in a study of minority women in Washington, DC who traded sex for drugs and money, mobile vehicles were taken into the community to recruit participants (Klein et al., 1999). This was a study that focused on increasing the likelihood of these women using the female condom. It is encouraging that most of the women were receptive to condom usage for several reasons. The women reported liking the increased control with the female condom, the advance insertion available with the female condom, and the potential for use of it without detection by their partners and clients. The study used peer educators who had used the female condom and who had extensive experience in the community where the study took place. Cultural congruence was enhanced due to the discussions between peer educators and the research participants.

Cognitive behavioral intervention has been used with ethnic minority participants to address substance abuse and HIV/AIDS (Fudge, 1996; Thomason, Bachanas, & Campos, 1996). Specifically, cognitive behavioral therapy may focus on dealing with any negative irrational beliefs that the individual (adult or teen) may have about his or her ancestry or race. Naturally, with this approach it would be necessary to first assess whether the person has negative irrational beliefs that need to be changed. Negative irrational self-attribution

Spotlight on Biology: The Stages of HIV Infection

The progression of HIV infection in adults is classified into three categories/clinical stages, according to the Centers for Disease Control. During the stage known as Category A, the infection may be asymptomatic or it may cause persistent swelling of the lymph nodes. Category B is characterized by persistent infections by yeast that may appear in the mouth, throat, or vagina. Other physical symptoms include shingles, diarrhea and fever, and certain cancerous or precancerous cervical conditions. Category C is the stage of clinical AIDS. The important AIDS indicators for Category C are yeast infections of the esophagus, bronchi, and lungs. Also, pneumocystis pneumonia, eye infections, tuberculosis, toxic invasion of the brain, and a rare form of cancer known as Kaposi's sarcoma are common. In addition to these categories, the CDC classifies the progress of HIV infection based on T cell count. T cells are a type of lymphocyte (white blood cell involved in specific immune responses). The normal population has a T cell count between 800 and 1000. A count that has dropped to 200 is considered diagnostic for AIDS regardless of the clinical category. The progression from initial HIV infection to AIDS typically takes about ten years in adults. During this ten-year period, large-scale cellular warfare takes place. T cells, antibodies, and other protective cells fight to try to clear the body of the viruses that are being generated daily. The HIV virus invades the host cell's DNA and begins the replication and destruction of T cells. Once a substantial amount of T cells are destroyed, the immune system collapses. Most HIVs are produced by infected T cells, which survive only for about two days, once infected. Each day about 2 billion T cells are produced to compensate for losses. However, over time there is a daily net loss of at least 20 million T cells, one of the main markers for the progression of the HIV infection. This allows opportunistic infections to enter the body and shut down the major systems of the body. An opportunistic infection ultimately results in the death of the AIDS patient.

Source: Tortora, Funke, & Case, 1998.

---

can occur in minority persons who have lived under impoverished conditions, been victims of negative stereotyping, been discriminated against, and have doubts of their self-worth. Cognitive behavioral therapy has been used to change these beliefs by bringing their thoughts to the surface in sessions, giving homework, and assigning positive culturally congruent readings to enhance racial conscience (Fudge, 1996). When there is greater internal locus of control, self-efficacy, and a strong positive racial/ethnic conscience, the client is less likely to show problem behaviors such as substance abuse. It has also been found that cognitive behavioral intervention that includes stress management works well with poor HIV positive African American women (Schneiderman, 1999).

For some African American males there is a need for aggressive HIV/AIDS education and prevention. It has been found that a significant number of substance abusing minority males may engage in high-risk sexual behavior (Morrison, DiClemente, Wingood, & Collins, 1998; Myers et al., 1997). One group that should be further studied is the bisexual male, due to findings of high numbers of partners, risky sex, and the often secretive nature of the bisexual activity that puts their male and female partners at risk (Myers et al., 1997). The form of intervention here should definitely include cognitively based approaches to address the negative beliefs of guilt and shame about bisexuality. The men also need stress management to learn how to cope with the various threats of prejudice that they experience due to race, sexual orientation, and possibly positive HIV/AIDS status. These issues are problems among highly traditional (African Americans and Latinos) males due to homophobia (Myers et al., 1997). For more traditional ethnic minority males, whether gay, straight, or bisexual, there is likely to be more sexual coercion of their partners, decreased sexual comfort with partners, and reduced impulse control when it comes to sex. All of these are sexually risky attitudes that need to be targeted for change. Overall, risky behaviors can be explained by several layers of social factors that must be addressed in interventions.

Conclusion

The risky behaviors discussed in this chapter are best described as being attributed to many layers of social factors. Since the numbers for substance abuse and HIV/AIDS infection continue to be disproportionately high in ethnic minority groups, there should be ongoing efforts to address the needs of ethnic minority persons. It is encouraging to learn that even hard-to-reach persons, when obtained for study, are receptive to interventions. In many cases these individuals are also actually able to benefit from interventions that are culturally congruent. Hopefully, as more health professionals become interested and knowledgeable about racial, ethnic, and cultural differences, interventions can increasingly focus on the minority client within his or her larger sociocultual and economic context. It is only with attention to this broad context that the best interventions will be developed.

Summary

For the risky behaviors of substance abuse and sexual risk taking, there are successive layers of societal influence on such behaviors in ethnic minority populations. It is necessary for health professionals to consider targeting such behaviors at early developmental stages, especially since risky behaviors are prevalent in adolescents. Teens who use gateway drugs, for example, are at risk for subsequent usage of illicit or hard drugs in the future. For minority teens and adults, the family has proven to be a strong significant factor. The family and other factors—such as strong ethnic identity, attachment, and affiliation—are all categorized as protective factors against health risky behavior. Although health professionals should be attentive to ethnic identification issues, it is still necessary to look for differences within the groups studied. Individuals may differ in how they are impacted by many different social problems in the environment, particularly issues related to structural strain.

Sexual behavior, like substance abuse, is also impacted by family dynamics. This is particularly so regarding the mother's sexual attitudes, sexual communication, and sexual behavior. The differences in survival rates with AIDS for African Americans and Hispanics compared to whites is attributed to socioeconomic factors and delays in obtaining diagnosis. This, plus the magnitude of social stressors in the lives of lower income minorities, may exacerbate the physical symptoms and progression of the disease, as shown with African American women who have suffered from victimization experiences. Another sociocultural variable related to sexually risky behaviors and attitudes is the individual's level of acculturation. This can be related to sexual comfort, sexual coercion, promiscuity, and a male's level of comfort with his same sex encounters.

Prevention efforts with ethnic minority groups should consider the broad social context as well as be culturally congruent, innovative, and aggressively directed toward the hard to reach at risk individuals. The therapeutic techniques used in cognitive behavioral therapy can be integrated with culturally congruent interventions to benefit a diverse group of ethnic minority clients.

Student Interview

Age: 19
Gender: Male
Country of Origin: Afghanistan
Years in United States: 16

1. **In the school system of your country, do the physical education courses discuss sexually transmitted diseases such as herpes, gonorrhea, HIV/AIDS?**
   No, they do not discuss that in the school system. Although I left when I was three, I am still aware of what goes on there and I know that would not be discussed in the schools there.

2. **In this country (United States) versus your country, what have you observed to be differences in sexual attitudes and behavior?**
   Well, first of all, there is no culture of dating for the Afghan people. Sex is not discussed because it is only to take place during marriage. They don't have the boyfriend/girlfriend stuff there because people usually marry at a young age. People in the United States are more open probably because they have sex on the TV, like in the commercials and stuff.

3. **Do you acknowledge any change in your behavior or thinking (i.e., about alcohol use or sexual issues) subsequent to living in the United States? If yes, how so? If no (not you personally), then consider others from your country with whom you interact.**
   The Afghan people that I know who have recently come here have changed a lot regarding views on sexual matters. They couldn't pursue stuff sexually in Afghanistan but here they can do more stuff openly. They have more sexual freedom. Regarding alcohol, well, for Afghan people they don't drink anything like they do here. Most of the Afghanis that I know here are not heavy drinkers maybe because of their traditional culture. But about the sex, in Afghanistan no sex before marriage but here they are doing it now before marriage (mostly the males).

4. **How important do you believe parents and peers are in influencing attitudes toward teen drug use and sexual behavior?**
   Within my culture, peers more than parents. My parents are very traditional Afghan people; they are not Americanized. Parents don't talk about drugs and sex in the Afghani culture. I guess there really isn't a drug abuse problem in Afghanistan. My parents never talked to me about sex and drugs even though I have grown up here in the United States They seem like they don't know that you will learn lots of stuff outside. They feel like it is okay if the school teaches it but they don't believe in talking about it. Most Afghan people my age and younger who have parents who are not Americanized probably don't discuss this with their parents.

5. **How prevalent are public service announcements in your country about substance abuse or STDs?**
   They don't have public service announcements like here. Few people there have a good TV, and the radio mostly has news and prayer.

continued

Student Interview   Continued

6. **If you were to experience having an STD or drug problem, who do you think you would turn to first about it? (i.e., parent, friend/significant other, personal physician, health clinic counselor, or no one)**

   If I were to have a drug problem, then I would probably keep it to myself. If I had to talk to someone about it, then it would probably be a friend. If I ever had an STD, then I would see a person at a clinic. You can't keep something like that to yourself. I wouldn't tell my parents because they wouldn't understand. They wouldn't be able to offer me any support.

7. **Would your answer to the last question be different if you were living in your country?**

   If I were still in Afghanistan, I would never have a chance for an STD or drug problem. People don't do that stuff there. They are already married and settled very young, like my Mom was married at 16 and my grandmother at 13.

8. **Has your knowledge of drug effects and STDs increased or remained about the same since living in the United States?**

   The Afghani friends and relatives that I have here who have lived here a shorter time than I have know more about that stuff now than they did before they moved here. I think that they are overwhelmed at first with all of the freedom and new stuff they can learn.

9. **What is the most significant difference between drug use and STDs here in the United States versus presently in your country, or do you perceive it to be the same?**

   The people here can freely talk to elderly people even outside of their family about sex or drugs. If I lived in Afghanistan, I wouldn't be able to talk to older Afghan people about stuff like that because of respect. Also another difference is that girls are treated differently here. In Afghanistan girls are treated very strictly. For example, Afghani girls would not be able to bring a guy home or even try to go out on a date. It is just not acceptable. Even here in the United States I don't go out with Afghani girls because of the Afghani parents. She wouldn't be able to bring me home. I like American girls because they can take you home to meet their family and you can have freedom. My parents know that I have a girlfriend who is not from Afghanistan, but they are not taking it seriously. They think and hope that I will marry an Afghan girl.

10. **From who or what source would you say that you learned the most about drug effects and sexuality?**

    Peers, school, and the media.

Key Concepts

African centrality
cultural congruence
ethnic affiliation
ethnic attachment
ethnic identity
familism
gateway drugs
immersion

machismo
marianismo
monitoring
primary socialization theory
problem behavior theory
social control theory
social interactional theory
structural strain
victimization experiences

Study Questions

1. How are the victimization experiences of urban minority women related to the progression of HIV/AIDS?
2. What is structural strain and how is it related to risky behavior?
3. Why is it so important to incorporate family-oriented programs in treatments with ethnic minority groups?
4. What would you tell a single female about the role she plays in the sexual behavior of her adolescent child?
5. Why should a health professional assess the ethnic minority client's stage of racial identity?
6. Is it possible for the adolescent from a positive family environment to still experiment with drugs according to primary socialization theory?
7. How does the acculturation status of a Latino male relate to his sexual attitudes and behavior?
8. What are some ways that HIV/AIDS education efforts and interventions can include cultural congruence?
9. What are the most significant reasons for focusing health promotion efforts on the bisexual ethnic minority male?
10. Give an example of ethnic attachment and ethnic affiliation. Why are these relevant to health behavior in minorities?

Student Activity

Interview someone who works in the field of HIV/AIDS and question him or her regarding his or her attitudes about the use of culturally congruent approaches with a diverse group of clients.

OR

Research the attitudes about and prevalence of homosexuality in more traditional Latino, Asian, and African American groups. How might these attitudes influence the cognitions and behaviors of gay and bisexual persons in these groups?

5

Exercise and Health

Health Benefits of Exercise

Throughout this chapter, the terms exercise and physical activity will be used interchangeably. The discussion of voluntary engagement in exercise is a particularly significant topic of interest for health researchers, and it is logical that health psychologists should attempt to gain understanding of the motivations for and barriers to regular exercise. An individual's degree of involvement in regular physical activity is related to the likelihood of experiencing a number of health complications. It has been reported that physical activity decreases overall mortality rates, as well as specifically decreasing the risk for cardiovascular diseases, hypertension, obesity, osteoporosis, osteoarthritis, various cancers, and non–insulin-dependent diabetes mellitus (Brannon & Feist, 2000). Also, coronary heart disease, the leading cause of death in the United States and all industrialized nations, is preventable and reversible through the implementation of a regular physical activity program instead of a sedentary lifestyle (Levin, Gans, Carleton, & Bucknam, 1998). Inactivity, therefore, can seriously compromise the quality of health across the life span.

Psychologically, there are also benefits to physical activity. Vigorous physical activity leads to acute reductions in anxiety and improvements in mood; research has revealed that following exercise, individuals may experience both reductions in anxiety and responsivity to stress, resulting in increased psychological well-being and coping ability (Steptoe, Kimbell, & Basford, 1998). Thus, it appears that exercise may be associated with a temporary inhibition of stress-related mechanisms. Steptoe and colleagues (1998) also state that this inhibition of stress related mechanisms may be a result of autonomic and neuroendocrine adjustments during the post-exercise period. Highly stressed individuals will likely benefit from regular exercise. Exercisers seem to feel as though they can tolerate a greater number of minor hassles of daily living without becoming stressed when they exercise on a regular schedule. Considering the prevalence of smoking and other substance use (often as reasons for coping with stress), research must be directed toward motivating clients to choose exercise over cigarettes, alcohol, and eating to possibly reduce anxiety and improve mood.

An emphasis on the health benefits of regular exercise must responsibly begin with elementary and middle school students. The emphasis should not be on weight loss or physical appearance during these formative years, but rather on health education and health promotion. Many children and teens show a high prevalence of body fat composition from sedentary lifestyles. It is important to educate youth and adults about the changes in body fat composition that can be achieved by regular intense exercise. It is important to implement exercise programs early, since young adults who are inactive and overweight are at risk for cardiovascular disease. Many also may be inclined to try dieting with the objective of effecting a change in body fat composition, while neglecting regular exercise. Beyond increasing awareness and early intervention, research will need to also focus on understanding factors that prevent exercise from occurring and how to overcome this in sedentary individuals.

In 1997, the Surgeon General produced *Physical Activity and Health: A Report of the Surgeon General*. The major purpose of the report was to summarize the existing literature on the role of physical activity in preventing disease and to report on the status of interventions to increase physical activity. In a one-year followup to the report, it has been noted that knowledge and attitudes are improving about the risks factors related to cardiovascular disease, but unfortunately specific large-scale traditional exercise interventions to promote physical activity have had limited success (Morrow, Jackson, Bazzarre, Milne, & Blair, 1999). National rates of physical inactivity are still rather high, since 24 percent of all adults report engaging in no physical activity during their leisure time. Of particular relevance to multicultural health, physical inactivity ranges as high as 43 percent have been cited for low-income, ethnic minority, and disabled populations (Taylor, Baranowski, & Young, 1998). Given this fact, it is necessary to understand the reasons or barriers related to the high percentages of inactivity in minority populations, particularly for ethnic minority women.

It is also important to focus on the ways to build upon the facilitators for exercise in such ethnic minority populations, while using the most culturally congruent interventions of initiating and maintaining exercise regimens for ethnic minority populations. Just as in previous chapters of this text, the personal and sociocultural factors need to be considered when attempting to understand the motivations and obstacles to physical activity in various groups.

Personal Barriers

In order to effect a change in the level of physical activity among ethnic minority groups, it is necessary to do a thorough assessment of the population (King et al., 2000). Research has found that the assessments should focus on gaining knowledge of the attitudes, preferences, needs, and any other personal barriers that prevent a routine exercise program (see Figure 5.1).

The reasons for physical inactivity may be attributed to both personal factors and social factors. For example, King and colleagues (2000) studied a racially mixed (Hispanic, African American, and Native American) sample of women aged 40 and over. They focused on leisure time activity, physical activity, occupational activity, and physical activity around the home. The study revealed the complex explanations for physical inactivity in these groups. Personal factors, social factors, and characteristics of the subjects' environment were all important to their level of physical activity. Specific differences across groups were also found. Native American women were most self-conscious about physical

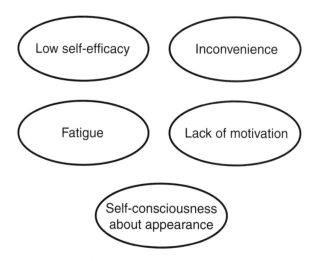

FIGURE 5.1 Personal barriers to exercise.

appearance, Hispanic women revealed the most discouragement from others about physical activity, and care-giving duties were significantly a barrier for African American women.

Researchers have specifically suggested that motivational interviewing should be utilized to identify barriers (Kelley, Lowing, & Kelley, 1998). **Motivational interviewing** focuses on asking the client questions in order to identify what the clients consider to be the major obstacles to initiating regular healthy activity such as exercise. It is especially important to gain an understanding of these factors for lower SES ethnic minorities because their levels of inactivity are relatively high (Taylor et al., 1998). For example, one of the Healthy People objectives is to increase blacks' vigorous physical activity from 12.8 percent to 17 percent and reduce the prevalence of a sedentary lifestyle from 28 percent to 20 percent in those aged 18 years and older.

Also in these groups we must consider the typical gender differences in levels of physical activity. The physical activity behaviors of men are often found to be greater than those of the women (Kelley et al., 1998). The varying socialization of men versus women may be relevant to this. Also, the magnitude of stressors for the ethnic minority female as wife and mother, single parent, or overworked and underpaid employee may be valid explanations for this (Taylor et al., 1998).

Motivational interviewing might reveal that physical inactivity is due to feelings of low self-efficacy for maintaining regular exercise. This is addressed in the stages of change model known as the transtheoretical model (Prochaska et al., 1992), which states that a person passes through five stages before being able to maintain new healthier practices. When it comes to changing one's behavior to engage in regular exercise, an individual may be a *precontemplator*, meaning he or she has no intent to begin any regular form of exercise for any reason. The reasons for being a precontemplator may result from a feeling that one cannot successfully initiate and sustain the behaviors, which is an example of low self-efficacy. For example, if a Latina woman in her 40s with a job, husband, children, and possibly no convenient place to exercise was presented with a suggestion to begin a physical activity routine, her response might be that she has no time for this (King et al., 2000). If she feels that she has no time, then she will not be inclined to even consider exercising because she will not be able to maintain it. In other words, she feels she will be unsuccessful in completing the progression to fitness. It is crucial to consider the workload of the client and the other work-related demands of the ethnic minority woman because lack of time due to work commitments has been reported as a barrier for more than half of working women who are in various early stages of change (Jaffee, Lutter, Rex, Hawkes, & Bucaccio, 1999).

In a study of African American women, it was reported that the women do understand the value of exercise in their daily lives. However, what is most prominent in influencing their level of physical activity is the identification of practical, convenient, and enjoyable forms of exercise that can be routinely performed (Nies, Vollman, & Cook, 1999). Thus, it is less likely that these women will initiate physical activity that requires purchasing expensive equipment (impractical), travel out of their neighborhood/work environment (inconvenient), or perform exercises that they derive no pleasure from. It is particularly important that programs include physical activities that are convenient for clients because the attributions given for unsuccessful behavior change in an African American sample of adults were related to personal causes such as time management, motivation, and fatigue (Minifee & McAuley, 1998).

The needs and preferences for physical activity in an ethnic minority sample may also vary. This is evident when comparing various groups of women, as well as when comparing women across all ethnic groups to men (Bungam, Pate, Dowda, & Vincent, 1999). Many people exercise to lose or maintain their body weight. This, however, may be of less importance in ethnic minority women. This can be attributed to the cultural differences in ethnic minority women versus white women regarding body image and norms of acceptance regarding thinness (see Chapter 2). Thus, unless the ethnic minority client makes it specifically known that weight loss or changing body fat composition is a goal, program planners and researchers should not assume that this will serve as a motivation for exercise. Weight loss or loss of body fat may eventually become reinforcers once they begin to occur, but initially it may be necessary to promote other issues. It is important to consider the cultural needs and preferences of the clients in order to tailor the exercise regimens. **Tailored health communications** support the development of strategies and messages that are highly individualized and thus meet the unique needs of the clients (Scharff, Homan, Kreuter, & Brennan, 1999).

Another personal factor that has been related to women's motivation to exercise may be concern about maintaining appearance after exercise (Jaffee et al., 1999). This factor, for some women of color, may have cultural relevance, regarding the complexity of hairstyle maintenance (Villarosa, 1994). When working with women of color, persons attempting to initiate regular exercise with them may need to ask questions about the women's concern for their physical appearance after exercise. This should be done during the motivational interview. Although women of any ethnicity may have concerns about this issue, black women have unique concerns that revolve around the effects of vigorous exercise on hairstyle maintenance. Vigorous exercise of any sort produces sweating that, particularly when profuse, can alter the appearance and condition of certain styles of African American hair. For African American women who wear naturally textured hairstyles, this would be less of an issue than it would be for the African American woman who chooses to wear a chemically treated hairstyle (which is negatively affected by moisture). Due to the cost associated with the maintenance of chemically treated hairstyles, some women may refrain from vigorous physical activity that affects the style of the hair and thus physical appearance following exercise (Jaffee et al., 1999). Although there is variety in the hairstyles worn by African American women, there are still substantial numbers of black women who adopt the styles that are negatively affected by some forms of exercising.

Social Factors as Barriers

Exercise motivation loads on two dimensions: a personal dimension and a social dimension (Steptoe et al., 1998). Barriers such as body image concerns, weight loss, anxiety reduction, and mood improvement are all personal dimensions of exercise motivation. Program planners must also acknowledge the social factors that are related to physical activity levels (see Figure 5.2 on page 86).

Social factors will underlie physical inactivity. Social factors are a lack of child care, no support, safety issues, social comparisons, and social identity. These issues may differ in their relevance for minority women versus Caucasian women (Harnack, Sherwood, & Story, 1999; Nies et al., 1999). Thus, when health professionals are working with ethnic minority populations, particularly those of lower income, it is necessary to ask questions about family and other social factors. For example, some women have children and need to structure their exercise schedules around either their children's activities or child care availability (Nies et al., 1999). Particularly if the women are of lower income, exercise programs scheduled for after work may be impossible since this would mean additional expenditure for extended child-care service. For persons who live with little to no excess money this would explain a willingness to sacrifice the exercise program. Also, low socioeconomic status alone may be a barrier to exercise if the individual is working both a full-time and part-time evening/night job to meet living expenses. For people who work two jobs and have children, there is less likelihood of their feeling that they have energy or time remaining for exercise.

For **contemplators** (Prochaska et al., 1992)**,** those who are thinking about becoming physically active, a major goal should be to move them forward to the point of making preparations to exercise and eventually actively engaging in exercise. For this group it is particularly important that they receive social support (Kelley et al., 1998). The social support may take various forms. For someone who is at the stage of contemplating exercise, the social support could come from someone providing encouraging words, someone acting as a role model with whom the person can identify, or persons acting as sources of **informational social reference**. Informational social reference refers to conforming to group behavior out of a need for direction and information (Huffman, Vernoy, & Vernoy, 1999). Social influence may move the contemplator forward into action (Laverie, 1998). This may happen as the contemplator follows the recommendation, suggestions, or persistence of similar persons perceived to possess greater knowledge of the relationship between physical activity and health outcomes.

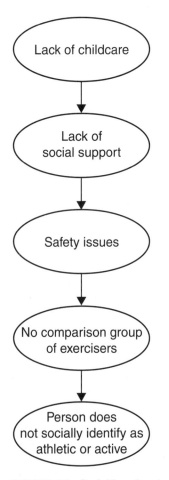

FIGURE 5.2   Social barriers to exercise.

For persons at varying stages of change, the type of social support needed may be different (Jaffee et al., 1999). For someone who is already active, the social support to maintain the behavior may need to be a workout buddy such as a friend or family member who is responsible for making a regular call to the newly exercising individual. For someone who is a contemplator with low self-efficacy, it is especially important for that person to have many forms of social support. The buddy idea is especially important for the ethnic minority female because in this population it has been found that "no person to exercise with" is a barrier along with "having no childcare" (Nies et al., 1999). The study participants were sixteen self-identified English-speaking African American women between the ages of 35 and 50. The study was a qualitative study using focus groups to describe the women's experiences with physical activity in their daily lives. The women were healthy, employed, and unemployed. They were also self-reported to be middle- to low-income level from the urban area of western Tennessee.

Another social dimension affecting levels of physical activity is safety. Unfortunately, in many urban communities of color, violence is still pervasive. Ethnic minority persons living in these communities are often stressed and could benefit from regular exercise. However, with a fear of the streets and few other options for exercising safely, many activities such as jogging, walking, or biking through the neighborhood may be avoided (Bungam et al., 1999). Since it cannot be assumed that all persons have access to exercise facilities in the workplace, the neighborhood, the community, and the home may be places for engaging in regular exercise. However, there may be limitations due to the lack of safety in the neighborhood or community. There may also be no financial resources for joining a health club. All of these reasons combine to make it likely that lower socioeconomic people have high rates of physical inactivity. This does not mean that lower socioeconomic people of color are doomed to a sedentary lifestyle, or that they should continue to be relatively neglected in the development of physical activity interventions. Instead, what must occur is an increased sensitivity to the specific needs of these populations, including attention to safety issues and some understanding of what would motivate activity.

Some suggestions for increasing physical activity are clearly written with mainstream suburban middle-class populations in mind. For example, study results based on surveys that question participants about their degree of interest in trying activities such as gardening, hiking, and badminton to increase fitness are not generalizable to diverse groups (Levin et al., 1998). What is the likelihood that urban city dwellers of lower socioeconomic status will have a garden, access to hiking trails, or places to play badminton? The problem with such suggestions is that even if more diverse populations are interested in these activities, there may be no safe or suitable places in which to do them. Researchers should be very concerned when they design programs/campaigns that only attract individuals who are already active (Levin et al., 1998). This is an indication that the program is not accomplishing anything for the sedentary hard-to-reach populations who are most in need of intervention. This highlights yet another example of the need for tailored health communications and motivational interviewing. For underserved sedentary populations, health professionals must identify and provide interventions that are more likely to be effective with these individuals.

Social comparison theory explains the common social behavior of comparing oneself to others in order to determine whether one's own behavior is normal or appropriate. Social comparisons will likely occur in association with one's choice of leisure time activity such as voluntary exercising (Laverie, 1998). Clearly, there is no such thing as race-specific forms of exercise, but due to cultural factors, environmental factors, and differences in media portrayals, persons of different racial backgrounds may have different preferences for leisure activities. Those who are contemplating beginning an exercise program are likely to compare themselves to others when selecting physical leisure activity. This is relevant to understanding individuals' motivations to continue participation in a fitness activity (Laverie, 1998).

Social comparison occurs in an upward or downward fashion. This is represented by the following example:

> Kutume occasionally goes walking on her lunch break at work. However, she does not have the time to really exercise consistently. The other women that she works with are not involved in any form of exercise. In comparison to them, Kutume feels that she is doing okay with her occasional walking during lunch.

Kutume's attitude represents an example of downward social comparison. As long as she has the inactive women at her job as her comparison group, her present level of physical activity will not increase very much. However, if she was to compare herself to other women who are similar to herself, but more physically active, then she would probably be more likely to increase her activity to match their level of activity. During upward social comparison the reference group acts as a motivator to the less active person.

The level of acculturation of ethnic minorities should also be acknowledged. Minorities who are low in acculturation are likely to compare themselves to others who are similar to them as opposed to comparing themselves to other races, or persons of a different socioeconomic level. When the person has similar others to compare himself to, he will look for something that indicates that the type of exercise he contemplates is common in his reference group. This could affect the choice of a particular organized team sport or individualized exercise. Research, for example, has revealed that there can be race differences in the degree of association of organized sport participation with vigorous physical activity (Bungam et al., 1999).

The **social marketing** of exercise uses many models that can formally and informally influence other groups of nonexercisers or minimal exercisers (Winett, 1998). Thus, for diverse populations, it is important to incorporate activities that the participants are likely to associate with themselves and others like them (Laverie, 1998). If the program planners are attempting to introduce a new activity that the participants have no experience with, then social marketing can be used that incorporates ethnic minority models with whom the participants can identify. For example, some persons may identify with Billy Blanks, the African American creator of Tae Bo:

> Billy Blanks overcame dyslexia, poverty, and medical complications (joint abnormality and pain in the hip region) to become a notable health and fitness expert. Blanks creatively combined boxing, dance, and Tae Kwon Do (Korean martial arts that teaches mental, physical, and spiritual discipline) to produce Tae Bo, which is a popular and creative full body aerobic workout. It has been praised for its ability to help users achieve and maintain fitness. Blanks states, "Tae Bo is more than just an exercise program. I created it to challenge not only your body but your mind, your spirit, and your will." (Price, 2000)

Social marketing using such celebrity models may be effective in social marketing.

Exercise programs for sedentary ethnic minorities should build upon the clients' existing interests. A good example of building upon existing sociocultural interests would be to use an activity such as playing "streetball." Many urban minority males engage in informal games on the basketball court that can be physically intense. These informal games are excellent forms of exercise with cultural codes/rules of the game. These informal games of basketball may not always be done with the objective of fitness, but may have a social nature or basis. The combined social and physical benefits make such activity especially beneficial. It would be helpful to inspire this form of exercise in a relatively inactive male, because he would have models for social comparison who indicate that this form of exercise can be enjoyable as well as beneficial to health.

Modeling is likely to have a significant impact on exercise behavior even via the media. Media portrayals such as television commercials are still not highly ethnically and racially diverse in the actors that are seen. For example, expensive and flashy health club commercials rarely portray people of color simulating working out. Once again, considering social comparison, people of color may not identify with the race of the persons in the advertisements, the body types of these individuals, or the activities being promoted.

Social identity may also affect the level of physical activity. **Social identity theory** considers whether the person associates who they are with being committed to exercise, whether the person has intrinsic motivation to participate in exercise, and the person's mindset while engaging in exercise (Laverie, 1998). According to this theory, social identity relates to what sport or activity the person will choose and how much time and energy he or she will put into it. Social identity determines whether an individual would view exercising as significant to him or her as a person.

Laverie (1998) classified exercisers according to four identities: totally immersed, socially influenced, outcome focused, and detached performers. The participants in this study were not, however, racially and culturally diverse. This means that the categorizations found here may not be generalizable to nonwhite middle to upper middle class populations. Persons categorized as totally immersed in exercise (aerobic dance classes) view the exercise as an important part of who they are; they also mention that the aerobics makes them feel better psychologically. Persons who are more individualistic are likely to be in this category, since it describes persons more likely to be motivated to exercise to promote their own psychological well being. Totally immersed persons report few to no social motives for engaging in the activity. This category might be less prevalent in ethnic minority individuals for two reasons (1) they may not be as individualistic, and (2) they may not see exercise as salient to who they are given other demands of their day-to-day lives.

Laverie (1998) found that the totally immersed persons focused on the atmosphere, music, instructor, dance, and structure of the aerobics class. It is likely that these same factors are also significant for ethnic minority populations. However, ethnic minorities are specifically likely to evaluate an exercise program for its degree of cultural congruence with their preferred cultural style of expression. The goal should not necessarily be to get sedentary ethnic minorities to become totally immersed in physical activity, but instead to get them to incorporate being a regular exerciser into their social identity. It may also be the case that instead of being in the totally immersed category, many ethnic minorities may be in the socially influenced category. This would make it even more important for them to have friends, family members, or racially and culturally similar role models in advertising to promote exercising.

Interventions

As indicated by Taylor and colleagues (1998), physical activity interventions that have been designed for specific ethnic groups have been limited primarily to African Americans and Mexican Americans, and even for these groups there is still a relative paucity of research on physical activity. Research and intervention for other groups of Latinos, Asians, and Native American tribes is lacking. Thus, this section will concentrate on suggestions for research and intervention with ethnic minority populations.

Having knowledge of the personal and social dimensions related to physical inactivity, program planners must creatively and successfully mitigate barriers. All interventions should include an educational component that is tailored to the participants' current knowledge of the relationship between physical activity and health. In addition, programs should be tailored to the participants' psychological readiness to begin an exercise program. Programs should also be accompanied by specific interventions that address self-efficacy and social dimensions.

For ethnic minority women of lower socioeconomic status, self-efficacy may be low regarding the initiation of regular exercise. Since it has been discovered that minority women report barriers related to no support, no child care, and no motivation, it is understandable that these women may also have low self-efficacy for their likelihood of initiating and maintaining regular exercise (Bungam et al., 1999; Harnack et al., 1999; Kelley et al., 1998). Persons low in self-efficacy can be assisted by workshops that teach them better time management and better communication about their needs. They may also need assertiveness training and problem-solving skills so that they can stick to their exercise program even when other life events or persons potentially interfere with their exercise schedule.

Lifestyle activities can also contribute to increased fitness. **Lifestyle activities** include brief activities like taking the stairs instead of the elevator or parking one's vehicle a greater distance from one's destination in order to walk further (Levin et al., 1998). These kinds of activities can be made a part of the daily routine and require very little time and effort compared to formal programs. And, unlike some other forms of exercise, lifestyle activities should produce little to no chance of failure. Self-efficacy should be high for the ability to conduct lifestyle activities.

However, even lifestyle activities may not be performed if the person's readiness for change is minimal. Particularly for someone who is a contemplator, the goal is to get that person to start thinking about becoming physically active on a regular basis in the next six months. Therefore, for precontemplators and contemplators, **consciousness raising** about the necessity for physical activity should be an initial part of the intervention. Consciousness raising refers to increasing the person's awareness about the benefits of physical activity through feedback, confrontations about inactivity, interpretations of life situations that may interfere with the motivation to exercise, and increasing the person's awareness of media campaigns (Kelley et al., 1998). Following this, perhaps individuals will be motivated to try basic activities such as lifestyle activities. Once the person has begun incorporating lifestyle activities into his or her routine, the next step might be to move forward to other slightly more vigorous activities.

For the busy person who says "I really don't have time to go to the gym," research has shown that we really do not need frequent long duration exercise (Winett, 1998). This is based on the belief that high intensity training principles are most appropriate for strength training and body composition change. **High intensity training** refers to high intensity efforts that require higher levels of power. This would include **aerobic power**, the ability to work very hard for a relatively short period of time. The use of high intensity training instead of high volumes of activity means that the duration of training sessions are only about 20 to 25 minutes and only twice a week or less to allow for recovery between sessions. This is partly good news for those who do not feel that they have time to exercise, although it should be made clear that this type of training is challenging and perhaps cannot be accomplished by someone just beginning to exercise.

Exercise promotes **maximal oxygen uptake,** which is the best measure of how efficiently the cardiovascular system transports oxygen to the tissues. This is increased with high intensity training. Each progression toward more vigorous activity should be positively reinforced, which will increase motivation to maintain the behaviors and advance in fitness. The timing for the delivery of the reinforcers and the types of reinforcers used can be decided by individual clients. The scheduling of reinforcers, and the type of reinforcer may vary by race, culture, gender, and age group. Health researchers can identify appropriate reinforcers during motivational interviews. When working with diverse groups, the reinforcers that are likely to motivate the ethnic minority client into action might not be the same as for whites. This is due to cultural factors and perhaps environmental and socioeconomic factors.

Sociocultural barriers are critical factors that can be creatively targeted for intervention. Exercise programs must address the unique and distinctive characteristics of targeted ethnic minority groups. Interventions need to be appropriate for the population. Because of the collective nature of Asians, Latinos, and African Americans, the approaches for increasing physical activity in these groups should involve the family, the community, cultural traditions, and social networks of both public and private agencies.

Sedentary ethnic minorities may be concerned about the exercise taking time away from family. It has been found for example, that elderly Korean women may not want to participate in exercise studies due to not wanting to take time away from their families (Shin, 1999). Findings such as this, as well as findings highlighting the lack of support and lack of child care, indicate that interventions should include family strategies. Ethnic minority mothers would benefit from programs that provide child-care services while the mother exercises. These mothers might also prefer exercises that involve the children, or even exercise such as walking the family dog. It is an interesting note that in one study, African American women but not Caucasian women reported that having a family pet was a facilitator to exercise (Nies, Vollman, & Cook, 1998). This is probably not because white women are less likely to own pets. Instead, it is more likely that this difference is due to the complexities of socioeconomic status, ethnicity, and other living circumstances.

Generally, programs with ethnic minority clients will probably work best if more than one member of a family can be encouraged to join the same exercise program. It may also be helpful if family members can exercise together outside of a facility/program. Having a family member or friend to work out with adds the element of social support (Kelley et al., 1998). Programs should offer incentives to individuals to join programs with a buddy or workout partner.

The Community Health Model

The community also has to be a part of interventions with ethnic minority clients. Involving the community means creating programs that can be implemented inside local schools during after school hours, on the campuses of community colleges during the weekends, or inside local churches and recreational centers. The **community health model** is a framework that is used to initiate the process of coalition development, to inspire future community participation, and to organize for increased community involvement (Taylor et al., 1998). Three different examples of community programs were described by Taylor and colleagues (1998). In one program, the community was involved through a coalition that studied the actual and perceived social and health problems existing in the target community and then decided the focus of the program. In another study, the community helped to define the needs, identify the strategies, and conduct the program. Organized communities (regularly scheduled meetings, good attendance at meetings, community leaders involved in activities to support the program) benefited substantially more from the community programs than unorganized communities. In a third program, community coalitions and subcoalitions selected their own priorities from a list of possible interventions, tailored the interventions, and implemented community-based interventions. Interventions of this type are particularly useful for ethnic minority clients because it means that the interventions are likely to be more culturally appropriate.

A community health approach allows clients to be a part of the program planning by offering information about what is needed. Clients are usually able to provide feedback on the efficacy of the program, and adjustments in the program can be made when necessary in order to meet the clients' needs. Members of the community are usually involved at all stages of the program. The community health model is particularly useful because it consists of persons inside the community who are familiar with the needs and characteristics of the targeted population. Using this approach also means that the persons recruited from the community to educate or conduct physical activities are likely to be similar to the participant.

Culturally Based Interventions

In several of the previous chapters, the significance of cultural traditions has been mentioned. These traditions can be important to the enjoyment of certain forms of physical exercise. Davis, Clance, and Gailis (1999) discuss the **TRIOS model**, which is an acronym for time, rhythm, improvisation, oral expression, and spirituality. Each of these reflects the basic ways in which individuals and cultures may orient themselves to living. Each is believed to possibly have implications for prevention and treatment. Using one example from the TRIOS model, the term *orality* refers to the value that speaking and hearing have as the preferred modes of communication versus writing or the written word alone. Among African Americans, orality can be used to capture attention, and the ways of speaking and being spoken to can be uniquely attention grabbing. Orality may be effectively used in developing culturally congruent exercise regimens (i.e., a call and response communication between dance/aerobic instructor and the class during exercise routines).

Davis and colleagues (1999) also reference the concepts **verve** and **movement**, which reflect the importance of newness and deviation from customary mechanically performed procedures. These aspects of African American cultural tradition can be easily used in an exercise program with diverse participants. African Americans and other people of color are likely to benefit from exercise programs that take the approach of incorporating their cultural traditions. Specifically, participants should take turns planning the physical fitness activities and aerobic routines for the entire group. Age-appropriate (depending on the group) rewards can be given for the best routine. Since African culture reflects expressive individualism/improvisation, encouraging African American participants to creatively develop exercise activities and routines is a way of incorporating the improvisation aspect of their culture. This, for dance aerobics classes, can include allowing the participants to select the music, format, style of dress, and movements for the routine. Each participant can be given an opportunity to creatively design a complete exercise session. Expressive individualism may result in participants demonstrating personal artistry and spontaneity rather than following strict guidelines. This will make the activities more enjoyable and perhaps decrease the rate of attrition. Allowing each individual to design an exercise session should promote flexibility and versatility. Orality, verve, movement, and improvisation can all be used together. Ethnic minority participants are likely to cease attending exercise classes that are not culturally congruent (they cannot relate to the aerobics instructor, do not like the music, etc.) (Davis et al., 1999).

Another cultural tradition for some groups that can be built upon is the use of martial arts. The martial arts or Wushu have existed for self-defense and survival throughout human history, and for some cultures Wushu may be regarded as a preferred style of physical conditioning and training. Presently, Wushu uses recent advances in sports medicine and nutrition because it is often practiced as a highly demanding sport and a delicate, complex art form, not just a system of self-defense. Correct Chinese Wushu training improves physical ability, health, and willpower (Shouyu, 2000). Therefore, it provides an individual with an excellent method of exercise. It is a personal art form, a competitive sport, and a basis for self-defense and sparring. The attempt to classify Chinese Wushu is very difficult because of the number and variety of styles in China. Consistent with the idea of building upon the individual's interest, finding a program that interests the client could likely be developed from the diversity of Wushu styles. For individuals who support the mind/body connection to optimal health, physical activities such as Kung Fu (North American term for the Chinese form of karate), Japanese karate, and Tae Kwon Do may be desirable due to their focus on mental, spiritual, and physical discipline (Gamache, 1995).

Social Networks

Social networks of private and public agencies can effectively meet the physical activity needs of large numbers of ethnic minority individuals in rural and urban areas. Interested professionals and researchers should write grants and seek funding from private foundations, as well as the federal government, to create culturally congruent programs. Depending on the scope of coverage planned, effective programs may require a small, medium, or large budget. Dance aerobics and walking are common and relatively easy forms of physical activity. Small-scale programs that use these forms of activity may be inexpensive to implement and yet still effective. This is particularly true if the programs are culturally congruent.

A good way to effectively reach many of the most sedentary ethnic minority persons would probably be through grants funded by nonprofit organizations. Research has shown that the use of personal trainers and financial incentives are effective for increasing exercise (Jeffery, Wing, Thorson, & Burton, 1998). However, lower income sedentary people of color in both urban and rural communities may not have the financial resources for a

Spotlight on Biology: Exercise Physiology

Physical training enhances the ability of the body and muscle cells to better handle oxygen. The muscles must be able to use oxygen efficiently to minimize the level of effort of anaerobic metabolism. Anaerobic metabolism is high intensity, lasts for a short duration, and produces lactic acid. The higher the anaerobic threshold, the better the body and muscles handle oxygen. Aerobic exercise requires oxygen to be present for the generation of energy from fuels such as glucose or glycogen. It results in no buildup of lactic acid as a result of metabolism. It is a more efficient process than anaerobic metabolism. While at a resting state and during aerobic exercise, carbohydrates and fats are used as fuels. A high degree of aerobic fitness requires a well-adapted ability to take in, carry, and use oxygen. Cardiac output is a major determinant of oxygen uptake. Muscle training and use of oxygen at the muscle also affects oxygen uptake. Training results in a more efficient heart (reducing coronary heart disease) and an increase in the maximum stroke volume. When maximum stroke volume is increased, the heart can work more efficiently at a given pulse rate. This lessens the necessity of an increased pulse and increased work for the heart during any given workload. The pulse will be lower while at rest as well as while the person is doing work. The changes in muscles following training are positive such as an increase in strength and the ability to extract and use oxygen. Muscle training also results in an increase in vascularity, which means a decrease in the amount of distance over which oxygen has to diffuse to be delivered to muscle fibers.

Source: Dr. Pribut on Exercise Physiology: www.clark.net/pub/pribut/spphysio.html.

personal trainer. Nonprofits that are funded by private and public agencies in most cases are able to provide trainers and monetary incentives free of charge to program participants. This is a plus for meeting the needs of people who are most in need with few financial resources.

Conclusion

Many in society are aware of the physical activity and health connection, yet that does not translate into persons changing from sedentary to active. One issue that is clear is that health psychologist can and should intervene on this matter. Regarding the relationship between physical activity and health, the barriers often are not physical but psychosocial and cultural. This means that there are many alternatives for intervention that can be creatively effective. It is necessary that those designing programs look beyond traditional recommendations. For more ethnically diverse groups, nontraditional recommendations for physical activity might be more effective. Martial arts, yoga, jazzercise (variation on traditional aerobics classes that uses more culturally congruent music and dance, used by some African American aerobics instructors), or organized walking groups may be motivating for clients. New approaches or variations on traditional methods may be especially effective if clients are able to provide feedback and make suggestions to program planners. It is important that health professionals obtain the clients' suggestions about program content as well as enhance the clients' internal locus of control and self-efficacy regarding their ability to make a change from sedentary to active.

Summary

A health and physical activity relationship has been specifically identified for several health complications. Cardiovascular disease, hypertension, obesity, osteoporosis, osteoarthritis, various cancers, and diabetes mellitus are a few health problems that can be affected by one's level of physical activity. There are also psychological benefits to regular exercise such as anxiety reduction and mood improvement. The significance of the health and physical activity relationship is in part evidenced by publications produced on the issue such as *Physical Activity and Health: A Report of the Surgeon General*. The levels of physical inactivity in ethnic minority populations has been highlighted and targeted for change. Generally, when discussing reasons for engaging in regular physical activity, personal and social dimensions are key. Personal dimensions include self-efficacy, convenience, needs, values and preferences, and physical appearance. Social dimensions include lack of child care, no support, safety issues, social comparisons, and social identity. Due to the various personal and social dimensions related to physical inactivity, program planners should design creatively effective programs that are culturally congruent for the ethnic minority clients involved. Tailored health communications that are culturally congruent can be developed following motivational interviewing that incorporates the clients' suggestions and preferences. The interventions should also utilize a community health model incorporating schools, churches, and recreational centers where the clients reside. Social networking between private and public agencies can result in funding for the creation of small or large culturally congruent programs in urban and rural environments. Many of these programs can be not only culturally congruent but also free of charge and thus better serve underserved and economically disadvantaged people of color.

Student Interview

Age: 24
Gender: Male
Country of Origin: Sudan
Years in the United States: 3 years, 11 months

1. **Do you regularly exercise? If yes, what form? If no, why not?**
   At the moment, no. I have not organized my time. Fifty days ago I regularly exercised. Before the end of the semester I plan to get organized. Weightlifting requires consistency in the form of a regular weight training program. School is blocking me from exercising and also Ramadan is blocking me from doing it. Ramadan (Muslim faith) lasts for thirty days sun up to sun down. During this time I am not eating as much and the prayers can be quite long. I get up early and eat before the sun comes up. Most of the time should be spent in worship and prayer, so I avoid the gym (it is not the atmosphere that I like to be in during that month).

2. **How knowledgeable are you of specific facts regarding the benefits of exercise?**
   I'm fairly knowledgeable of the health benefits of exercise. However, I'm not motivated only for that, but also for physical appearance (getting bigger). I learned when I was young that exercise will make for better health, strength, in old age. I observed my uncle who rode

continued

Student Interview   Continued

a bike for years and then when he stopped and became inactive he had numbing and loss of memory. I see older men in the gym who are active and capable. Luckily, I'm not exercising to avoid weight gain or because I'm worried about illness, I just enjoy it and I want to get bigger and more muscular.

3. **Do you presently have any fitness short-term or long-term goals? If no, what could motivate you to set some goals? If yes, how do you plan to obtain your goals?**

   I am planning to start my exercise routine again before the end of the semester and I want to try to build more muscle mass. I plan to accomplish this by weight training and I may do some track and field training.

4. **How important to you is having a regular workout buddy for exercising?**

   Having a workout buddy is very important for the support and motivation as well as when you need someone to spot you with the weights. I don't have a partner here, though. Not having a partner affects the frequency with which I work out. If I have an appointment with a workout buddy, then I know I must not stand my friend up.

5. **Are you satisfied with your present physique and physical health?**

   No, not at the moment. I just lost 13 lbs. in the past three months. I want to be bigger. I'm satisfied with my health, though.

6. **Is there a fitness craze or emphasis on exercise in your country?**

   Yes, in a sense, although not on a national level. There are only a few gyms there. If a gym is in a neighborhood, then the interest must be there. The gyms there are only for weight training and not many organized facilities with Nautilus and other amenities. Many guys are into Tae Kwon Do, football, and jogging. This, however, is all done in open fields or in a few community centers. Most exercise there is done without specialized equipment during mainly outdoor activities.

7. **Have you noticed a change in your motivation (increased or decreased) to exercise since living in the United States?**

   Yes. During the first two years that I lived here I did not exercise. During those two years I had to work to support my family and get settled. I had no time for the gym or for school. I only weighed 128 lbs. I used to be okay with that at first because I was lazy about counting grams, proteins, etc. Then I started going to the gym and I gained about 20 lbs. in 1 and $\frac{1}{2}$ month (weight training). At this time I became very concerned about food content and the amount of food that I ate. I liked my new muscle mass and size. My brother and a brother's friend had all gone to the gym together. They were getting buffed up. That is also what got me interested.

8. **How weight conscious is the society of your native country?**

   The society doesn't care about being overweight, although there may be individual persons who may be conscious about it. People from my home are not as concerned about it as those here in the west. Also one benefit for the body in Sudan is the weather. It is very hot there so most people drink lots of water. This takes away eating desire.

9. **Are males and females equal in their motivation/interest in exercise?**

   Males are more motivated to exercise. Women are not as interested and don't have organized sports really on a national level. Maybe there is a volleyball team for women, but that's it.

10. **Do you obtain exercise of any form in association with your daily living such as your work/job?**

    Yes. I run the stairs and I lift using my legs but not my back. Every day at work I have to do something strenuous.

Key Concepts

aerobic power
community health model
consciousness raising
contemplators
high intensity training
informational social reference
lifestyle activities
maximal oxygen uptake
motivational interviewing
movement
Physical Activity and Health: A Report of the Surgeon General
social comparison theory
social identity theory
social marketing
tailored health communication
TRIOS model
verve

Study Questions

1. Give an explanation of how social identity theory relates to one's choice of exercise and attitudes about exercise.
2. What would be an example of the use of motivational interviewing in a sedentary group of urban working mothers?
3. Physical activity decreases overall rates of morbidity and also decreases risk of what diseases?
4. If a health professional recommends high intensity training, what should you know about this before attempting it and what is the benefit of it?
5. Why would social comparison theory be significant regarding the likelihood of success of a new intervention effort?
6. Give a specific example of how self-efficacy could act as a personal barrier to exercise.
7. Ethnic minority women have higher levels of physical inactivity in comparison to whites and men; social dimensions are influential in this. What are some of the support and safety issues that may be unique to urban women of color?
8. Why is the community health model a particularly useful approach for ethnic minority clients?
9. How can the inclusion of "verve and movement" into an exercise routine produce a more culturally congruent intervention for specific clients?
10. For someone who is presently disinterested in exercise due to lack of time, fatigue, or general low self-efficacy, what are some relatively easy, high success rate activities that you would recommend?

Student Activity

Visit a local middle school or high school that has a large enrollment of ethnic minority students. Interview the physical education teachers and administrators about the content of class material and student interest/participation in physical activity (class-oriented or extracurricular organized sports). Summarize your findings and give commentary, stating pros and cons.

OR

Visit each of the following: a local school, church, or recreational center, each in the same urban community of color. Is there any evidence of use of the community health model? After obtaining knowledge from residents and via your observations, what social dimensions may affect residents' levels of physical activity?

6 Health Psychology and the Workplace

The Significance of Studying Health and the Workplace

In the previous chapter you learned that physical activity levels are significant to health. The workplace may be positively related to health by requiring physical activity as a part of the job. However, the workplace may also have a negative affect on health if the job decreases the workers' available time to exercise. Since approximately 70 percent of the adult population is employed (Taylor, 1999), it is feasible to study the workplace and the mental and physical strains of the job that may negatively affect workers' health.

Most people work out of necessity and not merely to pass time or as a means of recreation. Some are fortunate enough to have a job they love and would perhaps do their job free of charge out of a sense of intrinsic motivation. However, this category of individuals is considerably smaller than the number of persons who often complain of stress and fatigue in relationship to their jobs.

It is also worth considering that the average person who begins working a forty-hour week at age 22 and continues working until age 65 may well have worked over 80,000 hours in his or her life. Work, which is so pervasive in one's life, can be studied for its relevance to physical well being and psychological distress (see Figure 6.1 on page 100).

The literature in the field of health psychology distinguishes two terms when discussing health related behaviors: **illness behavior** and **sick role behavior**. Both are relevant to the subsequent behavior of employees who experience job stress and burnout. *Illness behavior* refers to the behaviors that an individual engages in before having an official diagnosis of the problem. This would include behaviors such as seeking medical information or scheduling appointments with a physician. *Sick role behavior* is the behavior that follows diagnosis that would result in a change in the individual's normal routine or typical level of physical activity such as exercise frequency or work attendance. For employers, illness behavior and sick role behavior may be targeted for reduction in order to produce cost-saving benefits for the organization as a whole.

Work-site intervention programs that are aimed at prevention of unhealthy behavior, as well as reducing already present behaviors, will save money for the organization. Reports have been cited that estimate that nearly 500 million workdays are lost annually due to risky health behaviors, illness, and disability (Taylor, 1999). Programs that address the poor health habits and stressful concerns of employees have the potential to save costs

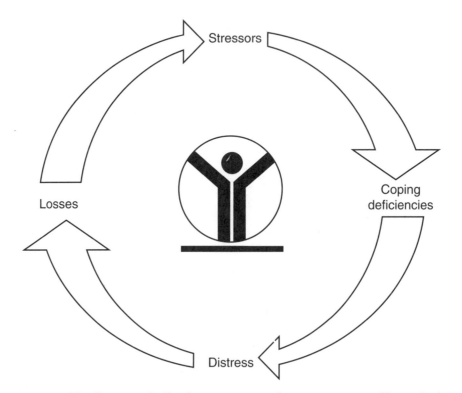

FIGURE 6.1   The distress cycle. Employees are exposed to many stressors. Those who have coping deficiencies rather than coping skills become distressed. Chronic distress, in turn, leads to social and financial costs—accidents, injuries, turnover, and poor productivity. But it doesn't stop there. These symptoms of distress become, themselves, stressors, and the distress cycle develops.

Source: USDHHS, 1987.

for organizations by reducing absenteeism, sabotage, and replacement costs for workers who quit (Karasek & Theorell, 1990; Taylor, 1999). It is also possible that such interventions may also increase employee morale and the self-image of some employees.

The job stress and health relationship is complex and worthy of study for both employees and their employers (see Figure 6.2).

Sixty-four percent of work sites have initiated some form of health promotion activities for their employees (Green & Cargo, 1994). Some studies in the workplace have focused on topics such as smoking and poor diet (French, Hennikus, & Jeffery, 1996), while others have focused on the effects of job demand combined with lack of decisional control on the job and how these factors relate to employee health (Contrada, Czarnecki, & Li Chern Pan, 1997).

The question, however, that most employers and their stressed employees ask is, just how successful are work site intervention programs? The answer to this question will depend on the population of employees being targeted and the type of programs being implemented.

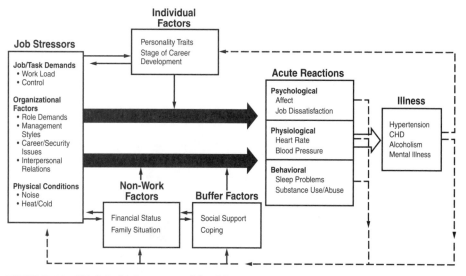

FIGURE 6.2   Model of job stress and health.

Source: USDHHS, 1987.

Diversity in the Workforce

A significant factor that employers need to be aware of when considering the implementation of health programs for stressed employees is the diversity of the workers. Employees of different race, gender, and cultures may differ in their needs, concerns, and experiences (James, 1997). The United States has been characterized as a place of struggle, opportunity, and change. The workplace in the United States is an environment where struggle, opportunity, and change take place daily.

Marsella (1994) describes the United States as an ethnoculturally pluralistic society in which the workplace is a critical agent for shaping a healthy and fully functioning society. Cultural biases in the workplace, conflicts in values, and lack of fit between the person and the work environment are a few challenges to a healthy and harmonious workplace. It can be an especially challenging task to create a workplace that is harmonious for all individuals within a diverse work environment.

Research in three separate studies indicated that minority workers may differ in how much their health is impacted by work conditions and their thoughts of self (James, 1994). In the studies, social identity theory was considered to be a central issue for work-related stress and minority workers' health. Social identity theory was believed to exert major influences on the behaviors directed toward minority workers by nonminority colleagues. It also was related to minority individuals' own perceptions of stress and their coping ability for stressful events. Several variables related to social identity were studied for their relevance to minority workers' stress levels and their significance across three studies:

■ Prejudice and discrimination resulting from in-group (one's own racial group) and out-group (others outside one's own racial group) comparisons

- **Collective esteem** (the individual's personal evaluation of his or her ethnic group) and self-esteem
- **Value conflict** (differences across employees in work-related and other attitudes that may affect the accomplishment of tasks)
- Social support at work

In the first, James (1994) investigated (1) the relationship between minority workers' perceptions of levels of prejudice and discrimination as relevant to subsequent health problems, and (2) the impact on health of the proportion of in-group (minority) members within an organization, and (3) whether the effect on health of in-group proportions within an organization was mediated by prejudice and discrimination.

Higher levels of prejudice and discrimination were associated with higher levels of health problems. It was also found that the more minority members within the minority worker's work unit, the less the number of health problems. Participants in this study were 58 professional- and managerial-level minority employees (Hispanic, 35, Asian American, 15, Native American, 5, and African American, 3) of both genders.

The second study primarily focused on the collective esteem and self-esteem of minority employees, prejudice and discrimination, differences in values of minority workers compared to supervisors and peers, and the relevance of all of this to blood pressure. Greater experiences of prejudice and discrimination were associated with higher blood pressure levels. Higher collective esteem and self-esteem were related to lower (healthy levels) blood pressure. An unexpected finding for differences in values was found. Minority employees who differed in values from white supervisors or peers had lower (healthy) blood pressure levels. James (1994) suggests that when minority employees differ in values from nonminority supervisors and peers, this may help to validate the ethnic identity of minority workers, yielding greater collective esteem. The participants in this study were 89 employed minority volunteers (males and females) from four organizations. Sixty-four percent were Mexican American, 18 percent were African American, 10 percent were Asian American, 3 percent were Native American, and 5 percent were individuals who indicated mixed heritage.

The third study highlighted differences between whites and African Americans. The participants were 102 technical and professional employees of a large university in the eastern United States. Groups were identified through personnel office records. The study showed that group-based components of social identity (collective esteem and values) are more important to the identity of minority individuals and distinctly relevant to minority health outcomes. African Americans also reported lower levels of social support on the job, which may be related to the degree of value conflicts with other members of the organization. Increased value conflict with supervisors and peers likely leads to less social support on the job.

Although the previous research is valuable, it is still primarily the case that many studies of issues in health psychology do not have diverse populations of subjects. Many studies fail to include information about the racial makeup of the subjects, and it is often difficult to discern the relevance of the findings to ethnic minority individuals (Carroll, Smith, Sheffield, Shipley, & Marmot, 1997). For example, in a study by Jeffery and colleagues (1993) age, gender, education, occupation, and marital status were identified, but no information was provided on race. Therefore, when regarding variables such as race and ethnicity, research results of some published studies might not apply to varying ethnic groups of workers.

When designing work-site health promotion activities, designers of such activities must be aware that for various racial groups there are different dimensions that affect health outcomes (Kato & Mann, 1996). An organization whose employees consist of a diverse group of African Americans, Hispanics, or Asians should design programs that take into consideration the cultural dimensions that are significant for these specific groups. Health promotion programs for working populations can only be successful to the extent that they incorporate this information, along with factors of particular importance for workers of low socioeconomic status in high-strain job positions.

Variation in Decision Latitude and Job Demand

Decision latitude has been defined as a person's ability to control his or her work activities (Weidner, Boughal, Pieper, Connor, & Mendell, 1997). **Job demand** refers to the amount of physical and mental stress encountered on the job. Decision latitude and job demands comprise what is known as *job strain* (Karasek & Theorell, 1990). Of course not all workers deal with the same level of job strain. This is due to the variation in the types of jobs that exist. Karasek and Theorell (1990) identify four different kinds of work experiences that exist due to the interactions of high and low levels of psychological demands and decision latitude. One of the four categories is the **high-strain job**, in which demands are high and decision latitude is low.

Job strain is prevalent. It has been found that organizational stress is a predictor of strain internationally, specifically in the United States, India, West Germany, Spain, New Zealand, Australia, and South Africa (Bhagat et al., 1997). The following is an example of a high-strain job:

> Luiz has been a trucker for the past fifteen years, and generally speaking he has enjoyed his work. Recently, however, the company has gone through some changes and he now works for the same company now under new management. With the new policies implemented, Luiz has less input into the routes he will travel for making deliveries. The company also now wants a 10 percent reduction in turnaround time for deliveries and restocking of inventory. This places greater demands on the truckers, especially since they now have less control over the delivery routes to be taken, and they have to work faster and harder with less rest.

High-strain jobs are the highest in psychosocial health risk, and in many cases they may also be associated with greater risk of physical injury and accidental death (see Figure 6.3).

Many high-strain jobs are female-dominated and include jobs such as nurse's aide, telephone operator, office computer operator, waitress, and garment stitcher. Other examples of high-strain jobs include many blue-collar occupations requiring shift work.

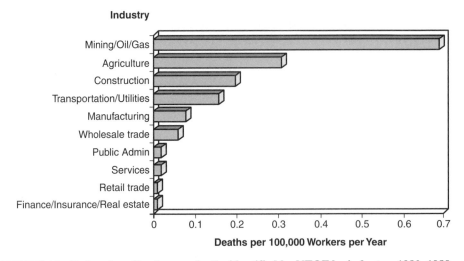

FIGURE 6.3   Rates of confined-space deaths identified by NTOF by industry, 1980–1989 (N=670).

Source: USDHHS, 1994.

Job Strain and Shift Work

Shift work has been studied in association with stress and health due to its high job-strain characteristics. Shift workers are usually defined as those who regularly work evening, night, or weekend shifts. Also, shift workers may rotate their work shifts every week or every two weeks, from day to evening, to graveyard shift (i.e., 11 PM to 7 AM).

Schechter, Green, Olsen, Kruse, and Cargo (1997) assessed the psychological demand and decision latitude of employees of a large telecommunications company, which included some shift workers. Workers were tested via mail out/mail in questionnaires. The type of job of the employee was compared against his or her responses to questions regarding self-reported stress levels, perceived general level of health, absenteeism, alcohol use, exercise level, and use of medications and drugs. This study found a number of associations between stress and stress behaviors and job types using the decision latitude and job demand model. Job types with high demand and low control were associated with increased stress, increased absenteeism, and poorer self-concept of health when compared to job types with low demand and high control. Also shift workers were found to have a poorer self-concept of health than nonshift workers. They were also more likely to report stress at home due to personal or family problems. Due to the findings of Schechter and colleagues (1997), shift workers should be considered a high-risk population for health problems. This has also been evidenced by the high rate of smoking associated with stress on the job for female shift workers in the occupation of nursing (Barak et al., 1996).

Although for some shift workers it may be difficult due to the nature of the work to reduce the job demand, managers can try to enhance decision latitude. Management should regularly implement programs that provide opportunities for education within the specifications of the employee's job. This would provide employees with the knowledge and confidence to be able to work more independently and should also enhance employee motivation and self-esteem. As a result of an increase in decision latitude, employees may feel less job strain and develop a more favorable attitude toward the work environment. Particularly for blue-collar employees, attending job-related educational courses and workshops can elevate self-esteem as well as reduce monotony. Job-related education and self-esteem both are not only related to each other, but also related to the experience of job strain (Kivimaki & Kalimo, 1996). It is also particularly important for blue-collar workers to experience feelings of reward for the effort they exert on the job, which may decrease job strain (Siegrist, 1996).

Sociocultural Factors and African Americans

For African Americans, there are individual, interpersonal, and societal influences on health outcomes (Jackson & Sellers, 1996). Occupation is an example of an interpersonal dimension. For African American employees' health, the workplace must be considered to be just as important as other interpersonal dimensions such as SES, family, and the neighborhood. Regarding interpersonal relations, African Americans may be faced with lower levels of social support on their jobs, coupled with higher levels of value conflict (James, 1997).

The resources that workers rely on to cope with value conflicts at work may not be the same for all employees. It can be expected that all employees will at some time during their job experience value conflicts, but the resources used to cope with the conflicts are not likely to be of the same significance for all. James (1997) found that although African Americans reported less social support on their jobs, the low levels of this coping resource were not significantly related to their health. What was more important as a health predictor for African Americans was their level of collective esteem. Social support, rather than collective esteem was only a significant health predictor for European American workers. The study also revealed that African Americans reported more health actions such as absenteeism and doctor visits (James, 1997). The results here support the inclusion of the work environment as an interpersonal dimension affecting African American's health differently from European Americans. Work environments that include programs and activities that build upon, reinforce, and support collective esteem in African American workers can result in a change in absenteeism rates, quality of performance, and negative attitude toward the workplace (James, 1997).

Many employers are motivated to design programs for their employees that foster corporate image, employee recruitment, good community relations, and a sense of corporate social responsibility (Taylor, 1999). However, it is also beneficial if organizations take an interest in the specific health concerns of their employees. Research into employee job stress can help employers identify the reasons for an increase in certain employee health actions such as absenteeism and doctor visits. In consideration of the behavior of African American workers, employers should have levels of collective esteem assessed. Programs should be implemented at the work site that address this coping resource, along with others such as self-esteem and social support levels. Each of these is related to worker social identity and is known to affect health-related costs for organizations. These costs might include factors such as premium increases, temporary worker replacement costs, and loss in productivity (Brannon & Feist, 2000).

Occupational health psychologists (psychologists who specialize in maximizing work conditions to promote the health of employees) and other psychological consultants to organizations must educate employers on the differences among employees when it comes to social identity issues. Diversity training seminars, for example, may help employers and employees change their perceptions. Many European Americans do not readily perceive themselves in relationship to a racial group as minorities do. European Americans may experience difficulty perceiving and expressing themselves racially due to less racial awareness in comparison to minority individuals (Pack-Brown, Whittington, & Parker, 1998). For the African American employee in a non-minority owned and operated company, the degree to which there are offerings (educational seminars, support groups, professional development opportunities) to sustain or enhance collective esteem may benefit the employee and the company.

For businesses that have large numbers of African American females, an emphasis on collective esteem is even more significant. It is common for African American women to experience self-doubt and mental strain on the job as they question whether their treatment on the job is a result of race or gender (Pack-Brown et al., 1998). The status of double minority for African American women may make the workplace a major source of illness behavior. This contradicts findings based on European American females that have found that employment is associated with enhanced medical and physical well-being (Weidner et al., 1997).

Job stress is known to be a major psychosocial risk factor for African Americans and women. Mays, Coleman, and Jackson (1996) cite all of the following as sources of job stress for these groups: lack of advancement opportunities, lack of challenging work, underutilization of skills, lack of control over work environment, negative treatment and undesirable work atmosphere, inequities in rewards, high turnover, and lack of training and personal development. With all of these sources of stress it is no wonder that studies have shown African Americans to have higher absenteeism and doctor visits (James, 1997).

It has been shown that factors such as age, education, and type of work may be significant variables that affect African American job stress (Mays et al., 1996). This is another finding that health psychologists should incorporate into **applied research** (research conducted in a real-world setting as opposed to a laboratory study). According to Mays and colleagues (1996), for the employer whose African American employees consist of large numbers of young males and females (24 to 29) or highly educated women, there may be more job-related problems/stressors interfering with productivity and motivation. Without attention to the significance of these variables, the average employer may be baffled as to why problems are reoccurring.

Perceptions of discrimination have been identified as the explanation for job-related problems/stressors in younger and more educated African American women. Therefore, for the employer interested in understanding and meeting the health needs of the employees, employee-perception of discrimination should be ascertained and addressed. Discrimination and other pertinent issues should be raised in focused group discussions where workers of similar employment status, gender, and race come together. Such focus groups are advocated to decrease feelings of job-related stress and increase sources of support (Pack-Brown et al., 1998).

African Americans' health may also be differentially affected by pressure on the job. **Pressured drive** has been defined as hard-driving, achievement-oriented, and time-pressured behavior; this, in conjunction with a repressive coping style, may have health damaging effects (Contrada et al., 1997). Personality differences result in individuals' responding differently to pressure. Some personality types will naturally express their frustration and dissatisfaction, while others will feel negative emotions, yet keep them bottled up inside. Oftentimes, it may not be a passive personality that causes this but instead a "never let them see you sweat" attitude. Such individuals may use emotional defensiveness and **verbal-autonomic dissociation** to maintain self-control and environmental control. Verbal-autonomic dissociation refers to showing sympathetic system arousal, although verbally and behaviorally reporting no signs of distress or arousal (Contrada et al., 1997). A coping style such as this may be particularly relevant for African American women in the workplace who are dealing with status as a double minority and who must develop coping mechanisms to prevent physiological arousal and reduce negative behavioral decisions with respect to work-related pressure. Intervention in this area should focus on restructuring such health-damaging coping mechanisms, since ultimately such coping mechanisms can lead to an increase in illness behaviors and sick role behavior (Contrada et al., 1997).

Related to pressured drive for the African American is a phenomenon known as **John Henryism**. The literature defines John Henryism as a behavioral pattern of hard work and determination against overwhelming odds (Anderson, McNeilly, & Myers, 1993). John Henryism is also often referred to as high-effort coping. Those who display John Henryism are more likely to believe that hard work, personal control, and initiative are the keys to success. It has been stated that blacks who display this type of determination, yet have few resources to help them achieve their goals, may be at greatest risk for developing hypertension (Anderson et al., 1993). In fact, African Americans who are high in John Henryism and low in SES show a higher percentage of hypertension than those who are low in John Henryism or those high in SES (Anderson et al., 1993). Also, in a study of 143 healthy employed African American and white men and women, racial differences were found in the relationship of John Henryism to blood pressure readings during work and laboratory challenges (Light et al., 1995). In African Americans, the combination of high-effort coping plus high-status jobs was associated with high work and laboratory diastolic pressure, as well as higher work systolic pressure. John Henryism was observed in the majority (71%) of the women and blacks in high status jobs, although seen in only a minority (36%) of white men in high status jobs. Also for white males, John Henryism was unrelated to an increase in their blood pressure. These findings suggest that there are increased psychosocial health risks for African Americans when high-effort coping is used in the workplace. The findings of the Light and colleagues study are particularly significant because they reveal the negative health impact of high-effort coping even for minority workers who are well educated (65.2% of the participants in the study had college degrees) and in high-status jobs.

Finally, regarding African Americans in the workplace, what occurs at work is definitely a significant interpersonal dimension affecting health outcomes. It is important, however, to acknowledge that in every case, studies have not shown job strain to be a variable significantly affecting health problems for African Americans (Curtis, James, Raghunathan, & Akser, 1997). This may be explained by the fact that African Americans are often struggling with issues related to family and community aside from their jobs (i.e., structural strain).

Sociocultural Factors and Hispanic Americans

It is very important to first acknowledge and mention here again the intragroup diversity of the Latino population. Discussions of this group should always consider that Hispanics may differ in at least six dimensions: language, color, economics, education, citizenship, and national origin (Shorris, 1992). Thus, the use of the word Hispanic is not meant to imply one culture or one nationality, but a general term often implying Spanish-speaking. Thus, it is important where necessary to make specific statements about intragroup differences. The stressors encountered in the workplace will vary depending on the type of work demands, the status of the job, and perhaps even the nationality and level of acculturation of the Hispanic individual. Shorris (1992) discusses Hispanics in the U.S. workplace as investors, civil servants, entrepreneurs, exploiters, and professionals. Barringer, Gardner, and Levin (1993) identified Hispanics in the United States as occupying the lower levels of prestigious occupations, which points to the likelihood that this group is likely to experience high levels of job strain and illness behavior stemming from high demands and low decisional latitude. Given this information, it is important for employers to acknowledge the impact that this may have on job performance and motivation. Health promotion programs can and should be devised for this population; however, before this is done, factors such as acculturation, family support, modesty, and traditionalism have to be assessed (Castro, Coe, Gutierres, & Saenz, 1996).

For Hispanics living in the United States, the degree of acculturation (acquisition of the language, behavioral norms, and values characteristic of the host society) can be just as varied as the makeup of the population of Hispanics. It has been stated that the blue-collar Hispanic employee is a loyal employee who will have an above average level of longevity on the job (Shorris, 1992). Such a description of these workers follows from acknowledgment of certain cultural manifestations. The employee's degree of acculturation should be assessed. Once this has been done, it is increasingly important for employers to implement programs that target the specific problem behaviors that may arise with increased acculturation and assimilation. It is important for employers to realize that although the worker may be physically present on the job each day and rarely comes in late or takes off for illness, the quality of the work being done could always be improved once workers are healthy mentally and physically.

In the areas of personality psychology as well cross-cultural psychology, emphasis is placed on the concepts of individualism and collectivism (Funder, 1997). Family support, another important variable in the study of Hispanic health, is related to collectivism. *Collectivism* is the belief held by members of some cultures that the importance of the group overwhelms the interests of the individual. *Individualism* is the belief held by members of some cultures that the individual is more important than the society of which he or she is a part.

There has been consistency in the research results on the significance of family support to Hispanic health programs. In many Latino families, there is strong emphasis on reciprocity and strong emotional ties among family members. Workplace health intervention programs with Latino workers may want to include some aspect of inclusion of employees' family members. Conditioning, education, or other intervention on the job may not be monumentally successful without the support of the employees' families. This may be particularly true for the female employee who may have an excessive amount of demands placed on her at work and from the family. Since family support is a direct result of the collectivist orientation, it seems logical to expect that family members will want to be supportive of the health promotion programs being implemented at the fellow family member's job.

Traditionalism as a variable has also been identified as important to specific Hispanic populations, particularly Mexican Americans (Castro et al., 1996). Traditionalism is characterized by nine domains, one of which is the value of traditions and ceremonies. Modesty in voluntarily engaging in certain health practices may be particularly prevalent in Hispanic women who are high in traditionalism. Behaviors taken for granted as routine and necessary (such as self breast examination) in some cultures may be regarded as inappropriate due to traditionalist attitudes about self-touching (Castro et al., 1996). Naturally, health-promotion programs for such groups should consider the traditionalism of the culture and how this may interfere with which programs might be successful.

A strong sense of community and family are also a part of traditionalism; therefore, organizations interested in positively affecting their employees' health behavior should consider hiring consultants who can implement programs on the job with provisions or extension to the community of the workers. This includes an interaction with the community through facilities such as churches and community health clinics. The joint efforts of the workplace, church, and community health professionals can provide the support necessary to positively reinforce the desired health-promoting behavior.

The *person environment fit (PEF) model* has been studied in relation to job stress and health outcomes for white and Hispanic employees (Gutierres, Saenz, & Green, 1994). The PEF model states that stress develops from situations in which incongruence exists between the person's attributes and the environmental configuration. In the workplace this may involve a misfit between the individual's needs or preferences and the organization's ability to provide rewards or resources to fulfill those needs. A misfit may also exist between the individual's work style or ability level and the organization's requirements or job demands. Gutierres and colleagues (1994) examined the impact of person-environment incongruence on the psychological and physical health outcomes of Hispanic and white employees in different job categories within a university setting. Hispanic and white participants were matched on income, gender, education, and marital status. For both white and Hispanic employees there were beneficial effects of both social support at work and family social support regarding coping with stress. Hispanic workers, in comparison to white workers, incurred a greater number of health problems when faced with discrimination in the workplace and an absence of social support. Prejudice and discrimination in the workplace were measured via a 16-item scale to assess discrimination against women and minorities in the workplace (e.g., "women are excluded from informal work networks by men" and "minorities must be better performers than Anglos to get ahead"). Health problems were assessed via a 62-item checklist of various health problems such as sore throat, diarrhea, change in blood pressure, depression, and headaches.

Sociocultural Factors and Asian Americans

Asian Americans are also a diverse group in the United States As with the previous discussion of Latinos, it is important to recognize the intragroup diversity of this population, which may speak several different languages and be from various countries of origin. The three largest groups of Asian Americans are Filipinos, Chinese, and Japanese. Significant numbers of Asian Indians, Koreans, Southeast Asians, and Pacific Islanders also make up this category of individuals.

The specific needs of professional Asian Americans in the workplace may be overlooked by researchers and program planners. This is primarily because labor statistics and research findings reveal that Asian Americans in the workplace have similar managerial and professional percentage levels to whites (Pollard & DeVita, 1997). This may lead some to mistakenly conclude that there are no specific concerns germane to this group that are separate and distinct from white employees. In some cases it has been reported that Asians and Pacific Islanders show usage of procedures of health insurance similar to whites (Carlisle, Leake, & Shapiro, 1997). However, it should not be mistakenly concluded that there are no specific concerns germane to this group that are separate and distinct from white employees. It is worth noting, however, that poverty rates for Asian and Pacific Islander families are twice as high as for whites. This may naturally be an explanation for why it has been reported that 21 percent of Asian and Pacific Islanders lack health insurance (Pollard & DeVita, 1997).

Comparatively, there is a scarcity of data on information concerning visits to physicians by Asian Americans. There are health studies, however, that have shown heterogeneity within Asian American populations and within other minority groups (Flack et al., 1995; Kim & Chun, 1993). For example, in studying Asian Americans, Filipinos in comparison to other Asians and Pacific Islanders have the highest percentage of hypertension. The percentages have been demonstrated to be comparable to blacks (Stavig, Igra, & Leonard, 1984). The same factors in Filipinos and blacks are likely to contribute to this occurrence. Dietary patterns that result in increased body weight and risk of hypertension are most significant (see Chapter 2). As with the discussions of Latinos and African Americans, acculturation, collectivism, and collective esteem are crucial areas to be addressed with Asian Americans and work-site health promotion programs targeting Asian Americans.

Level of acculturation is significant because it directly affects behaviors such as frequency of office-based physician visits and utilization of certain kinds of health professionals (Kim & Chun, 1993). Language, nativity, and ethnicity have been identified as barriers to health care access for Asians and Pacific Islanders. The degree to which these factors remain barriers is related to attitudes towards acculturation. Work-site health promotion programs must thus consider the level of acculturation of the employees. For example, it has been suggested that for Asian Americans and Pacific Islanders there are cultural underpinnings that explain differences in preventive care behavior and frequency of visits to surgeons and psychiatrists (Chun, Enomoto, & Sue, 1996).

The understanding of the psychological dimensions that contribute to behaviors such as excess alcohol intake, depression and boredom, and increased high blood pressure should be assessed in Asian Americans and Pacific Islanders. This should be done because attention has been given in the health psychology literature to somatization in ethnic Asians

(Chun et al., 1996). **Somatization** is the attribution of one's problems to physical complications, rather than to giving attention to significant psychological causes. Somatization may, in fact, if significant, be a result of cultural factors. It is more common in non-Western cultures to express somatic distress as opposed to psychosocial distress. The use of somatization can easily result in an increase in the amount of time away from work for the employee, as he or she may frequently schedule doctor visits to investigate physical complaints. The degree to which employers have employees who display somatization is relevant to what issues need to be incorporated in work-site health promotion programs.

Health psychological consultants may offer health psychology education to employees. When dealing with problematic behaviors existing as a result of cultural influences, it may be more difficult to effect change. Regarding somatization, however, a necessary first step is educating employees about basic health psychological principles and issues. Behavior modification techniques can also be incorporated into work-site health promotion programs. Similar to the information provided on other ethnic groups, employers attempting to implement change in the health of their Asian employees will need to consider factors such as level of acculturation. This is especially important since it has been stated that some Asian immigrants reach the status of white employees after just ten years in the United States (Barringer et al., 1993). Job status and subsequent levels of job strain are impacted by level of acculturation.

Program Type

It has been found that while employees may show more interest in participating in a work-site implemented weight loss program, more success is actually achieved in smoking cessation programs than weight loss programs (Jeffery et al., 1993). However, in some settings, the effectiveness of the program type may be based on whether the program meets the needs of the employees at the given time. Some examples of the types of programs implemented are health risk appraisal, blood pressure testing, exercise activities, nutritional education, stress assessment, back problem assessment, smoking cessation, weight management, accident prevention, and overall health education (Green & Cargo, 1994). Thus, it is important to have an assessment done of employees' needs and to implement programs that address as many of the employee needs and concerns as possible. It may also be important to have programs that have an organizational focus in addition to an individual focus.

Preventive Stress Management Programs

Organizational Focus
The design of a preventive stress management program may have an organizational focus or an individual focus. An organizational focus typically involves the overall system with the aim to design, change, or modify some elements of the organization as a whole, whereas individual programs typically focus on the care, treatment, and development of the individual employee. Organizational programs focus on designing structures, establishing goals, implementing technologies, and developing organizational cultures as a healthy context in which the employees can be more productive, serve, grow, and be valued. This may

have particular relevance for ethnic minority employees, who, as mentioned previously in this chapter, may deal with value conflicts, prejudice, and discrimination in the workplace. **Organizational culture** is the connective tissue that knits the people, structures, technology, and goals of the organization together into one, cohesive whole (Quick, Quick, Nelson, & Hurrell, 1997). Founders of the organization and key organizational leaders are most responsible for the creation and embedding of the organizational culture. Healthy organizational culture is beneficial in all work environments, but particularly in diverse work settings. It is a plus to have leaders and founders of organizations who prioritize human activity, people, and human relationships. The degree to which founders and leaders believe that people and profits in a challenging business are equally important, the more likely the organization will be a healthier organization in which to work (Cooper & Cartwright, 1994).

Quick and colleagues (1997) described Southwest Airlines as a company characterized by a sense of goodwill and humor, elements of its organizational culture. Southwest Airlines was also described as a company serious about work and service performance as a part of its organizational culture. Other aspects of organizational focus in preventive stress management programs are change of organizational structures and climate, promotion of organizational development, legal protection programs for the organization, and management consultation to address employee stressful concerns.

Organizational structure and climate are direct sources of stress on employees. The structure of the organization may include a task force for preventive stress management within the organization or an organizational health center under the responsibility of the company's executives. Healthy organizational structure leads to healthy organizational climate, which is relevant to the employees' levels of job strain. Healthy organizational climate is concerned with workers' perceptions and features of the workplace such as whether workers have autonomy, pride in their work, good working relations with colleagues and supervisors, and other conditions of the workplace.

In a study of 266 teachers from ten schools in a New York City school district, empowerment, achievement, and affiliation were organizational climate factors studied for their relationship to worker strain. It was found that a sense of empowerment was strongly related to feelings of work strain, and the findings were promising for affiliation and achievement dimensions (Michela, Lukaszewski, & Allegrante, 1995). Examples of the items presented to the teachers to measure the organizational climate factors were the following:

- Empowerment: "I often have the opportunity to influence the goals or actions of my unit."
- Affiliation: "People in this unit don't really trust each other very much."
- Achievement: "In our unit, we set very high standards for performance."

The results of this study are reflective of worker strain in women and minorities because the teachers in both the primary study and the followup study were predominantly female; also, for the primary study, participants were 41 percent nonwhite. In the followup study participants were 49 percent nonwhite. The high number of women in the sample was consistent with the proportion of teachers who were women in the district. The school district was located in a community with a predominantly minority population, which accounted for the high proportion of nonwhite teachers in the sample.

Individual Focus

Worker programs that focus on the individual for preventive stress management may include medical, psychology, and health departments of the organization. The programs may vary from specific stress management programs and physical fitness programs to comprehensive health promotion programs that teach individuals to manage their health risk factors while reducing vulnerability. Programs such as these are often a part of the employee benefit package, although they may also be considered by some as preventive maintenance costs for the company's human resources. Since these are often a part of employee benefits packages, the availability of such programs to all workers is not the same. Unfortunately, employees in lower-status jobs (often with high job strain) may lack quality benefits packages such as these.

Many companies also now have an individual focus that includes Employee Assistance Programs (EAPs). EAPs historically were developed to help employees with alcohol and other substance abuse problems. Presently EAPs are more comprehensive and include other issues that may also hinder an employee's performance on the job. A few large companies that offer EAPs are Ford Motor Company, B.F. Goodrich Company, and General Mills (Quick et al., 1997). The EAPs within an organization may be found in the medical, psychology, human resource management, health, or employee relations departments. From the previous sections on program type, it is apparent that preventive stress management will vary across organizations and preferences and needs of the employee.

Spotlight on Biology: Job Strain, Neuroendocrine Activation, and Immune Status

Immune system parameters have been studied in relationship to job strain. In general, negative relations between the stress factor and the assessed immune system parameters have been found. Stress, such as that found in high-strain jobs, seems to be related to immunosuppression. There are several processes that mediate the relationship between stress factors and immune functioning. Among these processes are the nature and duration of the stressful emotional stimulus and the role of neuroendocrine mediators. As presented in this chapter, increased job demand and decreased decision latitude are job characteristics that negatively affect workers. Specifically, it is believed that low decision latitude may be related to lower counts of several important immune cells in peripheral blood. In a study of male cargo handlers (shift workers), the following hypotheses were investigated: (1) the higher the level of (perceived) job demands, the lower the values of the immune cell counts, and (2) the lower the level of (perceived) decision latitude, the lower the values of the immune cell counts. Interindividual differences in the perception of workload and control over work activities were related to some immune parameters such as the percentage of lymphocytes. A higher perceived workload in combination with a lower perceived control was related to a lower value of these immune parameters. There was also a weak relation found with urinary excretion rate of adrenaline. This and the reduction in lymphocytes for the workers with low decision latitude and high demand suggest immune system suppression due to job strain.

Source: Meijman, van Dormolen, Herber, Rongen, & Kuiper, 1995.

Conclusion

Health psychology and the workplace has become an important and necessary concern for employers and their employees. Increasingly, as the workforce becomes more diverse, it is necessary to understand the needs and concerns of this changing workforce. How to specifically structure work-site health promotion programs highly depends upon the makeup of the various employees and the organization's goals. This includes addressing factors such as gender, race, and ethnicity. A significant component of this chapter has been diversity in the workplace and how this relates to the climate of an organization and the composition of health programs in the workplace. The first step in creating work-site health promotion programs should be to assess the needs of the employees and then subsequently assess the employees' opinions of change in themselves and change in the work environment. The unique strengths and offerings of each individual employee contributes to a thriving ethnocultural workplace.

Summary

Work is pervasive. Employers are in a position to improve the health of workers by implementing work-site health promotion programs. These programs can reduce poor health habits of workers and have the potential to save costs for organizations by reducing absenteeism, sabotage, and replacement costs for workers who quit. The success of a work-site program depends on the type of program being implemented and the population of employees being targeted. When designing work-site health promotion activities, designers of such activities must be aware that for various racial groups there are different dimensions that affect health outcomes. Dimensions that may differ may be the degree of decision latitude and job demands of the worker. An organization whose employees consist of a diverse group of African Americans, Hispanics, or Asians should have programs designed that take into consideration the dimensions that are significant for these specific groups. Following the assessment of the workers within an organization, the next task is to decide upon a focus for stress prevention management programs. The focus may be on the organizational structure or culture as a whole, or specifically on the individual. Whether the focus is on the organization as a whole or the individual, the objective should be to create a productive and healthy workplace for an increasingly diverse workforce.

Student Interview

Age: 32
Gender: Female
Country of Origin: El Salvador
Years in the United States: 15

1. **How stressful would you rate your work on a scale of 1 to 10?**
   My work is very stressful. I am a supervisor of a shipping company and it is the third major shipping company. Sixty percent of all of our work is with independent contractors. We have turnover with the small company independent drivers. We have standards that we have

to meet, but we can't discipline the drivers if they are tardy because they don't work for us. It is stressful with the turnover in drivers, something will be lost (customer) when new drivers have to go through training. My job requires long hours. In this area, people scrutinize people in a "polite way."

2. **How do you deal with job stress?**
   I like to spend a lot of time alone, traveling (spring and summer) to get away from everything. I do photography for a hobby (relaxing something to do). I get in my car and go.

3. **Are you ever conscious of your race/ethnicity as an employee in the United States?**
   Sometimes from the customers I can tell that they think (because of my accent) that I don't know what I'm talking about. They sometimes say that they want to speak to someone in charge, and I am in charge.

4. **Due to concerns about stress and health, what type of work would you avoid?**
   I don't want to retire from the type of work I'm doing. I want to do something more rewarding (helping people). I wouldn't want to do work just for the paycheck.

5. **What kind of work do or did your parents do?**
   My father is a tailor and my mother is a housekeeper.

6. **Do you perceive your parents as experiencing work-related stress and health problems?**
   Yes, my Dad. He was the sole breadwinner of the family. He was stressed if there was no work. I saw him worrying about not having money to pay for my school.

7. **Do you ever experience negative health effects that you would relate to your job (hours, stress, physical exertion)?**
   Oh yes. I sometimes work more than 10 hours and sometimes as many as 14 hours. I would like to sleep 6 to 7 hours but sometimes it's hard. Sometimes I think my blood pressure is getting high. I like to do a good job, and if things don't go well I feel responsible, which makes me lose sleep. This happens especially if it is one of our big customers. I also drink a lot of coffee and I am stressed. We (management) have to straighten everything out if something goes wrong. Seven years ago I didn't have trouble sleeping. I have been working my job for four years.

8. **How hard has it been for you to adjust to working in the United States?**
   I have been in the workforce since I was 15 or 16, even back in El Salvador. I haven't had too many problems adjusting. One thing that I had to get used to when I came here years ago was that the Hispanic population was not as large as it is now here, and I was the only Hispanic in the school. Language was the biggest adjustment as a teen. I didn't have many adjustment problems really, other than the weather.

9. **Do you rarely, sometimes, or often call in sick on your work days?**
   I never call in sick. I am a workaholic; work is good. I like to work. I feel like I owe them that much to work for the paycheck that I am getting. Besides, as a woman and a minority, the job opened doors for me.

10. **Describe the most common jobs in your country and the work ethic there. Are there many job-related health problems in your country of origin?**
    Most women have jobs as secretariés. The men may have a small business of some kind or work at a local business. People there are thankful to have a job, because there aren't that many jobs. Here people can change careers three or four times if they want to. It's not like that in El Salvador.

    The life expectancy there is not as high as in the United States The job-related health problems are not addressed there. People may be sick and may not go to the doctor. There are no emissions tests for cars there and the water is not good. There aren't any people there with jobs to keep those things up. They don't have regulations like they do here for selling foods such as health department rules.

Key Concepts

applied research
collective esteem
decision latitude
high strain job
illness behavior
job demand
John Henryism
occupational health psychologists
organizational culture
pressured drive
sick role behavior
somatization
traditionalism
value conflict
verbal-autonomic dissociation

Study Questions

1. What is the difference between illness behavior and sick role behavior? Give an example of each of these.
2. How could something such as verbal-autonomic dissociation have negative health effects?
3. What is an example of a task that might typify the work of a consulting health psychologist regarding organizational structure?
4. If someone were told that they displayed "somatization," would they be more likely to see a physician or psychologist for their health concerns?
5. What could an employer do to increase an employees' feelings of decision latitude?
6. Pressured drive can be bad if it is combined with what?
7. What is the difference in stress management programs that have an organizational focus versus an individual focus?
8. Give specific examples of two job characteristics that produce a "high job strain" situation.
9. Why might a Hispanic woman who is high in traditionalism be reluctant to participate in some work-site health programs?
10. What are on-the-job value conflicts?

Student Activity

Select two individuals (low job strain and high job strain) and interview them about their work. Based on the information that you obtain in the interview, what are the major differences in what the interviewees state about their work's affect on their health?

OR

Do research on the issue of somatization in less acculturated Asian populations. There is some debate on the validity of this issue in the descriptions of Asian health behavior. Write a thorough report on the topic (in your report you may want to interview employees from varying segments of the workforce).

7 Depression and Self-Injurious Behaviors

Statement of the Problem

The alarming fact that **suicide** is the third leading cause of death among those aged 15 to 24 underscores the need for health professionals to prioritize the issue of suicidal behaviors (Zimmerman & Zayas, 1995). A person's culture and worldview play an important role in determining whether a specific event or situation becomes a crisis (Herrera, 1996). Cultural and regional factors significantly influence whether a person will engage in suicidal behavior, which suicidal behaviors are displayed, and under what circumstances the acts will be performed (Kaplan & Geling, 1998; Roberts, Chen, & Roberts, 1997). And, particularly for teenagers, the type of suicidal behaviors displayed are based on imitation or identification with those they relate to from their culture, race, or peer group (Shaffer, Gould, & Hicks, 1994).

The unfortunate circumstances of life can sometimes lead to the desire and motivation to see one's life end. The culture and worldview may affect whether depression and suicide are discussed openly, or even whether self-injurious health behaviors are seen as related to underlying depression. For example, although the individual may not be aware of it, substance abuse and problems with impulse control, including conduct disturbance and sexual irresponsibility, may be the outward expressions of deeply rooted psychological dysfunction (Yamamoto, Silva, Justice, Chang, & Leong, 1993). This was demonstrated in a study of U.S. college students.

Barrios and colleagues (Barrios, Everett, Simon, & Brener, 2000) analyzed data from the 1995 National College Health Risk Behavior Survey. The sample was a nationally representative sample of 2,857 undergraduate college students, aged 18 years or older in two- and four-year public and private colleges and universities. The students answered two questions regarding suicide ideation: "During the past twelve months, did you ever seriously consider attempting suicide?" and "During the past twelve months, did you make a plan about how you would attempt suicide?" The students also answered several questions such as: "How often do you wear a seat belt when driving a car?" and "When you went boating or swimming during the past twelve months, how often did you drink alcohol?" The study found that suicidal ideation was associated with injury-related risk behaviors (see Table 7.1).

Specifically, many of the young people who reported suicidal ideation also engaged in behaviors that put them at risk for serious injury from motor vehicle crashes, drowning,

TABLE 7.1   Percentages and Adjusted Odds Ratios (OR) With 95% Confidence Intervals (CI) of Undergraduate College Students (*N*=2857) Who Engaged in Injury-related Risk Behaviors, by Suicide Ideation.

| | Planned/considered suicide† | | | | | | |
| | Yes | | | | No | | |
Risk behavior	%	CI	OR‡	CI	%	CI	OR
Seat belt use							
Rarely/never used as passenger	18.9	±5.2	2.26	1.54, 3.33	10.0	±1.8	1.0
Rarely/never used as driver§	15.3	±4.9	2.02	1.26, 3.25	8.9	±1.8	1.0
Drinking							
Rode with drinking driver‖	45.1	±5.9	1.48	1.14, 1.90	38.1	±2.9	1.0
Drove after drinking‖	34.3	±5.7	1.71	1.31, 2.22	26.9	±2.4	1.0
Boated/swam after drinking¶	32.9	±6.6	1.55	1.08, 2.22	27.6	±2.8	1.0
Weapons							
Carried weapon#	16.7	±4.6	2.98	1.94, 4.57	7.2	±1.4	1.0
Carried gun††	3.9	±2.6	2.15	0.93, 4.95	2.3	±0.8	1.0
In physical fight†	24.0	±5.2	2.78	1.98, 3.89	11.6	±1.3	1.0

†≥ 1 time during the 12 months preceding the survey;

‡controling for age, sex, race/ethnicity, and parental education;

§among those who drove a car;

‖≥ 1 time during the 30 days preceding the survey;

¶among the 81.4% who went boating or swimming during the 12 months preceding the survey;

#such as a gun, knife, or club on ≥ 1 of the 30 days preceding the survey, except for the job-related reasons;

††≥ 1 of the 30 days preceding the survey, except job-related reasons.

Source: Barrios et al., 2000.

or violence. Health-care providers and others who note the presence of injury-related or risky behaviors should screen for the presence of suicidal ideation (see Figure 7.1).

When a person is observed to be "acting out" in terms of health risky behaviors, the underlying explanations for this need to be ascertained. The following is an example:

> When Hasan entered college as a freshman, he was optimistic about his future in the medical field as a physician. He was not nervous about his likelihood of success in college, because in high school he typically found most course-work easy to pass. He had graduated at the top of his class. However, Hasan was admittedly underdeveloped in his social skills. He was a likable guy, but not socially comfortable at parties or around girls. Eventually, in order to fit in and relax more, he began drinking. Although the grades were still above average, his social life was not improving very much. Hasan's drinking on weekends was regular and heavy, and it eventually began to occur during the week. When he was drunk he was less inhibited and more outgoing. He could approach females. Hasan eventually became a

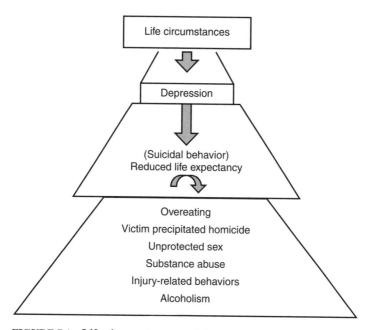

FIGURE 7.1   Life circumstances and depression may lead to suicidal behavior and reduced life expectancy from unhealthy behavior.

person who was drunk more than sober on any given day. He was also sexually promiscuous during his drinking binges. Eventually a friend suggested that Hasan see a counselor about his drinking and other obvious changes in his personality. Counselors suspected that Hasan was depressed. In addition, after a random visit to the campus health center, Hasan also discovered that he had contracted an STD. When he was asked if he could name others that he had been sexually involved with, he was not sure because oftentimes he had sex while inebriated. Hasan eventually obtained help to deal with the thoughts and emotions that led to his drinking, risky sexual behavior, and depressed outlook.

Hasan's behavior represents someone who engages in self-injurious behaviors due to social anxiety, depression, and stressful life experiences. Individuals who have alcohol dependence or abuse, cocaine use, and depression should be monitored closely because they are at increased risk for attempted suicide (Petronis, Samuels, Moscicki, & Anthony, 1990).

Social Factors

Sociocultural factors are often key to many aspects of self-injurious behavior. The method used to commit suicide, the number of attempts made, and the attitudes about the act in general are all influenced by sociocultural factors. Gender, for example, is a good sociocultural predictor of suicide mortality (Canetto & Lester, 1995). Men, as opposed to women, are more likely to commit suicide in the United States as well as in most other countries. There are also gender differences in what factors are related to suicidal behavior for men versus women. For men it is more likely to be alcohol abuse and for women depression (Canetto & Lester, 1995).

The degree of acceptance of suicide in the individual's culture is also significant. Therefore, discussions of stress and suicide should address gender, race and ethnicity, and treatment issues with diverse populations.

Gender Socialization

Toddlers can label themselves as boys or girls, but it is not until the age of 4 or 5 that most children develop a secure gender identity (Wade & Tavris, 2000). Socialization partly influences the adoption of either masculine or feminine gender identity. This socialization begins at birth. In some cases **gender socialization** can have negative health consequences: The gender socialization of males has been given attention by health researchers (Sabo & Gordon, 1995), who have found that socialization of males has partly resulted in their premature death compared to females. The worldwide trend is that males have shorter life expectancy than females. This shorter life expectancy begins prenatally and continues across the lifespan. In addition to socialization factors explaining this, there are also biological factors linked to hormone levels and the lack of immunoglobin M (Sabo & Gordon, 1995). Males also die more of HIV infection, homicide, the death penalty, and suicide. The socialization of men can also lead to smoking heavily, drinking excessively, and self-destructive aggressive behavior.

Generally, males are socialized to believe in displaying risky behaviors in order to prove one's manhood. This has been referred to as the **masculine mystique** (Staples, 1995). The masculine mystique is evident in the suicidal behavior of males because men use more lethal means to commit suicide (Sabo & Gordon, 1995). They are also more likely to carry through with a threat of suicide in order not to be perceived as weak (Canetto & Lester, 1995).

For women, coroners may be reluctant to label a death as suicide. This may be because suicide is less common for women compared to men in almost all countries. The likelihood of a woman committing suicide is influenced by factors such as her age, marital status, and socioeconomic status (Canetto & Lester, 1995; Nadelson & Zimmerman, 1993). Suicide in women is often associated with depression and abusive relationships. However, due to the perception that killing oneself is masculine, women's suicides are more likely to be misclassified (Canetto & Lester, 1995). The following is an example:

> Arati has been feeling down every since she suffered a miscarriage about one month ago. Although her friends and family know about this, she has not told anyone that this is the second time that this has occurred. She was not really devastated the first time, but this time it is hard to bear. Lately, Arati's motivation has declined significantly and she has difficulty focusing on tasks. She also feels frustrated with her job, her personal life, and financial worries. One night on her way home she intentionally drives more recklessly than ever (speeding, rounding curves dangerously) and she has a near-fatal accident. Although some people close to Arati may suspect attempted suicide, most of the family members and her healthcare providers do not seriously entertain the likelihood of such behavior. Although this is a suicide attempt, it is labeled as an accident.

Race/Ethnicity and Suicidal Behavior

Social Factors and African Americans

Black men have the lowest life expectancy of all racial and ethnic groups with the exception of Native Americans (Staples, 1995). The three leading causes of death for black males aged 20 to 35 are homicide, accidents, and suicide. Acquired immune deficiency syndrome (AIDS) and drug and alcohol abuse are also major contributors to the reduced life expectancy.

Unhealthy behaviors such as drug and alcohol abuse, and even the act of homicide, may be forms of suicide. Homicide is the leading cause of death for black males aged 15 to 34. Homicides may in actuality be forms of suicide in young black males because the victims may have arranged or demanded to be killed. A victim of homicide may also non-defensively provoke a confrontation with someone as a means of hastening one's death. Males may even in some cases deliberately confront authority figures such as the police in order to provoke an incident of violence. This is referred to as **victim-precipitated homicide**.

In 1990, black males had a chance of becoming a homicide victim at a rate of 1 in 21; for white males the ratio was 1 in 131 (Staples, 1995). This is a stark difference. The differences in life expectancy for black males compared to white males are attributable to sociopsychological factors such as lifestyle, hazardous occupations, low income, health-care availability, education, and diet.

Money and work define masculinity in mainstream society, and for those without either, this contributes to despair. Those who are unemployed or working in lower employment grades may be more depressed with lower subjective well-being (Juon & Ensminger, 1997; Stansfield, Head, & Marmot, 1998). Also, suicide rates are higher for black youth who do not attend college. This is further evidence that a sense of despair and low expectations for success are key to suicidal behavior in black youth (Staples, 1995).

Unfortunately, due to many of the circumstances for young urban African American males, suicide may be viewed as a way out of a hopeless life. Suicide among blacks reaches a peak in the early years, whereas among whites it increases in direct relationship to increased age.

Men and women of color in the United States commonly experience **social discrimination**. Social discrimination refers to the unfavorable treatment or action against an individual or group on the basis of ethnic or racial characteristics, gender, age, sexual orientation, or disabilities (Giachello, 1995). Black men in particular are accustomed to evoking suspicion, fear, and discrimination from others in society as they live their lives from day to day. Black men have the ability to alter public space just by their mere presence. Staples (1999) has written about black men and public space. He has noticed how some whites (men and women) seem nervous when alone with him on the street or the elevator. Staples (1999) describes himself as a clean-cut, erudite young black male. He writes that although he is far from a deviant, he is aware that because of being a black male, he has to sometimes whistle while walking in order to assuage the anxiety of whites. He has learned that where fear and weapons meet there can be a threat to the black man's life. So what does he do? He whistles a happy tune when approaching someone or when he is walking behind them. He refers to the whistling as a signal that lets others know that he is coming. He does this so that they will not be caught off guard, alarmed, or violently defensive against him. Imagine having to consciously display such a behavior (whistling) in order to protect oneself from someone who unnecessarily fears you. Although many people may have heard about such treatment of and attitudes about young black males, less often do we read about what these ongoing experiences do to the psyche/mental hygiene of the black male. Treatment such as this and the stressors of urban living are forms of **social restraint**. Social restraint refers to the external pressures from society that heighten the stress level of an individual (Nisbet, 1996). Social restraint can have two effects. It can result in the black male reacting aggressively against a source of the social restraint (i.e., the cause of homicides), or it can result in the internalization of the social restraint that leads to harm against the self, that is, suicide or substance abuse (Nisbet, 1996; Juon & Ensminger, 1997).

Some urban black males in the United States are often living in a state of anxiety. They have to worry about their families, money, or being shot on the streets by their rivals or shot by accident. Urban black males may have even internalized social restraint in the form of self-hatred. Self-hatred, mental confusion, depression, and obsessions about death are often expressed in popular culture via hip-hop music (Gonzales, 1999). Rappers such as DMX, Tupac Shakur, Naughty By Nature, and The Ghetto Boys have all demonstrated how suicide has become the subject of lyrical poetry. The topic of suicide has been dealt with poetically by rap artists.

It was predicted that as many of 70 percent of black males would be incarcerated, dead, addicted to drugs, or victims of alcohol abuse by the year 2000 (Staples, 1995). This percentage is striking evidence for the need to focus on the psychological influences on African American males and the relevant health risky behaviors that they may display as a result.

African American females have the lowest suicide rate of all racial and gender groups in the United States. (Nisbet, 1996). Suicide is the sixth leading cause of death for black females aged 15 to 24. Women of color carry the status of **dual minority** due to both gender and race. Their status as a dual minority relates to their experiences of higher rates of medical indigence (Giachello, 1995). They experience financial, cultural, and institutional barriers in obtaining health care. These issues account for many of the health and social problems of women. Specifically, African American women may regularly experience poverty, violence in the home and community, and poor housing (Alston & Anderson, 1995).

Women are socialized to discuss their feelings and to have more extensive social ties. For black females, their involvement with marriage, church, family, and other social organizations may be protective from suicidal behavior (Nisbet, 1996). Another reason for the lower suicide rates for African American women may be due to the sanctions that the African American community imposes on overt suicidal behavior based on religious interpretations and church affiliation, which is a protective factor against suicide (Alston & Anderson, 1995).

Alston and Anderson (1995) state that black women are more likely to choose methods of attempting suicide that are never intended to really bring about death. Instead, the self-injurious behavior is carried out to draw attention to their depression that has resulted from stressful life situations. African American women's **nonfatal suicide behavior** is a response to powerlessness and hopelessness. Nonfatal suicide behavior is a suicidal act that does not result in death but is willful, self-inflicted, and life threatening (Alston & Anderson, 1995).

Particularly for lower SES African American women, occupational and economic disadvantage, external locus of control, poverty and depression contribute to suicidal behavior. Research has also found that another primary impetus of nonfatal suicidal behavior in African American women is desperation over being abandoned by a lover (Alston & Anderson, 1995). The women reportedly have often experienced severe and repeated experiences of neglect and abuse that began in childhood. The stressful living damages healthy well being. Subsequently, a variety of negative behaviors may follow such as nonfatal suicide attempts and a disregard for one's health and overall well-being. The disregard for one's physical health can stem from depression, powerlessness, hopelessness, and poor self-esteem (Giachello, 1995).

Social Factors and Hispanics

This section will focus on Hispanics who experience acculturative stress, which is stress caused by a clash between the native culture and adaptation to U.S. culture. This section does not apply to Hispanics in general. As stated in previous chapters, Hispanics are diverse in socioeconomic status and ethnicity and cannot be discussed as one homogenous group.

Acculturation plays a major role in the lifestyle behaviors and well-being of those who have recently immigrated. A sense of loss experienced by the culture clash can contribute to increased depression (Hovey & King, 1997). The rates for depression are higher for acculturating Hispanics than for non-Hispanic whites, and the suicides occur at a younger age (Organista & Dwyer, 1996). The risk of suicide is higher when the accustomed relationship between the individual and his or her society is shattered. The individual is more likely to feel caught between the influence of traditional values and norms and their experiences in the mainstream society. The acculturative stress that results may lead to a particular set of emotions and behaviors such as anxiety, feelings of isolation, psychosomatic illness, and identity confusion.

In an extensive report that summarized findings from community-based studies, suicide and risk factors for suicide were explored among immigrant Mexicans and Mexican American groups (Hovey & King, 1997). These studies have found that acculturative stress is especially prevalent for some Latino youth. For example, Mexican American adolescents in comparison to adolescents in Mexico report higher rates of current suicidal ideation, depressive symptoms, and illicit drug use (Hovey & King, 1997).

Also, when we study the behaviors of some youth we see self-destructive behaviors that are sometimes culturally influenced. A study of inner-city adolescent Latinas (Puerto Rican and Dominican descent) revealed that their suicidal behaviors might be a reflection of issues of acculturation, specifically mother-daughter conflict over the acculturation (Zimmerman & Zayas, 1995). Crucial to the girls' development was a sense of **self-in-relation.** Self-in-relation refers to the idea that the self is organized and developed in the context of important social relationships. Research has shown that one of the most important social relationships for the adolescent Latina is her relationship with her mother (Zimmerman & Zayas, 1995). Research has found that the mother may be ambivalent because she wants her daughter to make progress in the new country by acclimating, but the mother may also fear that the daughter will become culturally distant from the family. This causes distance and strain in the mother-daughter relationship. It was stated that the girl needs the mother to support her as she is dealing with acculturative stress. As the adolescent Latina is dealing with all of this, her emotional well-being is being negatively affected. The resulting actions may be suicidal behaviors, sexual promiscuity, or substance abuse, all of which are health compromising.

More traditional Latinas may also be socialized to be submissive, self-sacrificing, and enduring of suffering from the men in their lives, which further complicates health problems and depression (Organista & Dwyer, 1996). Organista and Dwyer (1996) state that the manner in which some Latinas cope with family problems and the way that they hold in emotions may negatively affect their emotional well-being. In a discussion of clinical case management and cognitive behavioral therapy for depressed Latino primary care patients the authors reported that Latinas commonly report the use of *guardar* or holding in of anger. Clinicians regard this as problematic because such behavior exacerbates any existing physical illness (Organista & Dwyer, 1996). In addition to the use of *guardar*, Latinas were reported as demonstrating depressed thinking related to remaining married despite the quality of the marriage and giving help but not requesting help. Most of the female patients being treated for depression were overextended with family responsibilities.

In a review of contemporary research issues in Hispanic/Latino women's health, it was reported that for Latinas, depression is related to socioeconomic status (Zambrana & Ellis, 1995). Although Latinos do maintain traditional family structures, households headed by women with no male spouse present are six times more likely to be Latino than non-Hispanic white (Zambrana & Ellis, 1995). Within these households, the woman is also likely to earn below-poverty wages. It was also reported that being female and having low socioeconomic status predisposed Mexican Americans to depressive symptomatology.

Latino males are likely to deal with their issues of acculturative stress in ways that are distinct from Latinas. In their book, *Working with Latino Youth (Culture, Development, and Context)*, Joan Koss-Chioino and Luis Vargas (1999) state that adolescent males too, however, have the self-in-relation issues mentioned previously with Latinas. The authors state that instead of the same type of suicidal behavior as adolescent Latinas, young males may express their need for affiliation by gang involvement and more outward expressions of aggression. The authors state that if young males have difficulty relating to their more traditional parents, they may not attempt suicide to gain the connection, but instead they may seek to affiliate with peers who are going through similar crises. Sometimes as a result of the masculine mystique, or *machismo* as it is known in Latino culture, the males will engage in risky behaviors such as victim-precipitated homicide, substance abuse, sexual risk taking, as well as gang activity (Koss-Chioino & Vargas, 1999).

Many times the depression of these males may be incorrectly noted as conduct disorder. Gang involvement may become a means of separating themselves from their families of origin in order to resolve their identity crises resulting from acculturative stress

(Koss-Chioino & Vargas, 1999). If the family cannot meet the psychosocial needs, and the youth is not connected to the community and positive role models, then older gang members may serve as role models (Koss-Chioino & Vargas, 1999). Fellow gang members are counterparts who validate and legitimize each other's concepts of masculinity. Affiliations with gangs provide the youth with a reference group that allows them to integrate any aspects of themselves that they do not like into a newly constructed identity. Sometimes due to affiliation with gangs males begin health-damaging behaviors such as drinking, smoking, and substance abuse (Koss-Chioino & Vargas, 1999).

A review of community studies has revealed that, culturally, Mexican Americans may learn at an early age to believe in **fatalism** (Hovey & King, 1997). Fatalism is the belief that the good or bad fortune of the individual is predestined and every occurrence in human existence comes to pass because it was fated to do so. Fatalism is a belief that is an example of external locus of control. This is the belief that one cannot control what happens in one's life.

Although cultural beliefs such as fatalism may have negative physical and mental health consequences, other cultural beliefs of Latinos may be protective against behaviors such as suicide. For example, many Latinos practice Catholicism, which may serve as a deterrent to suicide (Hovey & King, 1997). In Catholicism, it is considered a sin to take a life under any circumstance. The belief is that suffering while waiting for the afterlife makes the suffering more endurable, therefore the person may be willing to suffer with the emotional pain instead of ending his or her life. While this is protective against suicide, it may also promote willingness to suffer with an illness. This may be counterproductive to seeking timely medical advice and treatment for ailments.

Social Factors and Asians

The levels of acculturative stress that Asians experience and the subsequent depression and suicidal thoughts may be different for different ethnic groups of Asians. Here again, the focus in on Asians who are most likely to experience greater acculturative stress, not all Asians. This includes immigrants and those U.S.-born Asians who may have ties to their culture of origin (i.e., contact with more traditional family members).

Southeast Asian refugees seem to face the greatest stress in adjusting to a new life in the United States (True, 1995). This is due to the traumatic experiences and the major losses that they experienced prior to the immigration. Following their immigration they may experience posttraumatic stress. Also, refugees from rural areas such as Laos and Cambodia may experience significant acculturative stress when they have to adjust to modern urban living (True, 1995).

Male and female Asian immigrants both experience the strains of adapting to new culture; however, the strain may be manifest as physical complaints and not psychological complaints. Asians may be more likely to believe that psychological problems should be handled by talking to friends and relatives. However, they may believe that professionals should treat physical complaints. Regarding depression and suicidal ideology, Asians may not perceive themselves as having problems. There is a cultural stigma among some Asian groups about mental illness. For example, in the Chinese language there are few terms to describe emotional pain, and it is more socially acceptable to discuss physical pain instead of psychological pain (Ibrahim, 1995). For this reason depression and suicidal ideology may be expressed as physical ailments (Gaw, 1993). Some Chinese may be ashamed to acknowledge having a psychiatric illness and may be reluctant to seek help from a professional. A challenge for the health professional would be to help the client to understand how physical complaints and general health problems may be the result of psychological disturbances.

Some Asian American women who live in a patriarchal system may be frustrated because the patriarchal system prevents them from having any power over their own lives (Kim, 1993). They also may be influenced by Confucianism, in which there is an obligation to the family that is reinforced by shaming the woman who violates family and cultural norms. Because collectiveness is very important to Asians and other ethnic minorities, the threat of losing familial or community ties due to nonconformity may deter women from violating cultural norms. When they do violate cultural norms, they may experience extreme feelings of guilt, which have been found in the behavior of Korean American women (Kim, 1993).

Also from very early in life, some girls may learn to accept a position of inferiority. Many traditional Asian cultures emphasize the unquestioned authority of men over women, and female children may be viewed as burdens, whereas male children are valued because they are expected to provide economically for the family (Ibrahim, 1995). If a woman dares to break with social norms because she is more acculturated than other members of her family, she may suffer from depression and thoughts of suicide when she is isolated from her family (Ibrahim, 1995).

There is also a type of sociocultural suicide—known as death by **suttee**—that is condoned in some Asian and Indian cultures. Death by suttee is a type of suicide that is culturally sanctioned: A woman kills herself following the death of her husband in order to show honor and loyalty (Ibrahim, 1995). The difference in status of men and women is reflected in the fact that there is no comparable word or behavior that exists for men whose wives have died ahead of them. Suttee is an example of how some behaviors that one culture regards as abnormal may be condoned in another culture. Some Asian American females are under great stress, particularly if they are acculturated and their families are not. The stress is also more likely if the woman is elderly, unable to speak English, uneducated, and unemployed (Giachello, 1995; Ibrahim, 1995). In several Asian, Caribbean, and South American countries, women's mortality by suicide exceeds men's among individuals age 15 to 24 (Canetto & Lester, 1995). Specifically regarding gender differences, the correlates for mental health in Asian males tend to be work-related variables, and for females the correlates are family life satisfaction variables and ethnic attachment variables (True, 1995).

Treatment Issues

Ideally, it would be best to have clients enter a preventive program before their stressful life conditions and unhealthy mental state lead to self-destructive behaviors. It should not be surprising to learn that some clients may not realize that many of their physical complaints and persistent illness are attributable to disturbances in their psychological functioning. This is specifically the case for more traditional Chinese clients (Gaw, 1993). This may be because in traditional Chinese medicine there is an emphasis on close symbolic correspondence between human emotions and body organs. The traditional Chinese may be apt to express their distress through bodily organ symbols. The expression of physical complaints may be more socially acceptable to traditional Chinese clients than the expression of emotional complaints. The degree to which the Asian client is acculturated has an effect on the perception of mental vs. physical illness. For example, Japanese nationals associate the word "headache" with depression, whereas Japanese Americans and white Americans associate the word "loneliness" with depression (Fujii, Fukushima, & Yamamoto, 1993). Because these are well-established cultural attitudes, it could take quite some time to break through with a client and effect a change in his or her state of mental health.

When counseling Latinos, it may be best for professionals to utilize techniques that are concrete, active, practical, and oriented toward problem solving (Herrera, 1996; Organista & Munoz, 1996). Herrera (1996) states that treatment of this type meets the culturally based expectations of the Latino client and other ethnic minorities. Clinicians state that many clients will not want to feel that they are simply wasting time and valuable money for more abstract and indirect methods of solving their problems. Short-term directive problem solving therapies work better with minority individuals who may be of low-income groups (Organista & Dwyer, 1996). This is because they often have pressing life circumstances that frequently demand their immediate attention and may also interfere with long-term intervention plans (Organista & Dwyer, 1996).

During depression, both men and women may report to the therapist that they have low involvement in activities that they normally enjoy. Specifically, statements may be made that suggest that they need **cognitive restructuring.** Cognitive restructuring is a technique used in cognitive therapy to alter the client's thinking to become more rational and optimistic. A therapist may work to gradually shape the client's thinking, and ultimately the behavior that is health-damaging.

It has been reported that clinicians may fail to recognize depression in some ethnic minority patients (Yamamoto et al., 1993). Substance abuse and other risky behavior may not be thought of in association with emotional state and coping with stress. For example, a teenage female who becomes pregnant may be depressed. She may view having a baby as a tangible achievement in an otherwise gloomy and empty future (Yamamoto et al., 1993). Also, a young man who fathers a child may feel that this is what makes a man and will earn respect. Some clinicians fail to recognize such decisions in association with depression in ethnic minority clients. Specifically for African Americans, it has been found that the clients themselves may be prone to stoicism and denial of illness (Griffith & Baker, 1993).

Due to socialization, some men may be reluctant to express their feelings of despair (Sabo & Gordon, 1995). Also because of the masculine mystique and feelings of being invincible, a man may not choose to wear a condom during any of his sexual encounters. Indirectly, this is a form of suicide because if he or the woman contracts the AIDS virus, the disease may be quite progressed before the status is known.

Spotlight on Biology: The Neurobiology of Suicide

Suicide may be understood as an effort to seek relief from emotional pain. Stressors that may be associated with suicidal acts include psychiatric illness, acute use of alcohol, sedatives that disinhibit patients, acute medical illness that affects the brain, and adverse life events. One theory is that lower serotonergic activity contributes to suicide risk. Genetic factors, low cholesterol, and substance abuse can all be associated with or induce lower serotonergic activity. Evidence in support of this is that males commit suicide two to three times more often than females and have lower serotonergic activity than females (females are more likely to attempt suicide, however, for psychosocial reasons). The deficiency in serotonergic function results in greater impulsivity and aggression that also includes self-directed aggression in the form of suicidal behavior. It is plausible that increasing serotonergic activity may be a valuable therapeutic approach that can work in a variety of circumstances to reduce the risk of serious suicidal behavior.

Source: Mann, 1998.

Conclusion

Health professionals need to consider the client's state of mind when addressing important health issues. It is likely that when a person displays unhealthy behaviors such as poor eating habits, excessive drinking, or other reckless behavior, the individual is in an unhealthy state of mind due to stress and depression or suicidal ideation. Unhealthy coping with stress can cause depression and hopelessness that is so extreme that it leads to suicide. Health professionals and the clients may overlook the influence of psychological disturbance on physical illness and self-injurious behavior. Varying socialization experiences can cause a buildup of stress and pressure that damages the psyche in both men and women of color. If the problems are not dealt with via a focus on the mental, then sometimes health-risky behaviors may exacerbate. An improvement in emotional well-being can subsequently contribute to general feelings of well-being and protection from injury, suicide, and disease.

Summary

The rates of suicide are high in young persons aged 15 to 24. Increasingly, attention needs to be given to suicidal ideation that is related to health-risky and life-threatening events. Suicide is self-injurious behavior that results in death. Gender differences in suicide exist across racial and ethnic groups. Gender socialization begins at birth; however, there can be negative health consequences of gender socialization for both men and women. Two examples of this are the masculine mystique for men and the failure of many people to expect suicidal behavior from women. Cultural and regional factors significantly influence whether a person will engage in suicidal behavior, which suicidal behaviors are displayed, and under what circumstances the acts will be performed.

Black men have low life expectancy. The leading cause of death for young black males is homicide, which in some cases may be suicides in disguise. Victim-precipitated homicide is an example, where some males may have actually wanted to be killed in order to escape despair. The lifestyles of black males and the treatment that they receive in society can be very damaging to the psyche. The social restraint or external pressure from society, coupled with the masculine mystique, can result in a silent depression and suicide. African American women have low incidence of suicide compared to other groups. They have social supports that likely buffer their stress and suicidal ideology.

Acculturation for Latinos is a key factor in the mental health of men and women. Particularly for Latino youth, there may be conflict with the family due to differences in acculturation. The males and the females may engage in self-destructive behavior as a means of coping with the stress.

Asians may suffer from stress and strain of the psyche but they may not be aware that their pain is psychological and not physical. Specifically, Asian women may be depressed due to conflict within the family over issues of acculturation. The prevalence of suicide among these women is high.

Interventions to promote optimal health will need to consider gender, age, ethnicity and race of both the client and the therapist. Explanations of self-destructive thinking and behaving (i.e., sexual promiscuity, drinking excessively, binge eating, substance abuse) may be deeply embedded in the experiences of the individuals, so it may take time to change certain attitudes and patterns of responding to mental anguish.

Student Interview

Age: 28
Gender: Female
Country of Origin: African American

1. **What is your attitude about the use of therapy to deal with emotional pain?**
   I think that therapy is effective and I would be okay with going for myself.
2. **If you had a serious problem that was making you sad or depressed, whom would you first consider talking to about it?**
   A minister. I'd try to deal on the spiritual aspect first and then if that didn't work I would see a therapist because I would think that it might be something biological.
3. **What is your impression of the biggest health problem facing men in the United States? And women?**
   Men: Cancer, based on my family (prostate and lung).
   Women: Diabetes and not eating properly.
4. **As a woman living in the United States today, what health issue is of most concern to you personally?**
   The health issue of most concern to me is sexually transmitted disease. People don't take the time to do research to find out about the transmission and about how much they are at risk.

continued

Student Interview   Continued

5. **Have you ever been concerned about sadness that you may have thought was serious depression?**
    Yes. Actually I was depressed for a while. And I spoke to a minister and I read about depression. My psychology class has helped me learn about depression.

6. **What kinds of things do you do in your life that help you maintain your peace of mind?**
    I go to worship service every Sunday, I read, and I meditate. I read the Bible a lot. I'm a Christian, I attend the Church of Christ.

7. **When you talk to male friends/female friends what things seem to be common issues that they are upset about or worrying about?**
    Child support and financial problems. Everyone wants to become financially stable. We can go on for hours about that.

8. **Do you expect certain things of men that you don't expect of women when it comes to coping with problems?**
    No, I expect men and women to handle things the same. Most of the time women seem stronger in dealing with things because they often have the children on top of everything else, whereas men don't have the single parent stress.

9. **Do you expect a difference in how men and women deal with depression?**
    Yes. I think that men don't want to communicate and talk things out. Women want healing and resolution and are more willing to talk so that they can move on. I think that my father was depressed, which led to alcoholism that he almost died from. Now he goes to church to find healing for the depression that he was carrying around.

10. **What are your views on people who commit suicide?**
    I think that it is the same underlying factors for men and women. There are usually signs. I always wonder, "Why didn't people see the signs?" I tried twice in my life before I had kids to commit suicide. I think, if they don't hurt themselves they will hurt someone else like when people "go postal." It will come out some kind of way whether it is suicide, murder, or drinking too much.

Key Concepts

cognitive restructuring
dual minority
fatalism
gender socialization
masculine mystique
nonfatal suicide behavior
self-in-relation
social discrimination
social restraint
suicide
suttee
victim-precipitated homicide

Study Questions

1. What is something that you could possibly learn about suicidal ideation from listening to hip-hop lyrics from some popular African American rap artists?
2. What was one explanation given in the chapter for why some young Latinas might attempt suicide?
3. What is your understanding of the masculine mystique? Can you think of examples?
4. What is one explanation for why African American women may carry commit suicide less often than other groups?
5. What was the explanation given for why a less acculturated Chinese American may seek a physician's intervention instead of a psychologist?
6. What is the an explanation for why someone might engage in victim-precipitated homicide?
7. Why would a woman engage in an act of suttee?
8. Explain the following: "A black man can alter public space sometimes merely by his presence." How does this likely affect a black male's emotional well-being?
9. What would be an indication that a client may need cognitive restructuring?
10. How might fatalism play a role in coping with an injury or disease?

Student Activity

Read *The Joy Luck Club* by Amy Tan, which focuses on Asian female characters. Write a paper on the main characters in this novel. In your paper, focus on the emotions, thoughts, and behaviors of the women as they pertain to cultural issues and conflict within the family.

OR

Popular culture hip-hop releases such as "The Crossroads" by Bone Thugz in Harmony or "So Many Tears" by Tupac Shakur express the sadness and suicidal ideation of many young urban males. Listen to the lyrics from these artists or similar artists and write a paper about the emotions being expressed that have relevance to the thoughts and actions of some young men of color in urban America. (The lyrics of some songs may be explicit and usually have warning labels indicating such.)

8 Personality and Health

Personality and Health Relationship

Personality is defined as the relatively stable pattern of thinking, behaving, and expressing emotions that makes a person unique. Theories linking personality and health are not new. For example, regarding the two leading causes of mortality in this country, heart disease and cancer, the link to personality dates back many years. The belief that personality is linked to heart disease is dated back 2000 years to Hippocrates; the personality link to cancer dates back several centuries (Hafen, Karren, Frandsen, & Smith, 1996). An interesting link between personality and health occurred in the 1940s when a doctor who was a proponent of psychosomatic medicine noticed a difference in two of his patients who had received mastectomies (Friedman, 1991). Two years following their surgeries, one of the women was well and the other was dying, although they were similar in every other way. The differences were attributed to differences in personality, that is, the way that the women coped with the situation. You may believe in a relationship between personality and health if you, for example, believe that an irresponsible or anxious person is not as likely to follow doctors' suggestions, thereby experiencing a decline in health.

There is variation regarding what personality characteristics are indeed most significant to the likelihood of illness and disease. This is not surprising, since for many years personality researchers could not agree on what traits were universally significant to the human expression of personality. This chapter will present the following: (1) the five-factor theory of personality and the specific traits within this theory that have been studied in health research, (2) the debate over the existence of disease-prone personalities, (3) self and identity issues, (4) stress and coping, and (5) the relationship between sociocultural issues, personality, and health.

Five-Factor Theory

Although virtually ignored for nearly twenty years, the five-factor model of personality is presently a recurring and comprehensive theory in psychology (McCrae & Costa, 1987). The theory was originally proposed in the 1960s but became popular in the 1980s. Although not all psychologists have agreed with the emphasis on trait models of personality (Mishel, 1968), or on the specific wording used for the five traits, the following are generally agreed upon as the continuums for each of the five factors in the **five-factor model** of personality traits:

1. *Neuroticism vs. Emotional Stability:* Worrying, insecure, self-conscious, and temperamental describe neuroticism; this trait is generally regarded as negative affect that may include anger, depression, and anxiety.
2. *Extraversion vs. Surgency:* Sociable, funloving, friendly, and talkative describe the extraversion trait, and, generally speaking, this trait could be described as lively sociability; unlike neuroticism, extraversion is regarded as positive emotionality. These individuals may be quite fond of being around people even if people are not too fond of them.
3. *Openness to Experience:* Original, imaginative, broad interests, and daring.
4. *Agreeableness vs. Antagonism:* For agreeableness, issues like trust and ease in getting along with others is significant. Antagonism is a highly negative trait that is characterized by mistrust/skepticism, as well as being callous, unsympathetic, uncooperative, stubborn, and rude.
5. *Conscientiousness vs. Undirectedness:* Purposefulness and adherence to plans, schedules, and requirements, dutiful, and scrupulous would all describe the conscientious trait, whereas the other extreme would be someone who might be described as undirected and lazy.

These five traits are commonly discussed in the literature on personality and have been supported by research that has been based on peer ratings, self-reports, and questionnaire scales (McCrae & Costa, 1987). To some degree, it is believed that all personalities can be measured along continuums for these five factors.

Because the five-factor theory is a popular theory, it is worthwhile to examine how the five factors relate to health and **subjective well-being** (see Figure 8.1). Subjective well-being refers to individual reports of life quality. Specifically, extraversion and neuroticism have been proposed as the primary determinants of subjective well-being (DeNeve, 1999). The degree to which a person has a sense of well-being following a surgery or illness is related to the person's emotional tendencies such as emotional stability, positive affectivity, and tension. DeNeve found neuroticism to be one of the strongest negative correlates of subjective well-being. Recall from the five-factor description of neuroticism that it is generally regarded as negative affect. Thus to the degree that a person can refrain from negative and pessimistic attributions, he or she will have higher subjective well-being (Ingledew & Brunning, 1999). Extraversion is positively related to subjective well-being because it is an expression of positive emotionality.

In another study, the relationship between negative affectivity, self-reported medical condition, and somatic complaints were assessed in relationship to personality (Vassend & Skrondal, 1999). This study found that neuroticism was clearly the most important variable in all the models that were tested. Neuroticism showed substantial direct effects on distress level and medical condition and a significant indirect effect on the subjects' somatic complaints. Individuals who are high in neuroticism are likely to report more somatic complaints, which are consistently linked to the occurrence of illness.

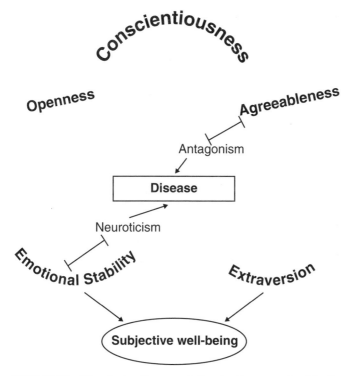

FIGURE 8.1 **Five-factor theory relation to disease and subjective well-being.**

Neuroticism has also been linked to individuals who are more prone to homesickness (Van Tilburg, Vingerhoets, Van Heck, & Kirschbaum, 1999). Homesickness is associated with lowered mood, increased health complaints, and more cognitive failures. The reason for neuroticism's significant role in health is the fact that persons high in neuroticism are highly self-critical, critical of others, and critical of situations. Those high in neuroticism emphasize the negative aspects of the events that occur in their lives, including their health conditions.

Neuroticism is not the only trait among the five factor traits that is negative. Antagonism is also a negative trait. In the description of antagonism, the word hostile is also appropriate. Antagonism/hostility may be related to increased susceptibility to disease and ill health. Both antagonism and hostility are linked through their characteristically high levels of interpersonal distrust and anger. Typically, someone high in antagonism or hostility is not a likable person. Highly hostile/antagonistic persons also do not perceive themselves to have high levels of social support. Social support is a health protective resource, therefore a lack of social support can be especially health compromising for hostile persons (Hart, 1999).

In addition to considerations of antagonism/hostility, personality characteristics that may be related to antagonism/hostility should also be addressed. Two such possibly related characteristics are defensiveness and style of anger expression. **Defensive hostility** exists when an individual endorses a cynical and distrusting view of the world, yet wishes to be viewed in a positive manner by others. Researchers have studied whether defensive hostility may be a better predictor of coronary artery disease and cardiovascular reactivity than hostility in isolation (Mente & Helmers, 1999). Mente and Helmers found that defensively hostile males displayed heightened diastolic blood pressure reactivity on a cold pressor task; these responses were significantly greater than for nondefensive hostile males.

Style of anger expression is also relevant to the antagonistic trait. A person's style of anger expression may have health-related consequences (Martin, Wan, David, Wegner, Olson, & Watson, 1999). The two primary styles of anger expression are **anger-out** and **anger-in**. People who readily express anger characterize the anger-out expressive style. Anger-in refers to experiencing anger, but not expressing it (holding the anger in). Martin and colleagues (1999) specifically found that the nonexpression of anger was positively related to physical symptom complaints and linked to neuroticism.

Persons who are categorized as anger-in are less likely to show emotional expressivity for all of their emotions. **Emotion suppression** is the inhibition of overt emotionally expressive behavior, although the person may intensely feel an emotion (Richards & Gross, 1999). Anger-out, on the other hand, has been found to yield a more promising picture with regard to health (Martin et al., 1999).

The link between style of anger expression and health outcomes such as cardiovascular disease has a biological explanation. The relationship is explained by the arousal of the sympathetic nervous system during anger. Even someone who suppresses his or her emotions will experience increased sympathetic activation from holding the negative emotions inside. If the sympathetic system is aroused for prolonged periods (during anger-in or anger-out), this can lead to physiologic wear and tear and an increased likelihood of disease. Both styles of anger management, however, may be related to cardiovascular disease, depending on how a person appraises a situation.

Generic Disease-Prone Personality Theory

After reading the previous section, you may still wonder if generally there is a certain type of personality that is more prone to disease and whether you yourself possess this type of personality. You may also be curious about what kind of person is more likely to have ulcers, heart disease, or migraines. Some psychologists support the view of a "generic disease-prone personality," while others believe that there may be "specific disease personalities," meaning one personality type can be specifically linked to a certain disease (Hafen et al., 1996).

Researchers who support the generic disease-prone theory say that some personality traits, such as depression, anxiety, anger, and hostility, are regarded as health damaging. These are all traits that are taxing on the sympathetic nervous system. Those who support generic disease-prone theories assert that if we were to search for a specific personality that causes a specific disease, we may not find that there is such a thing. The premise of the generic disease prone personality theory is that a personality may have risky characteristics that can predispose a person to various diseases. Related to this viewpoint is the opinion of some researchers that several personality traits may make a person susceptible to a cluster of health conditions (Rodgers, 1989; Stanwyck & Anson, 1986).

Disease-Specific Personality Theory

Another point of view is the disease-specific personality theory. This theory suggests that specific traits of the personality can be linked to the development of a specific disease. Advocates of this view do believe that there is such a thing for example, as a **coronary-prone personality** and a **cancer-prone personality**. The coronary-prone personality has been defined as the hard-driving and competitive personality that is hostile, angry, and suspicious. The coronary personality—or Type A pattern of behavior, as it is commonly known—is a common discussion in the study of behavioral health (Hafen et al., 1996; Kirkcaldy, Cooper, & Furnham, 1998). This pattern of behavior was identified in the mid-1950s by a cardiologist. Although it is discussed in association with heart disease, it is important to know that not every aspect of this personality is harmful. For example, when the Type A behavior was originally described, researchers referred to it as "hurry sickness." This was in reference to the individual's constant rushing around, coupled with the need to do everything quickly. Hurrying or rushing is less harmful to the development of disease than some other characteristics of Type A individuals. Free-floating hostility, anger, cynicism, and mistrust/skepticism are potentially more harmful than just being in a hurry.

The cancer-prone personality has been defined as the person who demonstrates little emotion and is ambivalent toward self and others (Hafen et al., 1996). Physicians many centuries ago referred to melancholy, deep anxiety, hopelessness, and disappointment as characteristics related to cancer (Locke & Colligan, 1986). Research has identified a nonexpression of emotions among some cancer patients. This is because some cancer patients may not openly express their feelings but instead may try to mask their feelings of anger, hostility, and pain.

One study, in which melanoma patients were interviewed, discovered that cancer patients were actually too nice, such that they were passive about everything. They could not express negative emotions, admit their needs, or assert themselves (Locke & Colligan, 1986). The verdict on personality and cancer seems to be that although not caused by depression, cancer may be related to those who feel lonely, are loners, and are unemotional and bland on the exterior. Regarding these characteristics, however, it is difficult to know whether such characteristics precede the illness (along with poor diet, genetic influences, and lifestyle) or are caused by it. The coronary-prone personality and the cancer-prone personality are not the only diseases studied in association with personality. Researchers have also addressed the issue of personality as related to health problems such as arthritis, ulcers, and asthma (Hafen et al., 1996).

Sense of Self/Identity

You may identify where you fall on the continuums of the five personality factors, or you may simply describe yourself to someone. Think of how many times someone has said to you, "So, tell me about yourself." By revealing how we define ourselves and how we view ourselves relative to others, we are revealing our **sense of self/identity.** Personality researchers' reliance on a person's self-judgment is a common and valid method of obtaining information about personality (Funder, 1997).

In the field of health psychology, self and identity are particularly important. A person's self-concept following diagnosis with a life-threatening illness can be crucial to coping. Also important is how others affect the sick person's sense of self and identity. Being pitied or avoided by others following a newly diagnosed serious condition may alter the sick individual's sense of self. This may have consequences for whether the individual will be optimistic or pessimistic about recovery.

Sense of coherence and **hardiness** are two concepts related to self and identity and thus are also important to health (see Figure 8.2).

The sense of coherence is an orientation that expresses the extent to which one has a pervasive, enduring, and dynamic feeling of confidence that what happens in one's life is structured and predictable. The person who is high in sense of coherence also believes that he or she has the resources available to meet the demands of life and sees these demands as worthy challenges (Jorgensen, Frankowski, & Carey, 1999; Ouellette, 1999). A high sense

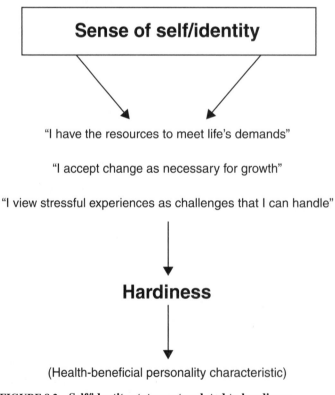

FIGURE 8.2   Self/identity statements related to hardiness.

of coherence is beneficial because it reduces the likelihood that negative life events (stressors) will lead to increased physical complaints (Jorgensen et al., 1999).

Hardiness is defined as the extent to which a person is able to express (1) commitment, (2) control, and (3) challenge in his or her feelings, actions, and thoughts (Manning & Fusilier, 1999; Ouellette, 1999; Ramanaiah, Sharpe, & Byravan, 1999). Hardiness is regarded as a key characteristic of the disease resistant personality (Kobasa, 1979). The three components of hardiness are defined as the following:

- Commitment: Having a sense of purpose and capacity to never give up even under pressure.
- Control: The belief that one has control over what occurs or does not occur in one's life.
- Challenge: Being comfortable with change because change is viewed as the potential for growth.

How specifically might hardiness be relevant to discussions of health? Consider two patients who are both seriously injured following an accident. Both patients may be told that the chance of walking again is minimal. However, if one patient is high in hardiness and the other low, the high hardiness patient may make more progress with the assistance of trained professionals. A person high in hardiness is expected to remain committed to making progress even though the situation looks bleak. The extensive training and exercising during rehabilitation following the accident is viewed more favorably in a high hardiness individual versus a low hardiness individual. The high hardiness individual is likely to feel that he or she has the ability to control the final outcome of the situation and will not accept fate or a doctors' conclusions. The high hardiness individual generally has a positive outlook regarding life's stressors.

Stress

Stress plays a significant role in disease (Nathan, Staats, & Rosch, 1987). Stress is defined as the nonspecific neurological and endocrine response of the body to an environmental demand that causes the body to have to adapt. Because the body begins the process of adapting in response to the stressor, the process is called the **general adaptation syndrome**. The process begins in people for different reasons (not everyone views the same event as stressful). There is, however, a general response that is about the same for everyone. When we experience unrelenting stress, we are forced into a situation of continuous adaptation to a chronic situation. This can be a threat to health because the body must devote a large percentage of its energy to coping with the stress. The constant excessive secretion of hormones in response to stress can impair the immune system and cause the body to be more susceptible to disease (Lamb, 1989; Sternberg & Gold, 1997).

Stress is relevant for discussing personality in relationship to health, because stress is pervasive. How we handle it is crucial. We cannot escape stress, especially those stressors commonly known as **daily hassles**. These are minor, annoying, or frustrating events.

Examples of daily hassles are being late for an appointment (i.e., traffic jam) or being unable to locate an item that we need (i.e., misplacing a pair of glasses).

We also may be exposed to significant life-altering stressors such as the death of a loved one or diagnosis with a chronic illness. Although some people would say that they wish they could avoid all forms of stress, this may not be beneficial because stress naturally accompanies positive changes and growth. Our personalities, which include how we view things, determine how stress will impact us. Personality factors ultimately shape how we appraise stressful events (Martin et al., 1999). In addition, it is important to understand how sociocultural factors influence personality expression and reactions to stressful events.

Sociocultural Factors, Personality, and Health

Diverse groups of clients vary in experience, behavior, and personality. It has been stated that the challenge to health researchers is to identify how the varying social contexts of individuals shape the individual thinking and behavior in ways that might either enhance or impair health (Williams, Spencer, Jackson, & Ashmore, 1999).

Race and ethnicity are significant among sociocultural factors that contribute to health behavior and attitudes. Race and ethnicity deserve attention because they are often visible characteristics that in some cases incite prejudice, discrimination, and racism. Why would this be important to a health discussion? This is important because ongoing exposure to prejudice, discrimination, and racism is stressful. These negative events may be so stressful that they affect the sense of self and identity and subsequently affect health behaviors (Lock, 1999). One's culture and ethnicity do not directly explain illness, disease, or self-destruction; however, social issues such as poverty, racism, violence, and discrimination experienced by ethnic minorities can lead them to the internalization of negative images (Lock, 1999; Wyatt, 1994). Once the negative images of self are internalized, this creates a fractured and conflicted sense of self, to the detriment of both physical and mental health (Lock, 1999).

It has been reported that closeness to one's racial/ethnic group appears to reduce the likelihood of major health problems (Williams et al., 1999). Previously, it was mentioned that sense of self is significant to health behaviors. For ethnic minorities, racial identification is often incorporated into their view of self. Although we may recognize the significance of racial identity for many ethnic minorities, we should not generalize this to everyone, nor expect that all ethnic minorities will respond the same way to stressors that occur. Even for frequently studied stressors such as racism, discrimination, and prejudice, we cannot expect all ethnic minorities to have the same reaction. However, the individual's perceptions of mastery or control over his or her life and self-esteem are generally recognized as important psychological resources for coping with stress (Williams et al., 1999). Some ethnic minority clients will have been exposed to a great deal of chronic stress in their lives (poverty, violence, racism) and will be more disease prone, whereas others may possess hardiness and a sense of coherence, thus resisting disease even in the face of such stressors. This reason may, for example, be relevant to why two children reared in the same family or neighborhood may be differentially affected by negative environmental factors. They may also show different recovery rates from injury or disease.

Personality factors such as hardiness and sense of coherence are related to the cognitive appraisal of a situation. Those who have more disease-resistant personalities are less likely to appraise situations as stressful. A person may view a stressor such as racism in terms of harm/loss, threat, or challenge (Outlaw, 1993). If stressors from the larger society cause feelings of threat or a loss of esteem, this could negatively affect health in a number of ways. It could lead to distrust of the health-care system and thus avoidance of its usage. It could also lead to a lack of concern about one's health (poor esteem).

Stein and Nyamathi (1999) studied stress, self-esteem, escapist drug use, risky sexual behavior, depression, and **active and avoidant coping** in male and female impoverished African Americans. Active coping is a problem-focused style of coping believed to be a stress buffer, whereas avoidant coping is a dysfunctional, counterproductive response to stress. The study was done to research the theory that stress is particularly a risk factor for the development of physical and psychological illnesses among impoverished minority populations. Although some gender differences were found, generally greater stress and lower self-esteem predicted greater depression in both genders. Stress was also significant for sexual risk taking in women, although not for men. The lives of the research participants were highly stressful, and they perceived the stressors to be uncontrollable. This lead to avoidant coping, learned helplessness, and powerlessness. Findings such as this underscore the need for self-esteem enhancement to promote hardiness, sense of coherence, and **internal locus of control** within health promotion programs. Internal locus of control refers to feelings that you can control what happens to you as opposed to fate, luck, chance, or other people.

The findings in the Stein and Nyamathi study are relevant to two social learning personality theories: Rotter's expectancy value theory of decision making (Rotter, 1982) and Bandura's social learning idea of reciprocal determinism (Bandura, 1978). Regarding the first theory, Rotter acknowledges the significance of expectancy for a behavior. An individual's **expectancy** for a behavior is his or her belief, or subjective probability about how likely he or she thinks it is that a behavior under consideration will actually pay off (Funder, 1997). Rotter believed that if an individual did not believe very strongly that a behavior would pay off, then he or she would not display the behavior. In the Stein and Nyamathi (1999) study, the research participants showed learned helplessness, powerlessness, and avoidant coping due to stressors that they identified as uncontrollable. Their expectancy was low regarding payoff for active coping. In a situation where a person is stressed by unemployment and poverty, discrimination, and a lack of safety in one's environment, there may be low expectancy for being able to do anything to change one's situation including one's health status.

Rotter also addresses the **reinforcement value** of an event. Reinforcement value refers to the subjective benefit of a reward (Funder, 1997). For example, in order to understand why a person engages in health-risky behavior, it might be helpful to know how much that person generally values good health. There may be no reinforcement value associated with the initiation of healthy behaviors. In highly stressful environments, such as in poor urban communities, reinforcement value may not be the same as in rural communities or suburban communities.

Bandura's reciprocal determinism is a theory that includes three significant components: choice, change of the social situation, and self-system. Bandura believed that each of us enters into different situations, and as a result of our stepping in, the social situation changes (we add something to that space). We evaluate ourselves in this situation, which determines how we will behave. According to Bandura, the environment shapes each of us, even as we shape it. When we affect our environment, the environment will react with consequences for our behavior. This further influences the self. All of this he refers to as reciprocal determinism. Now how does this relate to health and ethnic minority populations? In stressful environments, a minority youth may choose positive peer relations or negative peer relations. The following is an example of reciprocal determinism:

> Tameka chooses positive peer relationships and becomes a peer counselor. She is active in training sessions with other counselors. Once she enters the organization as a peer counselor, she may influence others there, who come to think very highly of her. She then evaluates herself in this new situation. Her peers and trainers compliment her on her behavior. The compliments represent the consequences for her good behavior. The social exchange will help her further define who she is and her competencies. She will likely be motivated to continue good behavior and also counsel others on health-enhancing behaviors.

Another health behavior relevant to Bandura's theory is **compensatory self-enhancement (CSE)**, which is the tendency to focus on one's positive traits in order to shift attention away from any negative health behavior, making it less salient (Boney-McCoy, Gibbons, & Gerrard, 1999). The fact that this occurs is an indication of how significant is our need for a positive self-image, which is relevant to Bandura's consideration of the self-system in his theory. Underserved populations that are particularly susceptible to the larger society's imposition of negative images may especially use CSE to attempt to boost their self-regard. For example, a male who is stressed and drinks heavily may feel that this is acceptable because he at least does not use any illegal drugs. If he has internalized a stereotypical attitude that other men of color and of his age group are using illegal drugs, then he may trivialize his drinking behavior, even though it is excessive.

Emotion Expression

Earlier you read that a person's style of anger expression and degree of defensive hostility may be related to health. These two issues may be particularly relevant to discussions of these feelings in people of color. The reason is that minority populations in U.S. society may experience discriminative treatment, unwarranted attacks, and other affronts to their character that dictate certain styles of emotional expression.

The specific situations are likely to be highly significant to how the individual expresses anger (Porter, Stone, & Schwartz, 1999). The person who instigates the anger and the location where the incident takes place may determine whether the person engages anger-in or anger-out. If a person finds himself in a situation in which he is being verbally assaulted or humiliated, yet feels powerless and defensive, he may feel that he has to suppress his expression of anger in order to avoid physical abuse. Unfortunately, emotion suppression can have negative health consequences (Richards & Gross, 1999).

In some areas, high crime exists and the police tend to be perceived as sources of arbitrary aggression. The actions and sometimes presence of the police arouse anger and hostility that often have to be suppressed in order to avoid life-threatening consequences. In a study of the effects of socioecological stress, suppressed hostility, and skin color on black and white male blood pressure, black high-stress males showed significantly higher blood pressure levels (Harburg et al., 1973). All of the men who were in the high stress condition reported more anger-in following an attack. This study is particularly informative due to the highly stressful conditions of the urban environment (Detroit) of the subjects. Living under such conditions can lead to increased sympathetic arousal, which could then lead to an increased susceptibility to coronary artery disease or cardiovascular reactivity (Velletri, 1996).

Research has revealed that when members of stigmatized groups such as ethnic minorities, the physically disabled, and gays and lesbians put their emotional upheavals into words, their physical and mental health improves markedly. Pennebaker and Seagal (1999) found that health improvements were more likely to occur in subjects who wrote essays that were more self-reflective, emotionally open, and thoughtful. The researchers of this study

Spotlight on Biology: The Biology of Personality

The biological approach to investigating personality focuses on two issues: (1) the anatomy of the brain and (2) biochemicals such as neurotransmitters and hormones. The health behaviors that an individual displays or fails to display can be related to that individual's personality. Certain personality characteristics can be linked to brain regions. A region of the brain that has particular significance is the limbic system. The limbic system is sometimes referred to as the emotion center of the brain beneath the cerebral cortex. The limbic system is the basis of emotion, motivation, appetite, fear, learning, and memory. When we discuss personality characteristics such as conscientiousness, neuroticism, openness to experience, and antagonism, we can relate these to fear, motivation, and aggression that are governed by the limbic system. A person's position on the scale of emotional stability versus neuroticism is believed to be a function of the way the limbic system responds to emotional stimuli. It is unlikely that specific personality characteristics can be related to the brain in a one-to-one fashion. It is more probable that there are varying neural pathways and systems of the brain that influence the personality. One theory involving personality and the brain asserts that the brain has excitatory and inhibitory neural pathways. Significant aspects of the personality rely upon the balance between the inhibitory and excitatory pathways. Another theory discusses high versus low anxiety and high versus low impulsivity. Brain-based theories about neural pathways and personality may be relevant to explaining the health-risky behaviors of a person who is high in impulsivity, extraversion, and neuroticism. Also, neurotransmitters such as norepinephrine and dopamine can increase blood pressure, energy level, arousal, and heart rate. These chemicals are involved in the expression of anxiety and anger. The levels of norepinephrine can affect whether a person is prone to anxiety, impulsivity, or social attachments, which can each influence the type of health behaviors displayed. Depletion of another neurotransmitter, serotonin, is related to irrational anger, hypersensitivity to rejection, pessimism, and worrying, which are all characteristics of some ill persons. It is important to understand that proper levels of neurotransmitters, plus levels of the hormone cortisol (stress hormone) can be crucial to health.

Source: Funder, 1997, pp. 151–178.

suggested that writing experiences can improve physical health by producing positive effects on blood markers of immune function. The people who wrote about their significant thoughts and feelings drastically reduced their doctor visit rates after the study compared to control participants who had written about trivial topics. Among members of stigmatized groups, writing about being a stigmatized group member changes one's level of collective self-esteem as well as providing health gains. The writing seems to be a way of confronting traumatic experiences, thereby producing a positive effect on physical health. This is evidence that an uncomplicated intervention such as a writing assignment can be significant to health enhancement when it focuses on expressing emotions related to stressful experiences.

Conclusion

Personality and health have a relationship. Psychologists' main objective in discussing the relationship should be to highlight the aspects of ourselves that we can adjust in order to improve our health. Discussions of issues such as the disease-prone personality may lead some people to believe that they are to blame for their chronic medical conditions. This could be quite depressing to anyone. Therefore, it is important for researchers to emphasize that disease is influenced by psychological factors, genetics, and social factors. However, the public should be informed about the link between disease and personality because research suggests that there is much that a person can do to protect and enhance his or her health. Issues related to health and the body are closely related not only to ideas about self and identity, but also to larger social and political issues. This includes the government, the community, the health-care industry, and the life experiences of disenfranchised persons. We must consider the historical and geographical context of diverse groups when we study health and body issues. This must be done whenever addressing individual personality factors and health (Lock, 1999).

Summary

Personality is the relatively stable pattern of thinking, behaving, and expressing emotions that makes a person unique. Personality can be linked to health behaviors and outcomes. The five-factor theory of personality consists of neuroticism, extraversion, openness to experience, agreeableness, and conscientiousness. To some degree, it is believed that all personalities can be measured along a continuum for each of these five factors. When evaluating health and subjective well-being, traits such as neuroticism and extraversion are significant. Antagonism, defensive hostility, and style of anger expression are all characteristics that may be related to the onset of illness or disease. Although expressing emotions in a hostile way can be bad for our health, suppressing our emotions also leads to increased sympathetic activation that is health damaging. Some researchers support a generic disease-prone theory that suggests that a personality may have flaws that lead to the likelihood of a variety of disorders. However, some researchers support the disease-personality theory, which suggests that there are specific personalities that lead to specific diseases. Two types of personality that may be specifically related to disease are the coronary-prone personality and the cancer-prone personality. How we view ourselves should also be studied as important to health behavior. Sense of coherence and hardiness are related to how we view ourselves. Sense of coherence and hardiness give individuals feelings of confidence, commitment, control, and challenge over life difficulties. One of the most pervasive of life's difficulties is stress. We may experience unrelenting chronic stress that weakens the immune system, or we may simply experience minor annoying and frustrating events known as daily hassles. Health professionals working with diverse groups of clients must acknowledge cultural variation in experience, behavior, and personality. Race and ethnicity are significant among sociocultural factors that contribute to health behavior and attitudes. Being a member of a stigmatized group exposes one to stressors that may for some individuals affect sense of self and identity. The stressors that members of stigmatized group have to deal with may be health damaging for those who are low in sense of coherence or hardiness. The personality determines how stressors will be dealt with. The coping that is used may be active or avoidant, and the locus of control may be internal or external. Personality theories about expectancy, reinforcement value, and reciprocal determinism explain some ethnic minority health behavior. The need for self-enhancement, the need to acknowledge and express feelings of anger and hurt, and the opportunity to write about emotional upheavals are all relevant to discussions of health in stigmatized groups.

Student Interview

Age: 23
Gender: Female
Country of Origin: Sweden
Years in the United States: 2 years, 6 months

1. **How would you rate yourself when it comes to anger expression?**
   a. I don't let people know when I'm upset.
   b. I never really get too angry.
   c. I let people know immediately and forcefully when I'm angry. I yell if I need to.
   My answer would be choice C. I've always been like that. I'm not a calm person.
2. **When negative things or stressful things happen to you, how do you tend to cope with them?**
   Right now my life is very stressful. I try to deal with it but I get very upset and emotional. I cry a lot. I do deal with it, though.
3. **Are you the type who normally takes preventive steps to ensure your health? What things do you do?**
   I don't go to the doctor that much for checkups. I don't think about it when I don't feel sick. I go to the doctor when I can't do anything about it myself. When I really need to, then I go to see the doctor. I go, but not for checkups. That's a lot of money to do that. Only if I feel really sick, not for prevention.
4. **How emotional are you? Describe.**
   I am very emotional. Especially now because there is a lot of pressure on me from back home. I don't know if I should stay here or go back home. I don't know if I should do what I want to do or what my parents want me to do.

continued

Student Interview   **Continued**

5. **Rate your overall health on a scale of 1 (poor) to 10 (very good).**
   Probably a 5. I'm not taking good care of myself. I eat poorly. I don't exercise. I only eat about once or twice a day. No breakfast at all. I eat dinner when I get home when I'm usually starving. I sit on my butt and I don't really do anything. I spend a lot of time in my car commuting to school. Traffic is heavy and stressful driving in the mornings.

6. **In your country, do people believe that they can influence their own recovery without help from a doctor? Explain.**
   Well, a lot of people are stubborn and want to help themselves, at least the people that I know (my family and friends). They try to help themselves.

7. **What personality characteristics do you feel are associated with healthier people?**
   I think that they are stressed out because they try to keep up with the way people want them to look. If you have a full-time job and then you go to work out, when do you have time to do other things? I think that really health-conscious people want people to look up to them and admire them for how they look.

8. **Do people in your family seem to be prone to getting sick often? Why or why not?**
   No, they don't seem to get sick often. My Grandma had cancer and my Mom has an anxiety disorder (she's been like that for a long time). My Dad is never sick, nor my sister. I get sick a lot here, probably due to the pressures on me. I've been sick a lot since I moved here.

9. **What has been the most stressful event for you since being in the United States?**
   Last year at this time I had to move out from with my roommate because I had no money. Now she and I don't speak any more and we were really close at one time. We were from the same hometown back home in Sweden. Now I'm glad I don't live with her; I'm happier. I don't miss the friendship and I don't even really think about her that much now.

10. **Are people of your country primarily in good health or poor health? Why or why not?**
    The health care system is good there compared to the United States. There, everyone gets health care no matter what. The government will always help. We don't need health insurance at home. You pay your taxes and you get health care. I could pay like $10 to stay at the hospital, but all the medicine would be free while I am in the hospital. Generally there, you pay only about $200 for medicines. Anything that costs more than that as treatment is free.

Key Concepts

active and avoidant coping
anger-in
anger-out
cancer-prone personality
compensatory self-enhancement (CSE)
coronary-prone personality
daily hassles
defensive hostility
emotion suppression
expectancy

five-factor model
general adaptation syndrome
hardiness
internal locus of control
personality
reinforcement value
sense of coherence
sense of self/identity
stress
subjective well-being

Study Questions

1. All personalities can be measured along continuums for what five factors?
2. What personality characteristic has been linked to increased somatic complaints and also the experience of homesickness? Why does this characteristic play a significant role in health?
3. What does it mean to be a person high in defensive hostility?
4. What is the difference in opinion of those who support a specific disease-personality theory versus a more generic disease-prone theory?
5. What is the relationship between a person's level of subjective well-being and personality?
6. Why is it that anger-out and anger-in can both be health damaging?
7. What is stress? Is there a relationship between stress, behavior, and personality? Explain.
8. Why is it important for health professionals to gain some understanding of a person's sense of self and identity when trying to understand the person's health behavior?
9. How do Rotter's concepts of expectancy and reinforcement value explain some negative health behaviors of impoverished minority populations?
10. What are the negative health consequences of compensatory self-enhancement?

Student Activity

Write down your stressful experiences (major or minor) for two weeks. For each event, record the thoughts and behaviors you displayed in order to cope with the event. Record whether you notice any changes in your sleep patterns, eating habits, or mood in response to these stressors.

OR

Locate newspapers from any two major cities in the United States and find stories pertaining to poverty and crime in urban communities where people of color may reside. Discuss in a paper how such events may impact the residents' reinforcement values, sense of self/identity, and expectancy regarding health promotion and prevention.

CHAPTER

9

Social Relations and Health

Social Support and Health

In the previous chapter you learned about the significance of personality to health behaviors and health outcomes. It is important, however, not to look solely at personality factors when studying health. We must also consider the individual's larger social context, which includes family, friends, community, and the economic and political climate. For example, we may be able to identify a person as a coronary-prone personality, and subsequently expect that person to show more severe coronary artery disease in comparison to a calmer, more relaxed person. However, consider this: The coronary-prone personality person, who has strong social support, may actually be similar in health to a Type B (relaxed/calm) person (Hafen et al., 1996, p. 280). This suggests that social support may actually act as a moderator of long-term health consequences, even in the face of health-damaging characteristics of the person. Social support combined with a positive personality characteristic such as hardiness (see previous chapter) may decrease the likelihood of poor health. Now let's consider exactly what psychologists mean by social support.

Social support is the positive psychological, emotional, and material resources provided to a person through interpersonal relationships. There are various types of specifically identified social support (Quick, Nelson, Matuszek, Whittington, & Quick, 1996). The four main categories of social support have been identified as:

- *Emotional:* Provided from family and close friends; includes caring, love, and empathy. Example: You are upset and you turn to a friend who is able to comfort you.
- *Appraisal:* Receiving evaluative information about ourselves that will be useful to us for making a change. Example: A colleague gives you some pointers on how to improve your job performance so that you can get a better job evaluation, thereby reducing your job stress.
- *Informational:* Advice, suggestions, and directives that will assist us to respond to personal or situational demands. Example: You confide to a relative about some physical complaints you've been having, and she tells you about an article that she read that sounds similar to your complaints; she strongly urges you to see a doctor.
- *Instrumental support:* Usually referring to giving of money or giving of time to someone. Example: A friend agrees to babysit for you so that you can attend your aerobics class.

There may be differences in the size of individuals' social networks, number and types of interpersonal relationships, and quality of resources. This has implications for health.

Social support across the lifespan (at any phase of our lives) can have important implications for health outcomes. Studies have shown that social support may be beneficial for reducing low birthweight and negative coping with arthritis, alcoholism, tuberculosis, and some forms of psychiatric illness (Hafen et al., 1996).

Perception is also significant to studying social support, such as the perceptions that a person may have about being loved or cared for by others. If a person perceives herself to be a part of a network of communication and mutual obligation, then this can be beneficial to health. Mutual obligation among individuals requires that individuals receive help and also give help to others. This is referred to as **level II attachment**, whereas **level I attachment** refers to only receiving assistance from others without giving help in return (Quick et al., 1996). Level I and level II attachments fulfill our love and belonging needs (see Figure 9.1).

Once our social needs are met, we are motivated to fulfill esteem needs and also our needs to become a fully functioning healthy person (Maslow, 1970). Social support appears to be beneficial not just for compliance with medical regimens, but it may also reduce the amount of medication required and accelerate recovery (Pilisuk & Parks, 1986). A primary reason for the beneficial effects of social support is its ability to act as a stress buffer.

Social Support

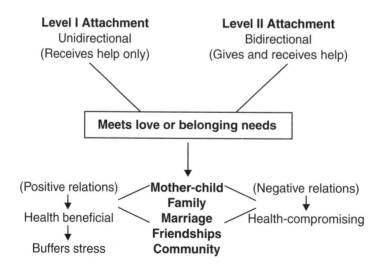

FIGURE 9.1   Types of social support and the relationship to health.

Relationships

Researchers have devoted rather extensive attention to the issue of social support and health (Hafen et al., 1996). Various types of relationships exist in the life of the typical individual. In order to understand health behavior, it is important to consider important relationships such as those of (1) mother and child, (2) family and marriage, (3) friendships, and (4) community relations. It is also important for researchers and health program developers to focus on important social relationships in the treatment and study of diverse groups.

Mother–Child Relationship

The emphasis on the mother in this section is not meant to suggest that there is no bond to fathers. However, the opportunity for a child to bond with the mother is primarily the first social opportunity for the child. It is significant to understand the attitude that a woman has about being pregnant and the health-beneficial effects of some aspects of mother–child interactions. A social bond between mother and child is important in many ways for the individual well-being of the parent and the child. Poor-quality relationships between mother and child may relate to psychological distress for parent and child, anxiety disorders in the child, aggressive behavior, withdrawn behavior, and learning disabilities (Hafen et al., 1996). Health professionals should be aware that poor-quality parent–child relationships might also have far-reaching consequences that affect the behavior of these children when they become adults.

Barber, Axinn, and Thornton (1999) did a thirty-one-year longitudinal survey of 1,113 mother–child pairs in order to determine the effects of **unwanted childbearing**. They defined unwanted childbearing as an uncontrolled and undesirable event; the mother did not want to have another child, but did anyway. The researchers wanted to follow up on results shown in the literature that children born from unintended pregnancies suffer more health problems than children from intended pregnancies. The health differences refer specifically to lower birthweight and greater infant mortality. The longitudinal study also focused on four specific factors that were thought to affect the mental health of mothers who experienced unwanted childbearing: postnatal depression, feelings of powerlessness, increased time pressures, and impaired physical health of the mother or the baby.

The results of this research showed that mothers who reported unwanted births had worse mental health in terms of self-reported depression and happiness. The researchers gathered information from the women about their marital status, income, educational level, and employment status. All of these factors were significant to how these women were affected by unwanted childbearing. The women who were happily married, of higher income, more educated, and employed outside the home were less depressed and physically healthier. Women who had younger children were physically healthier than mothers who did not have young children. In addition, although the women in this study were not physically less healthy, they were definitely more depressed than mothers who had intended pregnancies.

The results of unwanted childbearing are lower-quality emotional relationships with the children. The mothers reported having less shared leisure time outside of the home with their children and using more physical punishment of the children. They also shared less affection and social support of their children. The mothers' depression and frustration leads to the children receiving few hugs and kisses, which can have negative consequences for the growth and development of a baby.

The consequences of unwanted childbearing can also have negative consequences for the entire family. The mother's other children may even be affected by the birth of an unwanted child. These effects may linger for a very long time. Most of the women admitted that concerns about sufficient time and their health were the common reasons for not wanting to have an additional child. Having the unwanted child can thus be very stressful. It appears that women who have these concerns need to be given counseling to help them deal with these concerns during the pregnancy and after they have given birth.

Health Benefits of Breastfeeding

The benefit of breastfeeding for babies has been made known to the general public (Wolf & Crowe, 1992). Less might actually be known about the health benefits to the mother or more specifically why breastfeeding has health benefits for both mother and child. Chemically speaking, **oxytocin** is a peptide (chain of amino acids) regulated by the **hypothalamus** that is crucial to the health benefits of breastfeeding. The hypothalamus is a brain structure in the subcortex that regulates a number of actions such as hunger, thirst, and the release of hormones. A variety of types of stimuli that are associated with social interaction can result in the release of oxytocin. One such social interaction is breastfeeding. Oxytocin is released during lactation by breast stimulation, and its release can become conditioned to stimuli associated with the nursing infant.

The health benefit of oxytocin release is related to stress: Oxytocin release reduces anxiety by having a sedating effect. This occurs via its primarily parasympathetic action. Oxytocin can therefore reduce physiological reactivity to various stressors. The oxytocin release during breastfeeding leads to a reduction in the amount of stress hormones present. Women who breast-feed show a reduced responsivity to stressful experiences, which is an adaptive response that prevents the mother from overreacting to stressful stimuli and thus promotes successful lactation. This is good for the mother's mental and physical state, and it may actually even favor the interests of the infant over the mother. It promotes mother–child bonding because lactating women, in comparison to women who bottle-feed, interact more positively with their offspring in ways such as directing more touching and smiling toward their babies (Carter & Altemus, 1999).

Lactation and oxytocin oppose the more defensive behavioral patterns associated with stress and the release of another peptide known as **vasopressin**. Vasopressin is a peptide that is also regulated by the hypothalamus, but it is associated with more defensive behaviors such as enhanced arousal, vigilance, aggressive behavior, and a general increase in arousal of the sympathetic nervous system (fight or flight response). For more on the physiological and endocrine effects of social contact, see the "Spotlight on Biology" section.

Family Relationships

You can probably think of positive and negative health behaviors of your family members. Overall, you should be able to evaluate whether you believe your family has had a positive or negative impact on your behavioral choices, including your health behaviors. A reason for the advancement of the field of health psychology is the knowledge that major health problems in our society are often related to lifestyle and environment.

The family is one of the significant environmental influences on health and illness. The family is regarded as the first source of socialization for children and may be one of the first places where individuals learn about matters of health and illness (Danielson, Hamel-Bissell, & Winstead-Fry, 1993; Reutter, 1997). Social learning from the family may include how to cope with illness or attitudes about mastery over one's life situations. What one has learned from the family about health behaviors can lead to a higher prevalence of disease states. It may also affect the rate at which a person recovers from an illness. Specifically, the family can have an effect at a variety of stages: primary prevention, secondary prevention, and tertiary prevention (Danielson et al., 1993).

Primary prevention refers to lifestyle choices and behaviors such as immunizations that prevent illness in healthy people. The family can contribute to primary prevention. An example of this may be in the area of healthy eating. If your family primarily ate nutritious meals when you lived at home, you may continue this healthy style of eating as an adult. This reduces your chance of developing some forms of illness.

Secondary prevention refers to halting a disease while it is still in early and more treatable stages. The family may influence secondary prevention via the meaning that the family attaches to mental and physical symptoms of illness. The attitudes learned from family may influence your decision to seek health care. An example of this would be if your family members tended to trivialize or ignore signs of illness. In this case, they may not have made appointments to see doctors when they initially noticed health problems. This could cause you to behave similarly.

Tertiary prevention refers to actions that are taken to prevent further health decline following diagnosis with an illness. Families may influence how its individual members comply with treatment regimens given by doctors. An example of this would be if you learned an attitude from your parents or siblings that strict and consistent adherence to doctors' suggestions is not always necessary. This may influence you such that you do not adhere to medical advice about your condition.

In the United States, the population is becoming increasingly more diverse. This means that health professionals will need to be comfortable working with a wide variety of families. Especially in multicultural contexts, an awareness of the families' values will be essential to relating the appropriate health services to the family. The nuclear family that health professionals may work with today is quite different in many ways from the nuclear family many decades ago. The **nuclear family** has traditionally referred to a family that is composed of a mother and father and their children. Today the nuclear family should also be thought of as married couples who are childless, single parents, stepparents and stepchildren, unmarried couples who may or may not have children, gay and lesbian couples with or without children, and people who live as a part of communal societies.

The nuclear family is distinguished from the **extended family**, which refers to aunts and uncles, grandparents and cousins, as well as any other relatives that do not necessarily live with the nuclear family. The collectivism of many African American, Asian, Native American and Hispanic families is a part of the culture of these groups, which makes the extended family contacts numerous. Structure within the family is important as well. **Structure** is the organization of the family members and the patterns of relationships among them; it includes communication patterns, role relationships, value systems, and power structure (Reutter, 1997).

The above elements of structure can be seen in the example of a case study of a 74-year old African American woman (Outlaw, 1999). The woman, referred to as Mrs. M, suffered from chronic pulmonary disease, uncontrolled hypertension, insulin-dependent diabetes, and a history of major depression. Communication patterns within her family had negative consequences for her health. The family members (her adult children) were organized to participate in the management of Mrs. M's diabetes and hypertension. Specifically, she had two adult children who resided with her, and each of the children was responsible for a different task regarding Mrs. M's care. The problem regarding communication pattern was that the son and daughter frequently had conflicts with one another, resulting in a lack of communication between them. This constituted chaotic family dynamics. The son and daughter did not talk to one another at all, including failure to discuss the coordination of health care for their mother. Mrs. M's blood sugar was consistently fluctuating due to her children's lack of coordination and her own noncompliance with her dietary requirements. Mrs. M was not involved at all in the management of her hypertension and diabetes.

Role relationships were important in Mrs. M's case because of the role of another adult who was not biologically related to Mrs. M. A multilevel approach was used in Mrs. M's treatment, which incorporated the input of this other adult as well as Mrs. M's children. A **multilevel approach** includes developing a relationship with all family members or significant others who have a vital role in the management of the patient's health. The other significant adult in Mrs. M's case was her son's girlfriend. The nurse discovered that Mrs. M was very accepting of the girlfriend's input about her care. The son's girlfriend provided a necessary supportive function and Mrs. M seemed to view the son's girlfriend as another daughter.

The significance of the girlfriend's role also necessitated the need for the health professional to respect the family's value system. What if the nurse in this situation had not respected the girlfriend's role because she was not a blood relative? This could have had negative consequences for Mrs. M's treatment. It is always important that a health professional convey respect for the family, their home, and living circumstances. Outlaw (1999) reports that Mrs. M and her family had dismissed many nurses because they felt that the nurses were disrespectful.

In many families, it is also particularly important to understand the power structure as it relates to the elderly. Not only do most families of color have a collective focus, they also have a cultural norm that views the elderly as embodying the wisdom of the group; the elderly are to be respected. So although Mrs. M was the patient and in poor health, most of her children lived in her home or close by her home. Elderly persons in families of color may have a lot of power and influence over other family members, even if they are ailing. When dealing with the elderly, these are important considerations for health professionals.

The same structural dynamics will also be apparent for health professionals who work with **intergenerational families** (Kinsey, 1999b). Intergenerational families refer to single households that contain the elderly, their children, and their grandchildren. Kinsey (1999b) presented a case study of a pregnant African American woman in her early 20s, referred to as Ms. L. Ms. L had two sons who died of sudden infant death syndrome. She was described as depressed, a heavy smoker (2 or 3 packs of cigarettes/day), a single unemployed parent with no job skills, living in a challenging urban environment. She and her family experienced personal and community threats on a daily basis (drug gangs, murders, rapes, and drive-by shootings).

A health professional hoping to intervene with a client such as Ms. L would have to acknowledge the role relationships that are a part of her family. She lived in an intergenerational family in which she and her children lived with her grandmother. The grandmother was always present at Ms. L's meetings with the public health nurse. The grandmother was actively involved in the discussions, offering opinions on Ms. L's negative behaviors and Ms. L's pregnancy. The grandmother did not believe that Ms. L should be pregnant again. The nurse noted that because of Ms. L's dependence on her grandmother, she was not taking on the necessary parenting roles and responsibilities of an adult. Because the extended family ties are very close and common in families of color, it is not atypical for extended family members to assume parenting roles for other family members' children in times of crises. Ms. L was a parent by the standard definition of a parent, but she was essentially living as a child in the home of her grandmother. The grandmother cared for Ms. L and Ms. L's children. The fact that the grandmother was willing to do this is a part of their value system.

The grandmother, known as Mrs. S, reported that she had not seen her own doctor in two years, although she had been experiencing some physical complaints. She stated that she was too busy worrying about the kids and how they were doing in school. As you can see from the case study of this intergenerational family, both the health of Ms. L and Mrs. S suffered from their role relationships and value systems inherent in the family. The development of a health plan for either of these women needs to include the other, since their lives are so enmeshed. The role relationships and value systems of this family were damaging to both women's health. The health professional in this type of situation would have to respect this family dynamic, yet still work to have the clients make some changes towards better health (Kinsey, 1999a).

Marriage

Related to the previous discussion on family would also be the discussion of marriage. Couples with or without children are considered in today's definition of a nuclear family. The health benefits of marriage lend support to the significance of social relations to health. Studies have shown that married people generally enjoy better health than persons who are single, divorced, or widowed when all other factors are equal (Hafen et al., 1996). The health benefits of marriage may differ by gender, but, overall, marriage seems to be beneficial. Specifically, studies have shown marriage to be health beneficial to males (Hafen & Frandsen, 1987). Interestingly, those who are single and have never been married are second in health behind the married individuals, followed by those who are widowed, and last in poorest health are those who are divorced or separated. What do these rankings mean for the significance of marriage? When persons are happily married, they are experiencing quality support in areas that enhance their health status. For example, a spouse may be able to remind one of health appointments or actually attend meetings with the spouse and the physician. On the other hand, for persons who are divorced and separated, their immune system's functioning may actually be compromised by stress (i.e., financial status, loneliness).

Friendships

Closely related to the health benefits of marriage and the family is the social bond of friendship. Many of us perhaps do not think about the health benefits of having friends, but if you were to imagine how your life would be different without some of your best friends, then maybe you could begin to see how even your health could benefit from the presence of friends. The greatest benefit provided by friends is perhaps in the area of prevention of loneliness (Hafen et al., 1996). Our friendships help protect our health because we are able to confide many of our deepest feelings to our friends. Friendships are able to provide health benefits in a way that is quite different from the relationship we have with our family. When we confide troubling thoughts, feelings, and behaviors to our friends, we often receive support that helps us buffer the stress of the situation. You can probably recall incidents in which your friends were able to help you through major life-changing stressors, as well as through some of the minor stressful events of your day. Not all of the friendships that you have are equal in quality and significance to health. Close friendships are the most beneficial to your health and longevity (Sagan, 1987).

If you or someone you know has recently moved to a new city or country, many adjustments will have to be made. Having friendships will not only make the transition easier but will also produce health benefits (Sagan, 1987). Specifically, research has shown that people who are socially isolated are more likely to die of a wide variety of diseases compared to those who are happy with fulfilling social lives (Hafen & Frandsen, 1987). In many societies where people have very close ties to their family, friends, and community, they are protected from illness and a shortened life span (Hafen et al., 1996).

Community Relations

There is no doubt that social relations at the family level are highly significant to the study of the individual's health. However, in the field of public health, a systems approach emphasizes the need to look at how health problems may be based at a macro (larger) level instead of based solely inside the family (Kristjanson & Chalmers, 1991). It is plausible that external stressors at the macro level of the community can have detrimental effects on its residents' health. In Chapter 2 for example, it was mentioned that in many poor urban communities of color it might be difficult for residents to find a grocery that carries quality fresh produce.

In the previous case study of Ms. L, you read about how her community was plagued with murders, drug activity, and generally high levels of stress. Also, in some disenfranchised communities of color and other poor neighborhoods, residents experience illegal and unethical toxic dumping in their neighborhoods (Coleburn, 2000). The quality of the air and water and the location of toxic waste dumps may all differ by the socioeconomic characteristics of communities. Impoverished communities may have fewer healthy housing units, work environments, and recreational areas. There may also be an increased likelihood of exposure to pest infestation, lead paint, and asbestos. As in the case of the community where Ms. L lived, lower SES areas often have higher levels of actual and perceived crime, which can also have negative effects on health. Factors such as these impact the residents' health but are not directly related to the family dynamics. For people who have lived in such a community for longer periods of time—such as the elderly—the negative health effects are perhaps even greater. Although many health professionals emphasize the individual and family level factors that affect health, it is also important to understand the community context in which individuals and their families live (Robert, 1998).

In a study of the neighborhood social context and racial differences in women's heart disease mortality, the importance of examining the effects of neighborhoods was demonstrated (Leclere, Rogers, & Peters, 1998). This study was based on data taken from a national health interview survey and the 1990 Census of Population. The study found that in communities where women headed more than a quarter of the families, there was increased likelihood of death due to heart disease. The risk was greater in such communities compared to the risks for women who lived in neighborhoods with fewer female-headed families. Communities with substantial numbers of female-headed households may show greater heart disease mortality due to increased financial, physical, and emotional stress in such communities.

The study also revealed that black women were more likely to experience many factors that adversely impacted their health. Examples of these factors were identified as untreated chronic disease, work-related stress, family obligations, limited health care, and increased risk taking. According to this study, black women in particular may be significantly affected by the characteristics of the community in which they live. It is important to note here that family obligations were listed as a stressful factor. Thus far, the health benefits of family have been emphasized; however, it is important to also acknowledge that social ties such as the family are not always or necessarily health beneficial. Family, friends, and sometimes neighbors as well, may provide aid, but they are also examples of social obligations. When a person's family and neighbors require regular financial or emotional assistance, this can be stressful for the person being called upon for assistance. In poor communities with high percentages of female-headed households, there are likely to be significant reciprocal obligations among the residents (Leclere et al., 1998).

Finally, another area of community effects that should be acknowledged is the health behaviors that occur in rural versus urban areas or metropolitan versus nonmetropolitan areas. The definition of **rural** involves a combination of the number of people residing in a place, some aspects of geographical distance and space, and recognition of the distance of the place from other nearby health and human services. In population terms, many definitions of rural refer to a range from less than 100,000 persons to areas with densities of six or fewer persons per square mile (American Nurses Association, 1996). Areas with six or fewer people per square mile are probably better characterized as **frontier areas**, which are found almost exclusively in the western part of the United States. We often hear much about the frustration that leads to aggression, stress, and poor health in urban areas, but there can be stressors of rural life that also lead to poor health.

Common health characteristics are found in many rural areas. For example, there is a tendency towards independence and self-sufficiency; health is synonymous with being productive/able to work as opposed to other factors, and preventive health-care visits are infrequent. Rural residents may also prefer to continue to use more informal systems of health care. It has been reported that rural residents may be less healthy than urban residents due to the following (American Nurses Association, 1996):

- Low income
- Less access to Medicaid coverage compared to urban residents
- Less access to general health care due to economic, physical, and cultural barriers
- Lack of mobility (urban residents are more likely to have personal transportation and access to public transportation)

The health situation is even worse when the rural resident is poor and a minority (Beatty, 1997). Rural minority communities are some of the poorest communities in the United States (American Nurses Association, 1996). The rural resident, and particularly poor minority rural residents, have higher incidents of maternal and infant mortality, chronic illness and disability, diabetes, cancer, high blood pressure, heart disease, stroke, and lung disease (American Nurses Association, 1996).

Launching a community health program for rural populations, minority populations, and other disenfranchised populations requires going into the community to first find out what the community members want. Demographic factors determine what the needs and wants will be (Robert, 1998). Program planners will also need to find out from the residents what the residents believe to be barriers to improving their health. In some cases the health providers actually use an empowerment approach to provide community health education. This was done with a Native American population to build individual and communal self-esteem (Bragg, 1997).

The activities were held in the Native American community and involved community members of all ages. The activities promoted traditional Native American values of love, honor, and respect, and included Native American stories, myths, and legends. The community residents were allowed to participate in the design and execution of the activities. The outcome was that the community residents wrote a series of plays to be acted out that focused on healthy community behavior common to Native Americans prior to the European invasion. They focused on behaviors that enabled the individuals and tribes to survive and flourish. The activities and the education offered positive alternatives to negative behaviors such as substance abuse. This study provides an example of the necessity of doing a thorough assessment of needs and the necessity of allowing residents to take control over the formulation of activities.

Some populations may be particularly isolated even within their community. For these groups, health professionals will have much work to do to educate, build esteem, and empower these individuals. A good example of such a group would be gays and lesbians who reside in rural or small town areas such as those that are lacking in diversity (Cody & Welch, 1997). There is a paucity of research on gays and lesbians living in rural areas. Due to some themes that are relevant to these individuals, more research is needed. Cody and Welch (1997) studied twenty gay males in northern New England (Maine, New Hampshire, and Vermont) and found that nine themes were reflected in the subjects' specific experiences with life in a rural area:

- Early awareness of difference
- Internalized homophobia
- Some positive aspects of living in a rural area (enjoyment of the simplicity and comfort of small town living)
- Negative aspects of rural living (lack of a visible gay community, which reinforced feelings of difference, isolation, and aloneness)
- Positive family of choice (recreating a sense of family with chosen other gays, lesbians, or non-gays)
- Compulsory heterosexuality (attempts to conceal sexual orientation through heterosexual dating and marriage)
- Isolation
- Current life partner (50% had current significant long-term relationship)
- Family censorship (experienced censorship about homosexuality by families of origin)

The findings of Cody and Welch (1997) support other findings that gays and lesbians in rural areas often lack a community of gays and lesbians that can be relied upon for psychological,

Spotlight on Biology: The Neurobiology of Affiliation

Friendly or nonaggressive social contact has three subtypes: (1) approach and hunger, (2) interaction, and (3) relaxation or satiety. Each of these types occurs in sexual behavior and other social interactions that involve touch such as hugging, kissing, muscle massages, or breastfeeding. Nonaggressive social contact such as breastfeeding, sexual behavior, muscle massage, and even listening to pleasant sounds cause sensory stimulation that is positive. These sensory experiences are positive because they result in the conversion in cells of simple structures into complex molecular forms of living material. This leads to storage of energy and growth. Innocuous stimulation such as nonaggressive/friendly social contact promotes vagal nerve activity and subsequently digestion and the conversion of the simple cells to complex material. The evidence that innocuous stimulation is positive for storage of energy and growth has been demonstrated via the increased growth of premature babies in response to massage. The various types of innocuous stimuli such as touch, warm temperature, and breastfeeding increase oxytocin levels in the blood and particularly in cerebrospinal fluid. An increase in the levels of oxytocin brings about an antistress pattern. In humans, the administration of oxytocin always seems to be associated with decreased blood pressure. Depending on how much is released, oxytocin can induce an anti-anxiety effect/sedative effect. Oxytocin is released during breastfeeding and is good for the mother and the infant. The release of oxytocin during breastfeeding increases the blood flow to the skin over the mammary gland; the mother will show elevated chest skin temperature. The benefit for the mother is that after each suckling episode there is a fall in blood pressure and cortisol levels. The mother feels relaxed and sedated while nursing. The benefit for the child is that the warmth from the mother's skin is transmitted to the child, promoting a calming of the baby. The benefit of good relationships is that they are likely to promote the release of oxytocin that reduces anxiety and lowers stress hormone levels.

Source: Uvnas Moberg, 1999.

health, and educational resources (D'Augelli & Hart, 1987). Gays and lesbians may be living in shame and isolation due to their sexual orientation (Grossman, 1996; Mann, 1996; O'Hanlan, 1996). The health professional that wishes to target these individuals with community programs may have these and other issues to address (Grossman, 1996).

Conclusion

The need for affiliation seems to be a part of human nature. Therefore, it is not surprising that social support is important to health. Giving and receiving support has positive health consequences. It is particularly important that health professionals acknowledge the significance of family, spouses, friends, and the community of any client being treated. In acknowledging these influences it will become apparent to the health professional that sometimes the significant others in the patient's life may be health beneficial or health compromising. Both the patient and the significant others will need to understand how the dynamics of their social relationship relate to the patient's health behavior, health attitudes, and health status.

Summary

Social support is the positive psychological, emotional, and material resources provided to a person through interpersonal relationships. Level I and level II attachment exists. Level I attachment occurs when we receive assistance from others without giving help in return, and level II attachment refers to the mutual obligation among individuals to both give and receive help. Theories of motivation indicate that social needs are important and we are motivated to fulfill these needs. The bonds we establish with significant others are beneficial for our motivation to fulfill esteem needs that relate to concerns about health. The bond between mother and child is the first social bond of significance. Therefore, it is important to understand the mother's attitude about being pregnant and having an unwanted child. There are health consequences of unwanted childbearing for both the mother and the child. A positive health behavior is that of breastfeeding. Breastfeeding leads to the release of oxytocin; oxytocin release reduces anxiety by having a sedating effect. Women who breastfeed show a reduced responsivity to stressful experiences. The family plays a major role in an individual's health via primary prevention, secondary prevention, and tertiary prevention. Structure within the nuclear family and extended family is important to the family's function. The structure includes the communication patterns, role relationships, value systems, and power structure within the family. A multilevel approach is sometimes necessary with families and particularly with intergenerational families. Finally, health professionals may have different issues to confront when dealing with married versus single persons, those who are loners versus having many friends, and those who live in rural versus urban communities. The community of the individual may have unhealthy aspects that need to be addressed and changed in order to enhance the client's health. It is also necessary for health professionals to address the special needs of groups such as gays and lesbians who may be isolated within their communities.

Student Interview

Age: 26
Gender: Female
Origin: African American

1. **If you had a serious health concern, who would you likely talk to in addition to a doctor?**
   An herbalist and also my mother.
2. **What are the overall quality and quantity of friendships that you have?**
   The quantity is small but the quality is high. I highly value my relationships with my friends. Genuineness in people is very hard to find. I need someone who will tell me when I need to get my act together.
3. **Do you think that your family has mainly been a positive or negative influence on your health behaviors, i.e., eating habits, smoking, etc.?**
   Positive, meaning my Mom primarily. My Mom is the cornerstone of the family. My Mom is a vegetarian (she is a health nut, herbally she finds cures outside of going to the doctor). She has influenced me and it works for me.
4. **Are your friends health conscious?**
   Some of them are, but some are not. Some smoke, drink, and eat pork. I know what they don't know about what it will do to them.
5. **Do you think that marriage would be/is health benefiting or a negative influence on a person's health?**
   It depends on whether the spouse is health conscious. People who are married take care of each other more. They may cook for each other and encourage each other to go to the physician. My friend eats out every day (fast food, he is single). I rarely eat fast food although I'm single because I live with my Mom.
6. **Are you satisfied with the quality of grocery stores, and health facilities in your community?**
   Yes, I'm satisfied with the groceries and health clubs in my area.
7. **How important is family in your culture?**
   Well, I know that it is important for many African Americans and Hispanics, but it is not in my own personal experience. My Mom is an only child. Her only brother is deceased. It's just me and my Mom, and I have five brothers and sisters. I'm not close to my brothers and sisters though. My Grandma died, and I never knew my Granddads. I don't do the family thing. Except for me and my Mom, my family is not into that. My brothers and sisters are not even close to my Mom. It's a shame that my son won't get to experience the big family thing.
8. **What do you see as the most serious health issue facing your community (i.e., African American)?**
   Eating habits. Many African Americans seem to be unaware of what's going to happen to them from eating the way that they eat. Maybe it's a lack of knowledge of the ailments that come from eating that way. You are what you eat.
9. **What area of your own health would you like to improve?**
   I would like to cut out refined sugar completely from my diet and too much store bought prepackaged stuff. I would like to eat more fresh wholesome foods that are organic.
10. **Have you ever assisted anyone else in any way with a health problem that he or she had?**
    Yes. I offer suggestions to people who want to hear them about their diet (some don't want to hear them). I don't smoke or drink and I tell people why I don't. I am around much older people because younger people are not into the health consciousness as much. They tend not to like my lifestyle such as no partying, drinking, smoking.

Key Concepts

extended family
frontier areas
hypothalamus
intergenerational families
level I attachment
level II attachment
multilevel approach
nuclear family
oxytocin
primary prevention
rural
secondary prevention
social support
structure
tertiary prevention
unwanted childbearing
vasopressin

Study Questions

1. In what ways have families of today changed significantly from the families of the distant past?
2. What are regarded as major reasons for the health benefit of good quality friendships?
3. What are the four distinct types of social support that a person may receive from others?
4. How does marital status relate to the health of an individual?
5. What is an example of tertiary prevention as a family factor affecting the individual's health?
6. How was it that Ms. L and her grandmother were negatively impacting each other's health?
7. What kinds of issues might a health professional have to face in working with clients in rural areas?
8. Why is the issue of "unwanted childbearing" an important topic for health researchers to study?
9. What does it mean for a health professional to take a multilevel approach in treating a client?
10. How does the release of oxytocin and vasopressin differentially impact behavior?

Student Activity

Interview at least three women who breast-fed, asking them about their experiences and the physiological and emotional effects that they recall about the experience. Perhaps you can also inquire about their present bond with that child.

OR

Interview a recently arrived (5 years or less) person to the United States and ask him or her to describe their experiences with establishing friendships and maintaining ties to friends/family at home. During the interview, you should inquire about any major or minor health complications that they have experienced during the adaptation to the new culture.

10 Spirituality, Music, and Laughter: Health Benefits

In Chapter 9, attention was given to social relations, specifically as they pertain to significant others and the community. In addition, however, patients may believe in the possibility of a higher level of social support that transcends human relationships. This is referred to as *transcendence*, which refers to the attachment to God through faith. Some believe that, for health reasons, they not only need the relationships with family and friends that are horizontal, but they also need a vertical relationship with the Creator (Quick et al., 1996). In the vertical relationship the source of the support, the Higher Presence, is known by different names depending on the culture of the patient—for example, Adonai for Jews, the Holy Trinity for Christians, and Allah for Muslims are names used to refer to the source. It is not uncommon for some patients to defer to a Higher Presence during a time of need (i.e., life hardships, specifically illness).

In consideration of this type of attachment, the health professional's treatment approach must expand to include a biopsychosocial spiritual point of view. This point of view is consistent with the belief that there are four levels of dimension of human identity: the body, the mind, the soul, and the spirit (Fukuyama & Sevig, 1999). This chapter includes a discussion of the relevance of the spiritual dimension to multicultural health, the positive health effects of music (which often accompanies spiritual practices), and the health benefits of laughter. Regarding diverse groups of patients, health professionals and researchers will be best equipped if they are knowledgeable about these topics, and their significance to the health and lifestyle of the patient (Krause, Ingersoll-Dayton, & Liang, 1999).

Spirituality and Health

Spirituality refers to the human propensity to find meaning in life through self-transcendence; it is evident in a sense of relatedness to something greater than the self (James & Samuels, 1999). An individual is said to be on a path of spiritual development when he or she is searching for meaning and purpose that provides a sense of order and direction in life and a sense of connectedness with a higher power or God (James & Samuels, 1999). Once the individual establishes connectedness with the Higher Power, three faith-related coping styles can exist (Quick et al., 1996):

1) **Self-directing:** The individual is responsible for action but sees God as providing positive appraisal for individual problem solving. Example: The individual will take action to become healthier and will expect God to be a reinforcer of those actions.

2) **Deferring:** Outcomes are in God's hands and God is seen as the solver of problems; the individual waits for solutions to appear through God's efforts. Example: The individual is inactive and passively waits for God to intervene to take care of the sickness or disease.

3) **Collaborative:** God and individual are seen as active partners. Example: The individual expects that with God's help and support he or she can overcome any sickness or disease.

These three coping styles are not equally health beneficial. The self-directing and collaborative styles are more health affirming than the deferring coping style. The majority of U.S. residents describe themselves as spiritual and report that spirituality is an important aspect of their lives (Hill, 2000).

A sense of connectedness is enhanced by the consideration of spiritual issues and provides stability to the person (Chapman, 1996). This sense of connectedness and spirituality is significant in programs such as Alcoholics Anonymous. The program advocates that a consideration of spirituality is necessary in helping a client remain a recovering alcoholic. Alcoholics Anonymous operates according to a three-layered concept: affinity with others, affinity with self, and an affinity with a higher power. The alcoholism is seen as more than physical dependence—the addiction is acknowledged as involving the body, the mind, and the spirit. The spirit is believed to be important to recovery from alcohol dependence because it represents the client's harmonious relationship with the environment in which he or she lives (Chapman, 1996). The person believes that he or she is participating in the universe and in his or her own healing experiences.

In many cultures, a lack of attachment to a Higher Presence is believed to be a fundamental cause of human suffering, both mental and physical (Fukuyama & Sevig, 1999). There are multiple dimensions that contribute to a person's health status (i.e., physical, cognitive, emotional, social, and spiritual), and patients may have varying concepts of optimal health. Chissell (1996) defines **optimal health** as the best possible emotional, intellectual, physical, spiritual, and socioeconomic aliveness that one can attain and balance (see Figure 10.1).

Health professionals should be aware that there are some clients who may not only advocate this definition of optimal health, but may also even view spiritual development as integral to their optimal health (Adams, Bezner, Drabbs, Zabarano, & Steinhardt, 2000).

Human spirituality has not traditionally been a major focus of Western psychology. Historically, psychology has tended to equate any form of spirituality with pseudoscience, primitive superstition, lack of education, or even a form of psychopathology. This is changing, however, as journals now present reviews and research on the spiritual dimension of health (Perrin & McDermott, 1997). The spiritual dimension enhances an individual's health via (1) a personal belief or faith extending beyond the self (2) a locus of control and empowerment for self-realization, (3) unconditional meaningfulness that provides a personal sense of positive direction and fulfillment, and (4) peace and tranquility in the face of stressful situations (Perrin & McDermott, 1997).

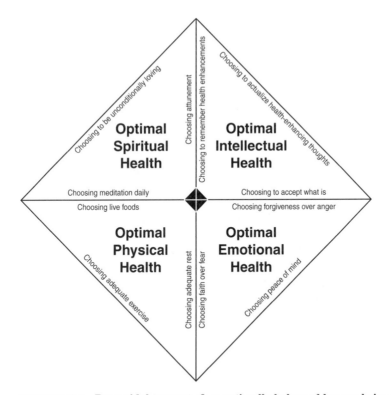

FIGURE 10.1   Pyramidal concept of an optimally balanced human being through positive life force choices.

Dark square formed by the black capstone represents Amun/God within/without

Source: Chissell, J. T., *Pyramids of Power: An Ancient African Centered Approach to Optimal Health*, p. 70, figure 10. Positive Perception Publications 1993. Used with permission.

Spirituality is also health affirming because of the vast number of health decisions that can be affected. For example, some religions actively promote healthier lifestyles such as eating less meat, no alcohol, avoiding caffeine-containing foods and drinks, no smoking, sexual abstinence, and no drug usage (Hafen et al., 1996). As a result of church affiliation and spiritual involvement, individuals may not only eat healthier, but get proper rest, exercise, spend more time with family and other social relations, and properly utilize the available health-care systems (Hafen et al., 1996).

Spiritual individuals may also be healthier people because of their construals. An individual's own particular experience of the world is called the person's **construal** (Funder, 1997). Construals are interpretations rather than reflections of reality, and they are freely chosen. The construal of individuals with a deep sense of spirituality causes them to see life differently (James & Samuels, 1999). They have a purpose, they enjoy a sense of meaning in life, and they have a broader perspective. Their spirituality can help them to buffer stress. For example, sometimes a stressful event such as a life-threatening illness will promote spiritual growth (James & Samuels, 1999). In addition, aspects of spiritual living such as prayer and forgiveness may actually have physiological effects that enhance health (Hafen et al., 1996). Prayer is believed to initiate the relaxation response in the body, and forgiveness prevents the buildup of stress hormones in the bloodstream (Hafen et al., 1996).

Multicultural Health and Spirituality

Health programs and research with diverse populations of patients will need to incorporate the worldview and value systems of the client's culture. This requires learning something about the client's history and showing respect for the information that is shared. It would also be a good practice for the health professional to acknowledge his or her own similarities and differences with the client in beliefs. This is a good initial position in order to reduce barriers to health improvements. The client's worldview and value system will likely include issues of spirituality. Generally, the spiritual or religious viewpoint of the client will be based on an Eastern or Western cultural perspective.

Eastern Tradition

In the Eastern tradition, God is known as the Impersonal Divine. Religions such as Buddhism, Advaita Vedanta, and Taoism emphasize the **Impersonal Divine** as a formless, nameless, impersonal spiritual reality that is ultimately revealed as the ground of being (Fukuyama & Sevig, 1999). The objective in these spiritual practices is to have the individual merge into the Impersonal Divine; this is accomplished through spiritual practices such as meditation, karma yoga, and devotion. Buddhism, which originated in India, is about enlightenment. The meaning of the word Buddha is "awakened one," hence the meaning of becoming enlightened. The enlightenment occurs when the individual experiences knowing oneness with the Divine source and with all beings. Eventually, what occurs is that the individual will no longer know separateness and will gain insight into the impermanence of life. The spiritual master or teacher is the healer of illness and suffering in the Buddhist worldview. The master or teacher uses various techniques for developing the consciousness within an individual. A developed consciousness brings the person into oneness or connection with the Impersonal Divine. In the Buddhist worldview, the cause of disease and suffering in the world is detachment from the Impersonal Divine. For the health professional attempting to work with a client or his or her family that practices Buddhism, there has to be some degree of understanding and respect for the belief system of the Buddhist tradition toward sickness and healing. The patient might also expect that the physician will meet or at least speak with the Buddhist healer at some point during the treatment process.

African American Tradition

Health professionals may also encounter Afrocentric spirituality as practiced by African Americans. The worldview from Africa (Western Africa) has contributed to African American cultures of today in several ways. Particularly with respect to worship style, Afrocentric spirituality emphasizes oneness with nature and the survival of one's people. For many

African Americans, as with Africans, religion/spirituality and life are inseparable (Taylor, Mattis, & Chatters, 1999). Just as with the Buddhist tradition, there is an emphasis on being connected. The individual is seen as belonging to an extended kinship system that includes people, animals, plants, objects, ancestors, and the unborn.

The Yoruban people of West Africa have had influence on Afrocentric spirituality today. The Yoruban value system includes a sense of relatedness to ancestors and community. The emphasis is on treating the family holistically from a spiritual base. The Yoruban religion focuses on balance in the universe by connecting to all things in the universe. Many African Americans today practice spirituality and religion from a Western perspective that views God as a Personal Divine, rather than as an Impersonal Divine as in the East. They often view God as theistic in nature, as is the tradition of Hebrews, Christians, and those who practice Islam. For those of a Western theistic position, the individual seeks a relationship with the Divine, and the soul exists in relationship to the Divine. When the soul cuts itself off from the Divine, the individual is subject to experiencing isolation, emptiness, depression, and poor physical and mental health. This point of view produces a way of thinking that leads the individual to seek a deeper communion with the Spiritual Power or Presence in order to combat and cope with illness and disease. For African American children with sickle cell disease, the religiosity of the child and parents, a personal relationship with God, and social connection to a community of worship were important resources in coping with the sickle cell disease (Barbarin, 1999). These factors also fostered healthy psychological development of the children.

Christian-based weight loss programs have also become widespread as thousands of overweight people have connected to God for help with their food obsessions and weight problems. In a plan called the "**weigh down diet**," the diet calls for people to substitute God for food (Brown, 2000). African American women affiliated with a church in Maryland used the weigh down diet to "eat the way God intended you to eat" (Brown, 2000). As a result of the weigh down diet, these women have gotten in tune with their body signals of hunger and they eat only when hungry. Their attitude is to cut their meals in half and focus the other half on God and prayer. Participants in the ten-week program use Biblical scriptures/teachings to guide them and gain power over food. Their attitude is that if you fail in the program, you don't let down Jenny Craig or Weight Watchers, your spouse, or yourself, but instead you have failed to abide by God's will. The participants admit that for some of them, the food was being used to fill a void that is now filled by their connection with God. Participants in the weigh down diet from the Maryland church-based class have lost 50, 60, and 100 lbs. within a matter of months (Brown, 2000). Health professionals may not advocate such drastic weight loss in short periods of time (particularly without a physician's approval and little to no exercise). However, a health-care provider should at least be open to listening to a woman who is spiritually inspired to attempt something such as the weigh down diet.

Latino Tradition

African Americans are not the only group of people who have been spiritually influenced by the Nigerian Yoruban people. There has also been an African influence among Latinos (Zea et al., 1997). Latinos differ in ethnicity but share a common cultural heritage. The roots of Latinos have an origin with the colonization of the Americas by Spain. There was a meshing of Spanish and indigenous cultures, and also the influence of African culture due to African slaves bought to areas such as Cuba, Puerto Rico, Brazil, and the Caribbean. In Cuba, Puerto Rico, and Brazil there has been a preservation of African practices. The Nigerian Yoruba traditions have influenced these regions and people via language and religion. These influences have flourished in parts of Latin America and the United States. Some Puerto Ricans, Cubans, and Caribbeans practice the religion of **Santeria**, which includes the worship of gods and goddesses (Fukuyama & Sevig, 1999). The practice of *Santeria* includes respect for the ancestors and a belief in the interconnection between the living and the dead. In the practice of *Santeria*, natural and supernatural forces are considered causes of physical suffering, emotional distress, and personal problems. Each of the *orishas* (gods/goddesses) is believed to control or represent a force of nature. *Santeria*, as influenced by Yoruban culture, suggests that life and death, health and illness are fluid processes and can be attributed to physical trauma or to supernatural forces punishing the sufferer for something wrong that was done. In working with clients from such a background of beliefs, professionals may need to become familiar with concepts and attitudes of significance in the spiritual practices of the client. If a client believes that a supernatural force is the cause of common diseases such as cancer or AIDS, then the health professional must respect this spiritual belief. The health professional may need to combine mainstream and indigenous practices of the client's culture. The health professional may need to familiarize herself with words such as **Dana**, a curse such as that brought on by a witch, or **Curandero**, which means indigenous healer (Zea et al., 1997). Depending on the degree of acculturation and age of the clients, the physician or counselor should be prepared for references to supernatural forces, folk explanations, and possibly a collective approach to treatment that involves the clients' family (Zea et al., 1997). Clients practicing *Santeria* may tell the doctor that they want to appeal to the *orishas* in addition to consulting the mainstream physician for health advice (Zea et al., 1997).

Native American Tradition

If treating traditional Native American patients, health professionals should be knowledgeable of shamans and the value of spirituality in the Native American culture (Matheson, 1996; Singh, 1999). Traditional Native American culture emphasizes that good health, mental, physical, or social is dependent on maintaining harmonious relationships with the spirit world. A **shaman** is a person who traverses the boundary between the physical and spiritual worlds. The shaman can compose special songs for healing. He or she can self-induce trances, travel after souls and objects, and diagnose and cure illnesses. Generally, shamanistic traditions teach ways to honor the spirit that is present in the earth, moon, sun, seasons, animals, rivers, mountains, and all other forms of creation. There are many forms of shamanism, as many forms as there are cultures in the world. Each type of shamanism has it own beliefs, practices, and rituals. The ways of integrating the shamanistic ideas into practice will be specific to each tribe, so no professional should assume knowledge of the specific practices of a client based on stereotypes about the shamanistic spiritual practices. There are many variations in myths and value orientations of Native Americans. The consistency among the beliefs of Native Americans includes connection with nature, cooperation, protectiveness of life, and unselfishness. Specifically regarding health, the spiritual practice includes the significance of the circle that is considered a symbol for life's processes and represents "reality" among Native Americans. The circle represents the cycles of life. The four compass directions (north, south, east, west) are included in rituals and are referred to as the Medicine Wheel. The four compass directions represent spirit, nature, body, and mind. The four directions each represent different issues such as birth, new beginnings, trust, wisdom, strength, and courage. Health is related to balancing the four directions. Traumas such as injury, sickness, or disease are believed to throw the person outside of the circle. In order for the person to be brought back inside the circle he or she must be healed. As a person is trained to become a shaman, he or she learns how to heal affliction of the body and mind.

Spiritual guides that exist in the cosmic world are called upon to assist the shaman's apprentice. The shaman's apprentice is taught to use physical and spiritual resources to heal the body, mind, and spirit. The shaman has power by learning to become one with all that exists and learning the balance of nature. Diseases are not considered to be individual afflictions but a disruption in the balance of life (i.e., the four compass directions and their meanings). Whenever there is imbalance, there will be pain and suffering, either mental or physical, or both. Serious medical conditions such as epileptic seizures may have a different explanation coming from a shaman versus the mainstream medical doctor. Shamans may explain the seizures by saying that there is an angry spirit draining the life force out of the individual, which causes him or her to drop to the ground and shake uncontrollably (Singh, 1999). The shaman will want to appease the angry spirit to restore balance and harmony, enabling healing to take place. Just as for groups possessing the spiritual beliefs of *Santeria*, likewise with shamanism, health professionals should remain unbiased and receptive to the spiritual beliefs of multicultural clients. If a client speaks of a shaman, then a health professional may consider meeting the shaman to gain further insight into the client's health attitudes and behaviors.

Women's Health and Sexual Minority Health

A discussion on multicultural health must also consider aspects of spirituality as they pertain to women's health and the health of gays and lesbians. The women's health and women's spirituality perspectives assume that fundamentally there is interconnection of all living beings and an interconnection of all dimensions within individuals such as the mind, body, and spirit (Lauver, 2000). The perspective is a holistic view. Both the women's health and women's spirituality perspectives aim to foster a sense of integrated well-being and thriving among women (Lauver, 2000). Women's spirituality enlightens women by teaching them that they are in a unique position to challenge oppressive thinking and foster balance and wholeness (Fukuyama & Sevig, 1999). Women's spirituality groups have created worship rituals using a circle of women together as a model for equality, sharing, and connectedness. A woman may benefit from being a part of a spiritual circle of other women who have had her same health experiences (Fukuyama & Sevig, 1999). The perspectives aim to empower women to feel positively about themselves in order to overcome negative emotions, thoughts, and poor health behaviors.

Spirituality and health may also be relevant for health professionals who work with gay and lesbian clients. A barrier to the treatment of gay and lesbian clients may be a client's internalized hatred and religious guilt about sexual orientation (Barret & Barzan, 1996). Barret and Barzan (1996) report that these clients may also be dealing with having been rejected by family members and church family. Counselors may have to deal with spiritual beliefs of some physically ill clients who believe God is punishing them for homosexuality. Negative attitudes may be heard and internalized from parents, teachers, members of the clergy, and peers (Cody & Welch, 1997). Both clients and professionals must ask themselves what their beliefs are on the matter of religion, suffering, and sexual orientation. Specifically, the health professional should ask him- or herself: "How best should I respond to a client who is suffering with pain or chronic illness and believes in God, but can't feel good about seeking direction and comfort from the Creator?" "How would I respond to a client who feels he or she is suffering and not worthy of God's attention and love, yet wants that love and attention?" These are serious issues that are relevant to the client's recovery and coping.

The previous discussion focused on spirituality and health. Relevant to this topic is the health benefits of music because religious and/or spiritual rituals may often include music. Music is a part of many of our social events including family gatherings, worship experiences, and other formal or informal settings. Now let's turn to a discussion of the ways that music can be health beneficial.

Music and Health

In all cultures, people rely upon some form of music to facilitate meditation, religious experience, and social activities (Merriam, 1982). Music can be used to quiet the mind and the body in preparation for meditation or worship. The music is able to quiet the mind and the body via actual effects on emotions and psychophysiology (Krumhansl, 1997). Specifically, when the music alters the physiological activity of the nervous systems, it facilitates a shift of consciousness, helping people to get in touch with the soul as an integral part of the whole self (Halpern & Savary, 1985). Music can enhance our lives at the molecular, cellular, and organismic levels, as well as the psychological and spiritual levels (Halpern & Savary, 1985).

Across numerous contexts, music is used in association with chanting, singing, drumming, and dancing (Nketia, 1974). During various ceremonies, music has been used to promote physical, emotional, and spiritual health (Simha, 1991). Participation in musical activity promotes the release of tension in the mind and body, promotes positive emotions, and also promotes interpersonal and transpersonal communication. Shamans, religious leaders, and faith healers have used music professionally and ceremonially. Music has been said to have the capacity to heal, inspire, console, and establish contact with cosmic forces (Halpern & Savary, 1985). Music, particularly when we are performing it or dancing to it, allows us to release spiritual energy and restore balance and harmony to our lives. Some believe that the most important remedy for the spirit is music (Ammann, 1998). Music, perhaps, has a strong effect because its medium, air, is of the same kind as the spirit.

In African American worship, the whole person, including the body, is utilized in praise of the Creator. Therefore, it is said that black spirituality involves the five senses, the emotions, and the limbs. A universal mode of spiritual expression for African Americans is music and dance. When one traces the roots of the culture via the study of slave songs or spirituals, there is a clear and intimate link in African American culture between music and spirituality. All forms of musical expression in black culture (gospel, blues, jazz, R&B, hip-hop, reggae) have been used as collective modes of cultural expression. These various forms of musical expression also serve vital spiritual functions. Music enhances the spiritual experience and has a powerful liberating and transforming effect in the African tradition. Clients can use music to express negative emotions, or the client can write a song of self-empowerment (Frame & Williams, 1996). This approach would be useful for clients who are recovering from substance abuse, suffering with a serious illness, or dealing with mental or physical pain (Frame & Williams, 1996).

Health professionals who decide to use music in the treatment of a client must be aware that the effectiveness of the music will depend on the piece of selected music and the individual client. Different compositions produce different effects on different people (Gregory & Varney, 1996; Halpern & Savary, 1985; Lewis & Schmidt, 1991; Sloboda, 1991; Stratton & Zalanowski, 1991; Terwogt & Grinsven, 1991). For example, Iwanaga and Moroki (1999) found that an excitative musical piece was able to arouse feelings of vigor and tension; a sedative musical piece eased tension. The study found that physiological responses were greater during excitative music than during sedative music. The same researchers also suggested that clients should select the specific musical recording from among alternatives instead of having the health professional select the music. The health professional may not select the music that will have the same meaning to the client (Iwanaga & Moroki, 1999).

Also, researchers have found that the culture of a listener may be related to his or her appreciation of the emotional connotations of a musical selection (Gregory & Varney, 1996). The periodic waves created by the vibration of music alters the environment. In the case of health and the body, the environment that is being altered by the sound of music is body tissue and the heart (Halpern & Savary, 1985; Krumhansl, 1997; Pujol & Langenfeld, 1999).

Relaxation has been described as being in harmony with oneself and with the world. Music can initiate the state of relaxation. How does this occur? When the body experiences vibrations from the outside that are nearly at the same pulse as some part of the organism (i.e., heartbeat), the body will experience **entrainment** (see "Spotlight on Biology" section). Entrainment to the rhythm of a relaxing piece of music can lower stress and foster psychological well-being. Some music fosters health automatically and effortlessly as the entire body responds to it. The breathing may slow down, the heartbeat becomes more regular, and the mind activity slows down to a state of relaxation.

The health benefit of music has been demonstrated in studies of guided imagery and music (McKinney, Antoni, Kumar, Tims, & McCabe, 1997). **Guided Imagery and Music (GIM)** is a depth approach to music psychotherapy in which specifically programmed music is used to generate a dynamic unfolding of inner experiences. A short series of GIM sessions can positively affect mood and reduce cortisol levels in healthy adults; these changes in hormonal regulation may have positive health implications for chronically stressed people (McKinney et al., 1997).

Music has shown positive patient responses such as relaxed muscles, sleep, regular deep breathing, and lowered blood pressure and pulse (Halpern & Savary, 1985). Music has also initiated pleasant memories and positive moods. These are some of the same effects as some prescription drugs. Unfortunately, medical students today still receive little or no training in the healing potential of sound and music and may be inclined to believe that this type of holistic treatment is unorthodox quackery. The use of music to facilitate healing is an alternative healing approach. Hopefully, the time will come when people will select their music with the same conscientiousness that they exhibit in selecting the foods that they eat. Patients should be informed that they could learn to follow a healthy diet of sound to facilitate optimal health.

Laughter and Health

Music is transmitted through the medium of air and is an auditory stimulus. Another auditory stimulus that has the potential to affect one's health is the sound of laughter. Laughter is an expression of the human soul that is manifest through sound vibrations in the human body. A scientific definition of **laughter** is

> A psychophysiological reflex, a successive, rhythmic, spasmodic expiration with open glottis, and vibration of the vocal cords, often accompanied by a baring of the teeth and facial grimaces. (Ornstein & Sobel, 1989)

The previous definition of laughter may not seem as though laughter would be a health-promoting experience. Laughter, however, is a complex physiological process that can relieve stress (du Pre, 1998). Regarding stress, college students were given a questionnaire that asked about the extent to which they used humor in dealing with anxiety-evoking events (Carroll & Shmidt, 1992). The students who reported using humor as a coping strategy reported fewer health problems than did those who scored low on using humor.

Health educators have also suggested that potentially embarrassing topics (i.e., responsible sexual health decision making and condom comfort) can be taught using humor (Fennell, 1993). Fennell states that programs incorporated into a curriculum that use humor can help educators deliver the kind of information about prophylactics that college students need to help them feel at ease about using condoms.

Think for a moment and try to recall the last time that you had a really good laugh. We have all heard people say, "I laughed so hard my stomach was aching." The aching feels similar to the sensation that you feel when doing exercises such as sit-ups or stomach crunches. In Chapter 5 you learned the health benefits of exercise. In the average laugh, the diaphragm, thorax, abdomen, heart, and lungs all get a brief workout (Halpern & Savary, 1985). The times when you have had a robust full body laugh, you may have experienced huffing and puffing, increased heart rate, increased blood pressure, increased oxygen consumption, and stomach and facial muscle movement. The hearty laugh is the equivalent to a total inner body workout (Hafen et al., 1996).

Additional health benefits of laughter stem from the fact that laughter boosts the immune system, increasing natural disease-fighting killer cells and lowering blood pressure (du Pre, 1998). Laughter also has been said to clear foreign matter from the respiratory system and stimulate the brain to produce **catecholamines**. Catecholamines are chemicals that function in the body's response to stress and affect many physiological and metabolic activities (e.g., heartbeat, nerve responses, muscle activity). Catecholamines may trigger the release of endorphins that can reduce pain or discomfort from health problems such as arthritis, allergies, headaches, and backaches (Hafen et al., 1996).

Although the use of laughter and humor among health professionals is still not widespread compared to more traditional approaches to treating patients, the benefit of laughter and humor is being recognized in publications of professional associations such as the American Psychological Association (McGuire, 1999). McGuire states that during sessions with patients, the physician or therapist's role is not to act as a stand-up comedian, but instead to be open to the inclusion of humor or laughter into the sessions. It is acceptable to allow for some lightheartedness during the session as long as clients do not feel belittled or that their problems are not being taken seriously.

Spotlight on Biology: Entrainment Using Music

Entrainment is a part of nature. It is a phenomenon that will result in the synchronization of movements or rhythms (i.e., heartbeat) from two distinct sources. Entrainment can occur as a result of listening to music. Listening to relaxing music can cause the onset of relaxation and relief from stress. Music causes entrainment/synchronization of our body rhythms such as the brain waves, respiratory rate, and heart rate. For stressed individuals with high levels of the stress hormone, cortisol, entrainment via music can reduce stress hormone levels. Individuals who are stressed experience increased heartbeat and respiration rate and low amplitude/high frequency brain waves. The heartbeat is the most significant target for entrainment to music because the heart rate increases in direct relationship to an increase in stress. If the stressed person can block out distractions sufficiently enough to concentrate and focus on the rhythm of the music, then entrainment can take place. The heart rate can decrease to match a slow regular rhythm of a musical recording. When a person is stress free, the parasympathetic and sympathetic nervous systems will be in harmony. Stress, however, throws the two out of harmony, resulting in a faster and inconsistent heartbeat (McCraty, Tiller, Atkinson, 1996). During entrainment, the rhythm of music contributes to the equilibrium of the sympathetic and parasympathetic nervous systems. The music causes a slowing of heart rate and brain activity in association with the listener's concentration on relaxation. Not only are the sympathetic and parasympathetic systems brought into equilibrium, but there is also a strengthening of the two-way communication between the brainstem and the heart rate. All of this results in a more consistent heart rate, which promotes a sense of calm, peace, and relaxation. The efficiency and equilibrium will be enhanced in the immune, cardiovascular, and hormonal systems resulting in reduced stress and enhanced cognitive ability (McCraty, 1996).

Sources: McCraty, 1996; McCraty, Tiller, & Atkinson, 1996.

Du Pre (1998) describes the use of humor as an invitation to greater social intimacy between the health professional and the patient. The humor can be used to buffer emotions such as anxiety, anger, fear, and embarrassment. When medical institutions are stiff and formal, humor can help caregivers dispel the stiffness and formality.

It is important, though, for health professionals to recognize that humor will not be appropriate at all times. When used in a sensitive and otherwise appropriate manner, humor and laughter can benefit the client and the health professional (du Pre, 1998).

Finally, Chinese culture states that laughter is especially healthy if one can learn to laugh from the center of one's being. The Chinese refer to such a laugh as the "**hara laugh**" (Halpern & Savary, 1985). Laughter, like music, is related to the leading topic of this chapter, spirituality, because laughter has been described as healthy spirit. It can bring balance and harmony to the body, mind, and spirit.

Conclusion

There are still many persons in the health field who would frown upon the content of this chapter. They would perhaps deem the content to be outside of the mainstream traditional interests of health professionals. While some aspects of these issues may be difficult to test scientifically, all health professionals who advocate a more holistic (bio-psycho-social-spiritual) approach to understanding and treating health problems should consider these issues to be relevant. This is especially true for professionals who work with a diverse group of clients in age, ethnicity, race, sexual orientation, and socioeconomic class. It is relatively easy for clients to integrate spirituality, music, and laughter into their lives as health behaviors, since all three can be integrated into the clients' lifestyle with little effort and possibly no additional cost. Attitudes about the health benefits of spirituality, music, and laughter have changed over the years, such that now we can at least find published research studies on each. For the future, more research and public information needs to be disseminated on these issues so that people can become more familiar with the practice of spirituality, music, and laughter as preventive health behaviors.

Summary

Transcendence refers to the feelings of attachment to a Higher Presence. In order to understand and treat a client's health holistically, the health professional should adopt a biopsychosocial-spiritual approach. Spirituality refers to the human propensity to find meaning in life through self-transcendence. It is evident in a sense of relatedness to something greater than the self. There are three faith-related coping styles—known as self-directing, deferring, and collaborative—that may be relevant to health actions. The inclusion of a spiritual dimension has been successful in programs such as Alcoholics Anonymous. As professional journals increasingly recognize the significance of the spiritual dimension, we have learned that spiritual beliefs can widely influence health decisions. For example, religious and spiritual practices may advocate abstinence from alcohol or sexual behavior. The construal of individuals with a deep sense of spirituality causes them to see life differently, and aspects of spiritual living such as prayer and forgiveness may actually have physiological effects that enhance health. In consideration of multiculturalism, the health professional should become familiar with both Eastern and Western spiritual practices and beliefs. This includes beliefs in an Impersonal Divine such as in the practice of Buddhism, or the Personal Divine as in the practice of Christianity. Practices such as the weigh down diet are based on the belief in the Personal Divine to assist with weight loss and food addiction. Practices such as *Santeria* and shamanism may also be significant in the treatment of traditional Latinos and traditional Native Americans. Women's health and the health of gays and lesbians may also involve special consideration of issues of spirituality.

Related to the topic of spirituality is the topic of music. Music generally accompanies many spiritual and religious practices. In health discussions, music is relevant because it can have health-enhancing effects at the molecular, cellular, organismic, psychological, and spiritual levels. Finally, laughter may also have health-beneficial characteristics. It has been referred to as a good form of physical exercise—especially a hearty laugh, because it produces a total inner body workout. Laughter also boosts the immune system by increasing natural disease-fighting killer cells and lowering blood pressure.

Student Interview

Age: 23
Gender: Female
Country of Origin: Philippine Islands
Years in the United States: 17

1. **What religions, if any, do you practice?**
   Roman Catholicism, that's what we say in the Philippines.
2. **Do you believe that during serious illness, patients really benefit from prayer?**
   Yes, definitely, you can receive strength from God through prayer. If you let God know, or ask God to keep you happy, then He will, if you are serious about asking in your heart.
3. **How was religion/spirituality introduced to you?**
   We took the classes and my first communion in second grade. It was a practice in my family, although now my family is not the reason that I go to church. This is something that I do independently.
4. **Why do you think it might be that religious/spiritual people may sometimes be healthier than nonreligious people?**
   They are not angry people, they seem to all have similar personalities. Religious people have a belonging feeling and say "peace be with you." They are all calm people. The atmosphere is soothing and relaxing around them. The prayers are helpful, and the people are very patient people.

continued

Student Interview   Continued

5. **Are there any aspects of your religious belief that you feel contribute to your leading a healthier lifestyle?**

   I never did smoke, but I did drink; I've stopped. I am now a vegetarian. The thought of red bloody meat is now disgusting and gory to me. I read things in the Bible about the sacrifices and it is gory to me. I also get more rest and sleep to be up early for mass. I eat no red meat in observance of Lent. I only eat fish.

6. **Describe some general religious practices of people in your native country.**

   We "walk the dead." This refers to walking the coffin around the town to give the people a chance to see and pay last respects. Also in the Philippines there is usually prayer every morning and meditation. The prayers usually last longer than prayers here, and they are really into the Virgin Mary. There is definitely less teen sex and teen pregnancy than here. In the Philippines, everyone practices Roman Catholicism.

7. **Do you surround yourself with others for whom religion and spiritually are important?**

   Yes, because people who are not spiritual don't understand the "hooplah" about church. My new boyfriend shares the same values and beliefs as I do. We read the Bible together. I try to stay away from those who don't understand because they ridicule me.

8. **If you were to become ill, do you belong to any church or other organization that would support you?**

   Yes. They would support me if I became ill. We have a moment of silence for those who are ill or who have died. They have a rosary in the Philippines for those who died. They would visit me at the hospital.

9. **Do you follow religious or spiritual principles that advocate helping others?**

   Yes, we had a class on charity work. We learn how to help others and learn to come away from ourselves to help other people.

10. **Describe how you feel immediately after attending prayer meetings or worship services.**

    I feel very relaxed, all my burdens and sins committed have been forgiven. I feel the soothing just to sit in a church, very light. Church is my stress management technique.

Key Concepts

catecholamines
collaborative
construal
Curandero
Dana
deferring
entrainment
Guided Imagery and Music (GIM)
hara laugh
impersonal divine
laughter
optimal health

relaxation
Santeria
self-directing
shaman
spirituality
weigh down diet

Study Questions

1. What are the three faith-related coping styles that an individual may use in dealing with an illness? Which one is not necessarily health affirming?
2. Prayer and forgiveness may have actual physiological effects. What are these effects?
3. What is meant by the statement that spiritual individuals are happier because of their construals?
4. Explain in detail the idea of the weigh down diet.
5. What is the role of the shaman in the treatment of illness?
6. What are the aims of women's spirituality?
7. How could the spiritual beliefs of some gays and lesbians act as a barrier to treating them?
8. How does music physiologically promote relaxation?
9. How might an activity such as dancing be health enhancing?
10. What are some possible explanations for why you may feel especially good following a robust laugh?

Student Activity

Locate and listen to a CD that has been recorded with music and natural sounds to produce relaxation or entrainment (try "Natural Stress Relief by Solitudes: Music for Your Health"). These CDs can typically be found in stores that sell stress-relief products such as scented candles, fountains, and music. Follow the directions for listening and then write a short paper about your experience of entrainment.

OR

Interview a pastor (or other religious leader) and physician. Talk to them about what you have read about the weigh down diet and record any differences in their opinions on it.

REFERENCES

Adams, T., Bezner, J., Drabbs, M., Zabarano, R., & Steinhardt, M. (2000). Conceptualization and measurement of the spiritual and psychological dimensions of wellness in a college population. *Journal of American College Health, 48,* 165–173.

Ahluwalia, I., Dodds, J., & Baligh, M. (1998). Social support and coping behaviors of low income families experiencing food insufficiency in North Carolina. *Health Education and Behavior, 25,* 599–611.

Ajzen, I. (1985). From intentions to actions: A theory of planned behavior. In J. Kuhland & J. Beckman (Eds.), *Action control: From cognitions to behavior* (pp. 11–39). Heidelberg, Germany: Springer.

Akan, G., & Grilo, C. (1995). Sociocultural influences on eating attitudes and behaviors, body image, and psychological functioning: A comparison of African American, Asian American, and Caucasian college women. *International Journal of Eating Disorders, 18,* 181–187.

Alaniz, M., Treno, A., & Saltz, R. (1999). Gender, acculturation, and alcohol consumption among Mexican Americans. *Substance Use & Misuse, 34,* 1407–1426.

Alston, M., & Anderson, S. (1995). Suicidal behavior in African American women. In S. Canetto & D. Lester (Eds.), *Women and suicidal behavior* (pp. 133–143). New York: Springer.

American Institute for Cancer Research. (1999). *Food, nutrition and the prevention of cancer: A global perspective* (1–7). American Institute for Cancer Research. Retrieved July 6, 1999 from the World Wide Web: http://www.aicr.org/report2.htm

American Lung Association. (1998). *American Lung Association fact sheet: Smoking* (1–3). American Lung Association. Retrieved August 8, 1999 from the World Wide Web: http://www.lungusa.org/tobacco/smoking_factsheet.html

American Nurses Association (1996). *Rural/frontier nursing: The challenge to grow.* Washington DC: American Nurses Publishing.

Ammann, P. (1998). Music and melancholy: Marsilio Ficino's archetypal music therapy. *Journal of Analytical Psychology, 43,* 571–588.

Anderson, N., McNeilly, M., & Myers, H. (1993). A biopsychosocial model of race differences in vascular reactivity. In J. Blascovich & E. Katkin (Eds.), *Cardiovascular reactivity to stress and disease* (pp. 83–108). Washington DC: American Psychological Association.

Bandura, A. (1978). The self-system in reciprocal determinism. *American Psychologist, 33,* 344–358.

Barak, Y., Achiron, A., Kimh, R., Lampl, Y., Gilad, R., Elizur, A., & Sarova-Pinhas, I. (1996). Health risks among shift workers: A survey of female nurses. *Health Care for Women International, 17,* 527–533.

Barbarin, O. (1999). Do parental coping, involvement, religiosity, and racial identity mediate children's psychological adjustment to sickle cell disease? *Journal of Black Psychology, 25,* 391–426.

Barber, J., Axinn, W., & Thornton, A. (1999). Unwanted childbearing, health, and mother-child relationships. *Journal of Health and Social Behavior, 40,* 231–257.

Barret, R., & Barzan, R. (1996). Spiritual experiences of gay men and lesbians. *Counseling and Values, 41,* 4–15.

Barringer, H., Gardner, R., & Levin, M. (1993). Employment and occupations. In *Asians and Pacific Islanders in the United States* (pp. 193–230). New York: Russell Sage Foundation.

Barrios, L., Everett, S., Simon, T., & Brener, N. (2000). Suicide ideation among U.S. college students (associations with other injury risk behaviors). *Journal of American College Health, 48,* 229–233.

Baum, A., Gatchel, R. J., & Krantz, D. S. (1997). In *An introduction to health psychology* (3rd ed.). New York: McGraw Hill.

Beatty, L. (1997). Introduction: Drug abuse among rural ethnic and migrant populations. In E. B. Robertson, Ph.D, Z. Sloboda, Sc.D., G. M. Boyd, Ph.D., L. Beatty, Ph.D., & N. J. Kozel (Eds.), *NIDA Research Monograph: Vol. 168. Rural Substance Abuse: State of Knowledge and Issues* (pp. 438–441). Rockville MD: U.S. Department of Health and Human Services, National Institutes of Health.

Becker, A., Grinspoon, S., Klibanski, A., & Herzog, D. (1999). Eating disorders. *The New England Journal of Medicine, 340,* 1092–1097.

Bhagat, R., O'Driscoll, M., Babakus, E, Frey, L., Chokkar, J., Ninokumar, B., Pate, L., Ryder, P., Fernandez, M., Ford, D., Mahanyele, M. (1995). Organizational stress and coping in seven national contexts: A cross-cultural investigation. In S. Sauter & L. Murphy (Eds.) *Organizational risk factors for job stress (93–105)*. Washington DC: American Psychological Association

Bliss, R., Garvey, A., & Ward, K. (1999). Resisting temptations to smoke: Results from within-subjects analyses. *Psychology of Addictive Behaviors, 13*, 143–151.

Bolin, L., Antonuccio, D., Follette, W., & Krumpe, P. (1999). Transdermal nicotine: The long and the short of it. *Psychology of Addictive Behaviors, 13*, 152–156.

Boney-McCoy, S., Gibbons, F., & Gerrard, M. (1999). Self-esteem, compensatory self-enhancement, and the consideration of health risk. *Society for Personality and Social Psychology, 25*, 954–965.

Bottorff, J. L., Johnson, J. L., Bhagat, R., Sukhdev, G., Balneaves, L., Clarke, H., & Hilton, B. (1998). Beliefs related to breast health practices the perceptions of South Asian women living in Canada. *Social Science & Medicine, 47*, 2075–2085.

Bragg, M. (1997). An empowerment approach to community health education. In B. W. Spradley & J. A. Allender (Eds.), *Readings in community health nursing* (5th ed. pp. 504–510). Philadelphia: J.B. Lippincott.

Brannon, L., & Feist, J. (2000). *Health psychology: An introduction to behavior and health*, (4th ed.). Belmont CA: Wadsworth Thomson Learning.

Brook, J., Balka, E., Brook, D., Win, P., & Gursen, M. (1998). Drug use among African Americans: Ethnic identity as a protective factor. *Psychological Reports, 83*, 1427–1446.

Brooks, A., Stuewig, J., & LeCroy, C. (1998). A family based model of Hispanic adolescent substance use. *Journal of Drug Education, 28*(1), 65–86.

Brown, D. (2000, April 11). Dieting faithfully. *Washington Post:* Health Section, pp. 14–16.

Brunswick, A. (1999). Structural strain: an ecological paradigm for studying African American drug use. *Drugs and Society, 14*, 5–19.

Brunswick, A., & Messeri, P. (1999). Life stage, substance use and health decline in a community cohort of urban African Americans. *Journal of Addictive Disease, 18*, 53–71.

Bungam, T., Pate, R., Dowda, M., & Vincent, M. (1999). Correlates of physical activity among African American and caucasian female adolescents. *American Journal of Health Behavior, 23*, 25–31.

Caetano, R., & Clark, C. (1998). Trends in alcohol consumption patterns among white, blacks, and Hispanics: 1984 and 1995. *Journal of Studies on Alcohol, 59*, 659–668.

Canetto, S., & Lester, D. (1995). Gender and the primary prevention of suicide mortality. *Suicide and Life Threatening Behavior, 25*, 58–69.

Canino, G., & Guarnaccia, P. (1997). Methodological challenges in the assessment of Hispanic children and adolescents. *Applied Development Science, 1*, 124–134.

Carlisle, D., Leake, B., & Shapiro, M. (1997). Racial and ethnic disparities in the use of cardiovascular procedures: Associations with type of health insurance. *American Journal of Public Health, 87*, 263–267.

Carroll, D., Smith, G. D., & Bennett, P. (1996). Some observations on health and socioeconomic status. *Journal of Health Psychology, 1*, 23–39.

Carroll, D., Smith, G., Sheffield, D., Shipley, M., & Marmot, M. (1997). The relationship between socioeconomic status, hostility, and blood pressure reactions to mental stress in men: Data from the Whitehall II study. *Health Psychology, 16*, 131–136.

Carroll, J. L., & Shmidt, J. L., Jr. (1992). Correlation between humorous coping style and health. *Psychological Reports, 70*, 402.

Carter, C. S., & Altemus, M. (1999). Integrative functions of lactational hormones in social behavior and stress management. In C. S. Carter, I. I. Lederhendler, & B. Kirkpatrick (Ed.), *The integrative neurobiology of affiliation* (pp. 246–260). Cambridge: The MIT Press.

Castro, F., Coe, K., Gutierres, S., & Saenz, D. (1996). Designing health promotion programs for Latinos. In P. M. Kato & T. Mann (Eds.), *Handbook of diversity issues in health psychology* (pp. 319–346). New York: Plenum Press.

Castro, F., & Tafoya-Barraza, H. (1997). Treatment issues with Latinos addicted to cocaine and heroin. In M.C. Zea (Ed.), *Psychological interventions with Latino populations* (pp. 191–213). Boston: Allyn & Bacon.

Centers for Disease Control (1996). *National and international HIV seroprevalence surveys—Summary of results*. Washington DC: Author

Chait, A., & Bierman, E. (1982). Diet and diabetes. In J. Rose (Ed.), *Nutrition and killer diseases, The effects of dietary factors in fatal chronic disease* (pp. 117–125). Noyes Publications.

Chapman, R. (1996). Spirituality in the treatment of alcoholism: A worldview approach. *Counseling and Values, 41,* 39–49.

Chissell, J. (1993). *Pyramids of power (an ancient African-centered approach to optimal health)*. Baltimore: Positive Perceptions Publications.

Christen, J., & Christen, A. (1990). *Defining and addressing addictions: A psychological and sociocultural perspective* (pp. 102–133). Indianapolis: Professional Teaching Monograph, Department of Preventive and Community Dentistry, Indiana University School of Dentistry.

Chun, C., Enomoto, K., & Sue, S. (1996). Health care issues among Asian Americans: Implications of somatization. In P. M. Kato & T. Mann (Eds.), *Handbook of diversity issues in health psychology* (pp. 347–365). New York: Plenum Press.

Clark, M., Hogan, J., Kviz, F., & Prohaska, T. (1999). Age and the role of symptomatology in readiness to quit smoking. *Addictive Behaviors, 24,* 1–16.

Cody, P., & Welch, P. (1997). Rural gay men in New England: Life experiences and coping styles. *Journal of Homosexuality, 33,* 51–67.

Coleburn, B. (2000, April 6). Lunenburgers oppose asbestos landfill expansion. *Courier Record,* 111(14), p. 7.

Contrada, R., Czarnecki, E., & Li Chern Pan, R. (1997). Health damaging personality traits and verbal autonomic dissociation: The role of self control and environmental control. *Health Psychology, 16,* 451–457.

Cooper, C., & Cartwright, S. (1994). Healthy mind; healthy organization—A proactive approach to occupational stress. *Human Relations, 47,* 455–471.

Corwin, S., Sargent, R., Rheaume, C., & Saunders, R. (1999). Dietary behaviors among fourth graders: A social cognitive theory study approach. *American Journal of Health Behavior, 23,* 182–197.

Curtis, A., James, S., Raghunathan, T., & Akser, K. (1997). Job strain and blood pressure in African Americans: The Pitt County study. *American Journal of Public Health, 87,* 263–267.

Dacosta, K., & Wilson, J. (1996). Food preferences and eating attitudes in three generations of black and white women. *Appetite, 27,* 183–191.

Danielson, C., Hamel-Bissell, B., & Winstead-Fry, P. (1993). *Families, health, & illness: Perspectives on coping and intervention* (pp. 3–17). St. Louis: Mosby Year Book.

D'Augelli, A. & Hart, M. (1987). Gay women, men, and families in rural settings: Toward the development of helping communities. *American Journal of Community Psychology, 15,* 79–93.

Davis, M. (1999). Oral contraceptive use and hemodynamic, lipid, and fibrinogen responses to smoking and stress in women. *Health Psychology, 18,* 122–130.

Davis, N., Clance, P., & Gailis, A. (1999). Treatment approaches for obese and overweight African American women: A consideration of cultural dimensions. *Psychotherapy, 36,* 27–35.

Davison, D. (1999, June). Black women's health: It takes a healthy village to raise a full woman. In *Black women in the academy II: Service and leadership.* Mental health and black women, Omni Shoreham Hotel, Washington, DC.

DeNeve, K. (1999). Happy as an extroverted clam? The role of personality for subjective well being. *Current Directions in Psychological Science, 8,* 141–144.

Diller, J. (1999). *Cultural diversity: a primer for the human services.* New York: Brooks/Cole-Wadsworth.

Dittus, K., Hiller, V., & Beerman, K. (1995). Benefits and barriers to fruit and vegetable intake: Relationship between attitudes and consumption. *Journal of Nutrition Education, 27,* 120–125.

Doljanac, R., & Zimmerman, M. (1998). Psychosocial factors and high risk sexual behavior: Race differences among urban adolescents. *Journal of Behavioral Medicine, 21,* 451–467.

Dressler, W. W., Bindon, J. R., & Neggers, Y. H. (1998). Culture, socioeconomic status, and coronary heart disease risk factors in an African American community. *Journal of Behavioral Medicine, 21,* 527–544.

Dugan, S., Lloyd, B., & Lucas, K. (1999). Stress and coping as determinants of adolescentsmoking behavior. *Journal of Applied Social Psychology, 29,* 870–888.

Duncan, C., Jones, K., & Moon, G. (1999). Smoking and deprivation: Are there neighborhood effects? *Social Science and Medicine, 48,* 497–505.

du Pre, A. (1998). *Humor and the healing arts: A multimethod analysis of humor use in health care.* Mahwah, NJ: Lawrence Erlbaum Associates.

Ellickson, P., Collins, R., & Bell, R. (1999). Adolescent use of illicit drugs other than marijuana: How important is social bonding and for which ethnic groups? *Substance Use & Misuse, 34,* 317–346.

Estrada, A. (1998). Drug use and HIV risks among African American, Mexican American, And Puerto Rican drug injectors. *Journal of Psychoactive Drugs, 30*(3), 247–253.

Farrales, L., & Chapman, G. (1999). Filipino women living in Canada: Constructing meanings of body, food, and health. *Health Care for Women International, 20,* 179–194.

Felix-Ortiz, M., Fernandez, A., & Newcomb, M. (1998). The role of intergenerational discrepancy of cultural orientation in drug use among Latina adolescents. *Substance Use & Misuse, 33,* 967–994.

Fennell, R. (1993). Using humor to teach responsible sexual health decision making and condom comfort. *Journal of American College Health, 42,* 37–39.

Flack, J., Amaro, H., Jenkins, W., Kanitz, S., Levy, J., Mixon, M., & Yu, E. (1995). Epidemiology of minority health. *Health Psychology, 14,* 592–600.

Ford, T. (1999, June). Eating disorders in African-American women. In *Black women in the academy II: Service and leadership.* Mental health and black women, Omni Shoreham Hotel, Washington, DC.

Frame, M., & Williams, C. (1996). Counseling African Americans: Integrating spirituality in therapy. *Counseling and Values, 41,* 16–28.

French, L. A. (2000). *Addictions and Native Americans.* Westport, Connecticut: Praeger.

French, S., Hennikus, D., & Jeffery, R. (1996). Smoking status, dietary intake, and physical activity in a sample of working adults. *Health Psychology, 15,* 448–454.

Friedman, H. (1991). *The self-healing personality.* New York: Henry Holt and Company.

Fuchs, C., Giovannucci, E., Colditz, G., Hunter, D., Stampfer, M., Rosner, B., Speizer, F., & Willett, W. (1999). Dietary fiber and the risk of colorectal cancer and adenoma in women. *The New England Journal of Medicine, 340,* 169–176.

Fudge, R. (1996). The use of behavior therapy in the development of ethnic consciousness: A treatment model. *Cognitive and Behavioral Practice, 3,* 317–335.

Fujii, J., Fukushima, F., & Yamamoto, J. (1993). Psychiatric care of Japanese Americans. In A. C. Gaw (Ed.), *Culture, Ethnicity, and Mental Illness* (pp. 318–319). Washington DC: American Psychiatric Press.

Fukuyama, M., & Sevig, T. (1999). *Integrating spirituality into multicultural counseling* (pp. 23–44). Thousand Oaks: Sage Publications.

Funder, D. (1997). *The personality puzzle.* New York: W.W. Norton & Company.

Furst, T., Connors, M., Bisogni, C., Sobal, J., & Falk, L. (1996). Food choice: A conceptual model of the process. *Appetite, 26,* 247–266.

Gamache, D. (1995). *Why karate tae kwon do?* Robert J. Tibbo's Tae Kwon Do Institute Inc. Retrieved July 13, 2000 from the World Wide Web: http://www.tiac.net/users/gamache/tkd/faq.html.

Gaw, A. (1993). Psychiatric care of Chinese Americans. In A. Gaw (Ed.), *Culture, ethnicity, and mental illness* (pp. 264–265). Washington DC: American Psychiatric Press.

Gelernter, J., Kranzler, H., & Satel, S. (1999). No association between D2 dopamine receptor (DRD2) alleles or haplotypes and cocain dependence or severity of cocain dependence in European and African Americans. *Journal of Family Psychology, 45,* 340–345.

Giachello, A. (1995). Cultural diversity and institutional inequality. In D. L. Adams (Ed.), *Health Issues for Women of Color* (pp. 5–26). Thousand Oaks California: Sage Publications.

Gil, E. F., & Bob, S. (1999). Culturally competent research: An ethical perspective. *Clinical Psychology Review, 19,* 45–55.

Gilbert, D., Crauthers, D., Mooney, D., McClernon, F., & Jensen, R. (1999). Effects of monetary contingencies on smoking relapse: Influences of trait depression, personality, and habitual nicotine intake. *Experimental and Clinical Psychopharmacology, 7,* 174–181.

Glanz, K., Patterson, R. E., Kristal, A. R., DiClemente, C. C., Heimendinger, J., Linnan, L., & McLerran, D. F. (1994). Stages of changes in adopting healthy diets: Fat, fiber, and correlates of nutrients intake. *Health Education Quarterly, 21,* 499–519.

Gonzales, M. (1999, November). Black and blue. *Code Magazine,* 77–81.

Green, L., & Cargo, M. (1994). The changing context of health promotion in the workplace. In M. P. O'Donnell & J. S. Harris (Eds.), *Health promotion in the workplace* (2nd ed.; pp. 497–524). Toronto, Canada: Delmar.

Gregory, A., & Varney, N. (1996). Cross-cultural comparison in the affective response to music. *Psychology of Music, 24,* 47–52.

Griesler, P., & Kandel, D. (1998). Ethnic differences in correlates of adolescent smoking. *Journal of Adolescent Health, 23,* 167–180.

Griffith, E., & Baker, F. (1993). Psychiatric care of African-Americans. In A. C. Gaw (Ed.), *Culture, ethnicity, and mental illness.* Washington DC: American Psychiatric Press.

Grossman, G. (1996). Psychotherapy with HIV infected gay men. In P. M. Kato & T. Mann (Eds.), *Handbook of diversity issues in health psychology* (pp. 237–260). New York: Plenum Press.

Gutierres, S., Saenz, D., & Green, B. (1995). Job stress and health outcomes among white and Hispanic employees: A test of the person-environment fit model. In S. Sauter & L. Murphy (Eds.), *Organizational risk factors for job stress* (107–125). Washington DC: American Psychological Association.

Gutmann, M. C. (1999). Ethnicity, alcohol, and acculturation. *Social Science & Medicine, 48,* 173–184.

Hafen, B., & Frandsen, K. (1987). *People need people: The importance of relationships to health and wellness.* Evergreen, CO: Cordillera Press.

Hafen, B., Karren, K., Frandsen, K., & Smith, N. (1996). *Mind/body health: The effects of attitudes, emotions, and relationships.* Boston: Allyn & Bacon.

Halmi, K. A. (1995). Hunger and satiety in clinical disorders. In K. D. Brownell & C. G. Fairburn (Eds.), *Eating disorders and obesity* (pp. 247–250). New York: The Guilford Press.

Halpern, S. & Savary, L. (1985). *Sound health: The music and sounds that make us whole.* San Francisco: Harper & Row Publishers.

Harburg, E., Erfurt, J., Hauenstein, L., Chape, C., Schull, W., & Schork, M. (1973). Socioecological stress, suppressed hostility, skin color, and black white male blood pressure. *Psychosomatic Medicine, 35,* 276–296.

Harnack, L., Sherwood, N., & Story, M. (1999). Diet and physical activity patterns of urban American Indian women. *American Journal of Health Promotion, 13,* 233–236.

Hart, K. (1999). Cynical hostility and deficiencies in functional support: The moderating role of gender in psychosocial vulnerability to disease. *Personality and Individual Differences, 27,* 69–83.

Herek, G., Gillis, J., Glunt, E., Lewis, J., Welton, D., & Capitano, J. (1998). Culturally sensitive AIDS educational videos for African American audiences: Effects of source, message, receiver, and context. *American Journal of Community Psychology, 26,* 705–743.

Herrera, R. (1996). Crisis intervention: An essential component of culturally competent clincial case management. In P. Manoleas (Ed.), *The cross cultural practice of clinical case management in mental health* (pp. 99–118). New York: The Haworth Press.

Hill, J. (2000). A rationale for the integration of spirituality into community psychology. *Journal of Community Pscyhology, 28,* 139–149.

Hirsch, J. (1997). The coming of genetics in the control of ingestion. *Appetite, 29,* 115–117.

Houtsmuller, E., & Stitzer, M. (1999). Manipulation of cigarette craving through rapid smoking: Efficacy and effects on smoking behavior. *Psychopharmacology, 142,* 149–157.

Hovey, J., & King, C. (1997). Suicidality among acculturating Mexican Americans: Current knowledge and directions for research. *Suicide and Life Threatening Behavior, 27,* 92–102.

Huffman, K., Vernoy, M., & Vernoy, J. (1999). *Psychology in action.* New York: John Wiley & Sons.

Humphries, D., & Krummel, D. (1999). Perceived susceptibility to cardiovascular disease and dietary intake in women. *American Journal of Health Behavior, 23,* 250–260.

Hyman, D., & Ho, K. (1998). Dietary intervention for cholesterol reduction in public clinic patients. *American Journal of Preventive Medicine, 15,* 139–145.

Ibrahim, F. (1995). Suicidal behavior in asian american women. In S. Canetto & D. Lester *Women and suicidal behavior* (pp. 144–156). New York: Springer Publishing Co.

Ingledew, D., & Brunning, S. (1999). Personality, preventive health behavior and comparative optimism about health problems. *Journal of Health Psychology, 4,* 193–208.

Iwanaga, M., & Moroki, Y. (1999). Subjective and physiological responses to music stimuli controlled over activity and preference. *Journal of Music Therapy, 36,* 26–28.

Jackson, J., & Sellers, S. (1996). African American health over the life course: A multidimensioal framework. In P. M. Kato & T. Mann (Eds.), *Handbook of Diversity Issues in Health Psychology* (pp. 301–318). New York: Plenum Press.

Jaffee, L. (1990). Tobacco smoking and nicotine dependence. S. Wonnacott, M. A. Russell, & L. P. Stolerman (Eds.), *Nicotine Psychopharmacology (Molecular, Cellular, and Behavioral Aspects)*, pp. 1–33. New York: Oxford University Press.

Jaffee, L., Lutter, J., Rex, J., Hawkes, C., & Bucaccio, P. (1999). Incentives and barriers to physical activity for working women. *American Journal of Health Promotion, 13*, 215–218.

James, B., & Samuels, C. (1999). High stress life events and spirituality development. *Journal of Psychology and Theology, 27*, 250–260.

James, K. (1994). Social identity, work stress, and minority workers' health. In G. P. Keita & J. J. Hurrell, Jr. (Eds.), *Job stress in a changing workforce (investigating gender, diversity, and family issues)* (pp. 127–145). Washington DC: American Psychological Association.

James, K. (1997). Worker social identity and health related costs for organizations: A comparative study between ethnic groups. *Journal of Occupational Health Psychology, 2*, 108–117.

Janson, H. (1999). Longitudinal patterns of tobacco smoking from childhood to middle age. *Addictive Behaviors, 24*, 239–249.

Jeffery, R., Forster, J., French, S., Kelder, S., Lando, H., McGovern, P., Jacobs, D., & Baxter, J. (1993). The healthy worker project: A work-site intervention for weight control and smoking cessation. *American Journal of Public Health, 83*, 395–401.

Jeffery, R., Wing, R., Thorson, C., & Burton, L. (1998). Use of personal trainers and financial incentives to increase exercise in a behavioral weight loss program. *Journal of Consulting and Clinical Psychology, 66*, 777–783.

Johnson, P., & Johnson, H. (1999). Cultural and familial influences that maintain the negative meaning of alcohol. *Journal of Studies on Alcohol, 13*, 79–83.

Jorgensen, R., Frankowski, J., & Carey, M. (1999). Sense of coherence, negative life events and appraisal of physical health among university students. *Personality and Individual Differences, 27*, 1079–1089.

Juon, H., & Ensminger, M. (1997). Childhood, adolescent, and young adult predictors of suicidal behaviors: A prospective study of African Americans. *Journal of Child Psychology and Psychiatry, 38*, 553–563.

Kaplan, M., & Geling, O. (1998). Firearm suicides and homicides in the United States: Regional variations and patterns of gun ownership. *Social Science Medicine, 46*, 1227–1233.

Karasak, R., & Theorell, T. (1990). *Healthy work: Stress, productivity, and the reconstruction of working life.* New York: Basic Books.

Kassel, J., & Shiffman, S. (1997). Attentional mediation of cigarette smoking's effect on anxiety. *Health Psychology, 16*, 359–368.

Kato, P. M., & Mann, T. (Eds.). (1996). *Handbook of diversity issues in health psychology.* New York: Plenum Press.

Keesey, R. E. (1995). A set point model of body weight regulation. In K. D. Brownell & C. G. Fairburn (Eds.), *Eating disorders and obesity* (pp. 46–50). New York: The Guilford Press.

Kelley, G., Lowing, L., & Kelley, K. (1998). Psychological readiness of black college students to be physically active. *Journal of American College Health, 47*, 83–87.

Khan, Y., & Montgomery, A. (1996). Eating attitudes in young females with diabetes: Insulin omission identifies a vulnerable subgroup. *British Journal of Medical Psychology, 69*, 343–353.

Kilbey, M. (1999, August). Feminist perspectives on smoking and nicotine dependence. In *Annual Meeting of the American Psychological Association. Symposium: Public Interest Miniconvention-Healthy Women 2000 and Beyond*, Boston.

Kim, L. (1993). Psychiatric care of Korean Americans. In A. C. Gaw (Ed.), *Culture, ethnicity, and mental illness* (p. 357). Washington DC: American Psychiatric Press.

Kim, L., & Chun, C. (1993). Ethnic differences in psychiatric diagnosis among Asian American adolescents. *Journal of Nervous Mental Disorders, 181*, 612–617.

Kimerling, R., Armistead, L., & Forehand, R. (1999). Victimization experiences and HIV infection in women: Associations with serostatus, psychological symptoms, and health status. *Journal of Traumatic Stress, 12*, 41–58.

King, A. C., Castro, C., Wilcox, S., Eyler, A. A., Sallis, J. F., & Brownson, R. C. (2000). Personal and environmental factors associated with physical inactivity among different racial ethnic groups of U.S. middle aged and older aged women. *Health Psychology, 19*(4), 354–364.

Kinsey, K. (1999a). The influence of family dynamics. In V. D. Ferguson (Ed.), *Case studies in cultural diversity: A workbook.* Boston: Jones and Bartlett Publishers.

Kinsey, K. (1999b). An intergenerational family. In V. D. Ferguson (Ed.), *Case studies in cultural diversity: A workbook.* Boston: Jones and Bartlett Publishers.

Kiple, K., & Himmersteib, V. (1982). *Another dimension to the black diaspora: Diet, disease, and racism.* New York: Cambridge University Press.

Kirkcaldy, B., Cooper, C., & Furnham, A. (1998). The relationship between type A, internality/externality, emotional distress and perceived health. *Personality and Individual Differences, 26*, 223–235.

Kivimaki, M., & Kalimo, R. (1996). Self-esteem and the occupational stress process: Testing two alternative models in a sample of blue collar workers. *Journal of Occupational Health Psychology, 1*, 187–196.

Klein, H., Eber, M., Crosby, H., Welka, D., & Hoffman, J. (1999). The acceptability of the female condom among substance using women in Washington DC. *Women & Health, 29*(3), 97–114.

Klonoff, E., & Landrine, H. (1999). Acculturation and cigarette smoking among African Americans: Replications and implications for prevention and cessation programs. *Journal of Behavioral Medicine, 22*, 195–203.

Ko, C., & Cohen, M. (1998). Intraethnic comparison of eating attitudes in native Koreans and Korean Americans using a Korean translation of the eating attitudes test. *The Journal of Nervous and Mental Disease, 186*, 631–636.

Kobasa, S. (1979). Stressful life events, personality, and health: An inquiry into hardiness. *Journal of Personality and Social Psychology, 37*, 1–11.

Koss-Chioino, J., & Vargas, L. (1999). *Working with Latino youth (culture, development, and context)* (pp. 43–72). San Francisco California: Jossey Bass Publishers.

Kotchick, B., Dorsey, S., Miller, K., & Forehand, R. (1999). Adolescent sexual risk taking behavior in single parent ethnic minority families. *Journal of Family Psychology, 13*, 93–102.

Koval, J., & Pederson, L. (1999). Stress coping and other psychosocial risk factors: A model for smoking in grade 6 students. *Addictive Behaviors, 24*, 207–218.

Krause, N., Ingersoll-Dayton, B., & Liang, J. (1999). Religion, social support, and health among the Japanese elderly. *Journal of Health and Social Behavior, 40*, 405–421.

Kristjanson, L., & Chalmers, K. (1991). Preventive work with families: Issues facing public health nurses. *Journal of Advanced Nursing, 16*, 147–153.

Krogh, D. (1991). *Smoking: The artificial passion.* New York: W.H. Freeman and Company.

Krumhansl, C. (1997). An exploratory study of musical emotions and psychophysiology. *Canadian Journal of Experimental Psychology, 51*, 336–352.

Kumanyika, S. K. (1995). Obesity in minority populations. In K. D. Brownell & C. G. Fairburn (Eds.), *Eating disorders and obesity* (pp. 431–437). New York: The Guilford Press.

Lafferty, C., Heaney, C., & Chen, M. (1999). Assessing decisional balance for smoking cessation among Southeast Asian males in the U.S. *Health Education Research, 14*, 139–146.

Laforge, R., Greene, G., & Prochaska, J. (1994). Psychosocial factors influencing low fruit and vegetable consumption. *Journal of Behavioral Medicine, 17*, 361–372.

Lamb, L. (1989). Your vital adrenal steroids (corticosteroids). *The Health Letter, 34*, 1–8.

Landrine, H., & Klonoff, E. (1994). The African American acculturation scale: Development, reliability, and validity. *Journal of Black Psychology, 20*, 104–127.

Lauver, D. (2000). Commonalities in women's spirituality and women's health. *Advances in Nursing Sciences, 22*, 76–88.

Laverie, D. (1998). Motivations for ongoing participation in a fitness activity. *Leisure Sciences, 20*, 277–302.

Lazev, A., Herzog, T., & Brandon, T. (1999). Classical conditioning of environmental cues to cigarette smoking. *Experimental and Clinical Psychopharmacology, 7*, 56–63.

Leclere, F., Rogers, R., & Peters, K. (1998). Neighborhood social context and racial differences in women's heart disease mortality. *Journal of Health and Social Behavior, 39*, 91–107.

le Grange, D., Stone, A., & Brownell, K. (1998). Eating disturbances in white and minority female dieters. *International Journal of Eating Disorders, 24*, 395–403.

Leibowitz, S. F. (1995). Central physiological determinants of eating behavior and weight. In K. D. Brownell & C. G. Fairburn (Eds.), *Eating disorders and obesity* (pp. 3–7). New York: The Guilford Press.

Lerman, C., Caporaso, N., Audrain, J., Main, D., Bowman, E., Lockshin, B., & Shields, P. (1999). Evidence suggesting the role of specific genetic factors in cigarette smoking. *Health Psychology, 18*, 14–20.

Leukefeld, C., & Leukefeld, S. (1999). Primary socialization theory and a biopsychosocialspiritual practice model for substance abuse. *Substance Use & Misuse, 34*, 983–991.

Levin, S., Gans, K., Carleton, R., & Bucknam, L. (1998). The evolution of a physical activity campaign. *Family Community Health, 21*, 65–77.

Lewis, B., & Schmidt, C. (1991). Listener's response to music as a function of personality type. *JRME, 39*, 311–321.

Lichtenstein, A., Ausman, L., Jalbert, S., & Schaefer, E. (1999). Effects of different forms of dietary hydrogenated fats on serum lipoprotein cholesterol levels. *The New England Journal of Medicine, 340*, 1933–1939.

Light, K. C., Brownley, K. A., Turner, J. R., Hinderliter, A. L., Girdler, S. S., Sherwood, A., & Anderson, N. B. (1995). Job status and high effort coping influence work blood pressure in women and blacks. *Hypertension, 25*(4), 554–559.

Llabre, M., Klein, B., Saab, P., McCalla, J., & Schneiderman, N. (1998). Classification of individual differences in cardiovascular responsivity: The contribution of reactor type controlling for race and gender. *International Journal of Behavioral Medicine, 5*, 213–229.

Lock, M. (1999). The politics of health, identity, and culture. In R. Contrada & R. Ashmore (Eds.), *Self, social identity, and physical health* (pp. 43–68). New York: Oxford University Press.

Locke, S., & Colligan, D. (1986). *The healer within: The new medicine of mind and body.* New York: E.P. Dutton.

Longshore, D., Grills, C., & Annon, K. (1999). Effects of a culturally congruent intervention on cognitive factors related to drug use recovery. *Substance Use & Misuse, 34*, 1223–1241.

MacLachlan, M. (1997). *Culture and health.* New York: John Wiley & Sons.

Mancuso, G., Andres, P., Ansseau, M., & Tirelli, E. (1999). Effects of nicotine administered via a transdermal delivery system on vigilance: A repeated measure study. *Psychopharmacology, 143*, 18–23.

Mann, J. (1998). The neurobiology of suicide. *Nature Medicine 4*, 25–30.

Mann, T. (1996). Why do we need a health psychology of gender or sexual orientation? In Pamela M. Kato & Traci Mann (Eds.), *Handbook of diversity issues in health psychology* (pp. 187–198). New York: Plenum Press.

Manning, M., & Fusilier, M. (1999). The relationship between stress and health care use: An investigation of the buffering roles of personality, social support and exercise. *Journal of Psychosomatic Research, 47*, 159–173.

Marin, B., & Gomez, C. (1997). Latino culture and sex: Implications for HIV prevention. In M. C. Zea (Ed.), *Psychological intervention with Latino populations* (pp. 73–93). Boston: Allyn & Bacon.

Marin, B., Gomez, C., Tschann, J., & Gregorich, S. (1997). Condom use in unmarried Latino men: Test of cultural constructs. *Health Psychology, 16*, 458–467.

Marks, D. (1998). Addiction, smoking and health: Developing policy based interventions. *Psychology, Health, & Medicine, 3*, 97–111.

Marsella, A. (1994). Work and well-being in an ethnoculturally pluralistic society: Conceptual and methodological issues. In In G. Keita & J. Hurrell (Eds.), *Job stress in a changing workforce: Investigating gender, diversity, and family issues* (pp. 147–159). Washington DC: American Psychological Association.

Martin, R., Wan, C., David, J., Wegner, E., Olson, B., & Watson, D. (1999). Style of anger expression: Relation to expressivity, personality, and health. *Personality and Social Psychology, 25*, 1196–1207.

Maslow, A. (1970). *Motivation and personality* (2nd ed.). New York: Harper & Row.

Matheson, L. (1996). Valuing spirituality among native american populations. *Counseling and Values, 41*, 51–58.

Mays, V., Coleman, L., & Jackson, J. (1996). Perceived race based discrimination, employment status, and job stress in a national sample of black women: Implications for health outcomes. *Journal of Occupational Health Psychology, 1,* 319–329.

McCrae, R. R., & Costa, P. T. (1987). Validation of the five factor model of personality across instruments and observers. *Journal of Personality and Social Psychology, 52,* 81–90.

McCraty, R. (1996). Entrainment. *IHM Research Update, 2,* 2.

McCraty, R., Tiller, W., & Atkinson, M. (1996). Entrainment: A preliminary review. Retrieved from the world wide web *www.heartmath.org/ResearchPapers/HeadHeart*

McDonald, L., & Sayger, T. (1998). Impact of a family and school based prevention program on protective factors for high risk youth. *Drugs and Society, 12,* 61–85.

McGuire, P. (1999). More psychologists are finding that discrete uses of humor promote healing in their patients (pp. 1–6). *APA Monitor Online.* Retrieved April 8, 1999 from World Wide Web: *http://www.apa.org/monitor/mar99/humor.html/.*

McKinney, C., Antoni, M., Kumar, M., Tims, F., & McCabe, P. (1997). Effects of guided imagery and music (GIM) therapy on mood and cortisol in healthy adults. *Health Psychology, 16,* 390–400.

McNair, L. D. (1996). African American women and behavior therapy: Integrating theory, culture, and clinical practice. *Cognitive and Behavioral Practice, 3,* 337–349.

Meijman, T. F., van Dormolen, M., Herber, R. F., Rongen, H., Kuiper, S. (1995). Job strain, neuroendocrine activation, and immune status. In S. L. Sauter, & L. R. Murphy (eds.), *Organizational risk factors for job stress* (pp. 113–126). Washington DC: American Psychological Association.

Mente, A., & Helmers, K. (1999). Defensive hostility and cardiovascular responses to stress in young men. *Personality and Individual Differences, 27,* 683–694.

Merriam, A. (1982). *African music in perspective* (pp. 155–166). New York: Garland Publishing.

Michela, J., Lukaszewski, M., & Allegrante, J. (1994). Organizational climate and work stress: A general framework applied to inner-city schoolteachers. In G. Keita & J. Hurrell (Eds.), *Job stress in a changing workforce: Investigating gender, diversity, and family issues (pp. 61–79).* Washington DC: American Psychological Association.

Miller, K. Forehand, R., & Kotchick, B. (1999). Adolescent sexual behavior in two ethnic minority samples: The role of family variables. *Journal of Marriage and the Family, 61,* 85–98.

Minifee, M., & McAuley, E. (1998). An attributional perspective on African American adults' exercise behavior. *Journal of Applied Social Psychology, 28,* 924–936.

Mischel, W. (1968). *Personality and assessment.* New York: Wiley.

Morrison, T., DiClemente, R., Wingood, G., & Collins, C. (1998). Frequency of alcohol use and its association with STD/HIV related risk practices, attitudes and knowledge among an african american community recruited sample. *International Journal of STD & AIDS, 9,* 608–612.

Morrow, J., Jackson, A., Bazzarre, T., Milne, D., & Blair, S. (1999). A one year follow up to physical activity and health: A report of the surgeon general. *American Journal of Preventive Medicine, 17,* 24–30.

Mott, J., Crowe, P., Richardson, J., & Flay, B. (1999). After school supervision and adolescent cigarette smoking: Contributions of the setting and intensity of after school self care. *Journal of Behavioral Medicine, 22,* 35–58.

Murrain, M. (1996). Differential survival in blacks and hispanics with AIDS. *Ethnicity & Health, 1,* 373–382.

Myers, H., Satz, P., Miller, B., Bing, E., Evans, G., Richardson, M., Forney, D., Morgenstern, H., Saxton, E., D' Elia, L., Longshore, D., & Mena, I. (1997). The African American Health Project (AAHP): Study overview and select findings on high risk behaviors and psychiatric disorder in african american men. *Ethnicity & Health, 2*(3), 183–196.

Nadelson, C., & Zimmerman, V. (1993). Culture and psychiatric care of women. In A. C. Gaw (Ed.), *Culture, ethnicity, and mental illness* (pp. 505–513). Washington DC: American Psychiatric Press.

Nathan, R., Staats, T., & Rosch, P. (1987). *The doctor's guide to instant stress relief* (pp. 41–43). New York: G.P. Putnam's Series.

Nguyen, H. H., Messe, L. A., & Stollak, G. E. (1999). Toward a more complex understanding of acculturation and adjustment. *Journal of Cross Cultural Psychology, 30,* 5–31.

Nies, M. A., Vollman, M., & Cook, T. (1998). Facilitators, barriers, and strategies for exercise in European American women in the community. *Public Health Nursing, 15*(4), 263–272.

Nies, M., Vollman, M., & Cook, T. (1999). African American women's experiences with physical activity in their daily lives. *Public Health Nursing, 16*, 23–31.

Nisbet, P. (1996). Protective factors for suicidal black females. *Suicide and Life Threatening Behavior, 26*, 325–340.

Nketia, J. H. (1974). *The music of Africa* (pp. 21–34). New York: W.W. Norton & Company.

Nuland, S. (1997). *The wisdom of the body* (pp. 112–118). New York: Alfred A. Knopf.

Oetting, E., Donnermeyer, J., Trimble, J., & Beauvais, F. (1998). Primary socialization theory: Culture, ethnicity, and cultural identification. The links between culture and substance use IV. *Substance Use & Misuse, 33*, 2075–2107.

Ogden, J., & Thomas, D. (1999). The role of familial values in understanding the impact of social class on weight concern. *International Journal of Eating Disorders, 25*, 273–279.

O'Hanlan, K. (1996). Homophobia and the health psychology of lesbians. In Pamela M. Kato & Traci Mann (Eds.), *Handbook of diversity issues in health psychology* (pp.261–286). New York: Plenum Press.

Organista, K. C., & Munoz, R. F. (1996). Cognitive behavioral therapy with latinos. *Cognitive and Behavioral Practice, 3*, 255–270.

Organista, K., & Dwyer, E. (1996). Clinical case management and cognitive behavioral therapy: Integrated psychosocial services for depressed latino primary care patients. In P. Manoleas (Ed.), *The cross cultural practice of clinical case management in mental health* (pp. 119–140). New York: The Haworth Press.

Ornstein, R., & Sobel, D. (1989). *Healthy pleasures (p. 218)*. Reading, MA: Addison-Wesley.

Ouellette, S. (1999). The relationship between personality and health. In R. Contrada & R. Ashmore (Eds.), *Self, social identity, and physical health* (pp. 125–154). New York: Oxford University Press.

Outlaw, F. (1993). Stress and coping: The influence of racism on the cognitive appraisal processing of African Americans. *Issues in Mental Health Nursing, 14*, 399–409.

Outlaw, F. (1999). An inner city multigenerational African American family. In V. D. Ferguson (Ed.), *Case studies in cultural diversity.* Boston: Jones and Bartlett Publishers.

Pack-Brown, S., Whittington, C. L., & Parker, W. (1998). *Images of me: A guide to group work with African American women.* Boston: Allyn & Bacon.

Pennebaker, J., & Seagal, J. (1999). Forming a story: The health benefits of narrative. *Journal of Clinical Psychology, 55*, 1243–1254.

Perrin, K. & McDermott, R. (1997). The spiritual dimension of health: A review. *American Journal of Health Studies, 13*, 90–99.

Petronis, K., Samuels, J., Moscicki, E., & Anthony, J. (1990). An epidemiologic investigation of potential risk factors for suicide attempts. *Social Psychiatry and Psychiatric Epidemiology, 25*, 193–199.

Phinney, J. S. (1996). When we talk about American ethnic groups what do we mean? *American Psychologist, 51*(9), 918–927.

Pilisuk, M., & Parks, S. (1986). *The healing web.* Hanover NH: The University Press of New England.

Polacsek, M., Celentano, D., O'Campo, P., & Santelli, J. (1999). Correlates of condom use stage or change: Implications for intervention. *AIDS Education and Prevention, 11*, 38–52.

Polednak, A. (1997). Use of selected high fat foods by Hispanic adults in the northeastern U.S. *Ethnicity & Health, 2*, 71–76.

Pollard, K., & DeVita, C. (1997). A portrait of Asians and Pacific Islanders in the U.S. *Statistical Bulletin Metropolitan Insurance Companies, 78*, 2–9.

Pomerleau, O., & Kardia, S. (1999). Introduction to the featured section: Genetic research on smoking. *Health Psychology, 18*, 3–6.

Porter, L., Stone, A., & Schwartz, J. (1999). Anger expression and ambulatory blood pressure: A comparison of state and trait measures. *Psychosomatic Medicine, 61*, 454–463.

Pribut, S. (1998). Dr. Stephen M. Pribut's sports pages (pp.1–3). Retrieved July 13, 2000 from World Wide Web: http://www.clark.net/pub/pribut/spphysio.html.

Price, J. (2000). The tae bo way (pp. 1–2). Retrieved July 13, 2000 from the World Wide Web: *http://www.taeboonline.com/book.html.*

Prochaska, J., DiClemente, C., & Norcross, J. (1992). In search of how people change: Applications to addictive behaviors. *American Psychologist, 47*, 1102–1114.

Pujol, T., & Langenfeld, M. (1999). Influence of music on Wingate Anaerobic Test performance. *Perceptual and Motor Skills, 88*, 292–296.

Quah, S. H., & Bishop, G. D. (1996). Seeking help for illness: The roles of cultural orientation and illness cognition. *Journal of Health Psychology, 1*, 209–222.

Quick, J. D., Nelson, D. L., Matuszek, P. A., Whittington, J. L., & Quick, J. C. (1996). Social support, secure attachments, and health. In C. L Cooper (Ed.) *Handbook of stress, medicine, and health* (pp. 269–287). New York: CRC Press.

Quick, J., Quick, J., Nelson, D., & Hurrell, J. (1997). *Preventive stress management in organizations.* Washington DC: American Psychological Association.

Ramanaiah, N., Sharpe, J., & Byravan, A. (1999). Hardiness and major personality factors. *Psychological Reports, 84*, 497–500.

Ramos Sanchez, L., Atkinson, D. R., & Fraga, E. D. (1999). Mexican Americans' bilingual ability, counselor bilingualism cues, counselor ethnicity, and perceived counselor credibility. *Journal of Counseling Psychology, 46*, 125–131.

Reutter, L. (1997). Family health assessment, an integrated approach. In B. W. Spradley, & J. A. Allender (Eds.), *Readings in community health nursing* (5th ed., pp. 329–337). Philadelphia: J.B. Lippincott.

Richards, J., & Gross, J. (1999). Composure at any cost? The cognitive consequences of emotion suppression. *Personality and Social Psychology Bulletin, 25*, 1033–1044.

Robert, S. (1998). Community level socioeconomic status effects on adult health. *Journal of Health and Social Behavior, 39*, 18–37.

Roberts, R., Chen, R., & Roberts, C. (1997). Ethnocultural differences in prevalence of adolescent suicidal behaviors. *Suicide and Life Threatening Behavior, 27*, 208–217.

Rodgers, J. (1989, February). Longevity predictors: The personality link. *Omni*, 25.

Rogers, A., Adamson, J. E., & McCarthy, M. (1997). Variations in health behaviors among inner city 12 year olds from four ethnic groups. *Ethnicity & Health, 2*, 309–316.

Rose, J. (1982). *Nutrition and killer diseases, the effects of dietary factors in fatal chronic disease.* Park Ridge, NJ: Noyes Publication.

Rotter, J. (1982). *The development and applications of social learning theory: Selected papers.* New York: Praeger.

Rozin, P. (1996). Sociocultural influences on human food selection. In *Why we eat what we eat: The psychology of eating* (pp. 233–263). Washington DC: American Psychological Association.

Sabo, D., & Gordon, D. F. (1995). *Men's health and illness (gender, power, and the body).* Thousand Oaks, California: Sage Publications.

Sabol, S., Nelson, M., Fisher, C., Gunzerath, L., Brody, C., Hu, S., Sirotta, L., Marcus, S., Greenberg, B., Lucas, F., & Hamer, D. (1999). A genetic association for cigarette smoking behavior. *Health Psychology, 18*, 7–13.

Sagan, L. (1987). *The health of nations.* New York: Basic Books.

Sanjur, D. (1995). *Hispanic foodways: Nutrition and health.* Boston: Allyn & Bacon.

Scharff, D., Homan, S., Kreuter, M., & Brennan, L. (1999). Factors associated with physical activity in women across the life span: Implications for program development. *Women and Health, 29*, 115–134.

Schechter, J., Green, L., Olsen, L., Kruse, K., & Cargo, M. (1997). Application of Karasek's demand/control model in a Canadian occupational setting including shift workers during a period of reorganization and downsizing. *American Journal of Health Promotion, 11*, 394–399.

Schneiderman, N. (1999). Behavioral medicine and the management of HIV/AIDS. *International Journal of Behavioral Medicine, 6*, 3–12.

Schwarzer, R. (1999). Self regulatory processes in the adoption and maintenance of health behaviors: The role of optimism, goals, and threats. *Journal of Health Psychology, 4*, 115–127.

Sellers, R. M., Smith, M. A., Shelton, N. J., Rowley, S. A., & Chavous, T. M. (1998). Multidimensional model of racial identity: A reconceptualization of African American racial identity. *Personality and Social Psychology Review, 2*, 18–39.

Serafica, F. C. (1997). Psychopathology and resilience in Asian American children and adolescents. *Applied Developmental Science, 1*, 145–155.

Serafica, F. C. (1999). Clinical interventions and prevention for Asian American children and families: Current status and needed research. *Applied and Preventive Psychology, 8*, 143–152.

Shaffer, D., Gould, M., & Hicks, R. (1994). Worsening suicide rate in black teenagers. *American Journal of Psychiatry, 151*, 1810–1812.

Shin, Y. (1999). The effects of a walking exercise program on physical function and emotional state of elderly Korean women. *Public Health Nursing, 16*, 146–154.

Shorris, E. (1992). *Latinos (a biography of the people).* New York: Avon Books.

Shouyu, L. (2000). An introduction to Chinese martial arts (pp. 1–8). Retrieved July 13, 2000 from the World Wide Web: http://www.nardis.com/~twchan/liang.html.

Shrimshaw, E., Siegal, K., & Karus, D. (1999, August). *Perceptions of available support, social conflict, and social integration in women living with HIV/AIDS.* Annual Meeting of the American Psychological Association, Boston, Massachusetts.

Shur, D. (1982). *Social and cultural perspectives in nutrition.* Englewood Cliffs, NJ: Prentice Hall.

Siegrist, J. (1996). Adverse health effects of high effort/low reward conditions. *Journal of Occupational and Health Psychology, 1*, 27–41.

Simha, A. (1991). *African polyphony and polyrhythm: Musical structure and methodology* (pp. 4–15). New York: Cambridge University Press.

Singh, A. (1999). Shamans, healing, and mental health. *Journal of Child and Family Studies, 8*, 131–134.

Sloboda, J. (1991). Music structure and emotional response: Some empirical findings. *Psychology of Music, 19*, 110–120.

Snel, J., & Lorist, M. (1998). *Nicotine, caffeine, and social drinking: Behavior and brain function.* Newark, NJ: Harwood Academic Publishers.

Snowden, L. R., & Hines, A. M. (1999). A scale to assess African American acculturation. *Journal of Black Psychology, 25*, 36–47.

Sorensen, G., Stoddard, A., & Macario, E. (1998). Social support and readiness to make dietary changes. *Health Education and Behavior, 25*, 587–598.

Spicer, J., & Chamberlain, K. (1996). Developing psychosocial theory in health psychology. *Journal of Health Psychology, 1*, 161–171.

Stansfield, S., Head, J., & Marmot, M. (1998). Explaining social class differences in depression and well being. *Social Psychiatry and Psychiatric Epidemiology, 33*, 1–9.

Stanwyck, D., & Anson, C. (1986). Is personality related to illness? Cluster profiles of aggregated data. *Advances, 3*, 4–15.

Staples, B. (1999). Black men and public space. In S. Barnet, M. Berman, W. Burto, W. Cain, & M. Stubbs (Eds.), *Literature for composition (essays, fiction, poetry, and drama)* (5th ed., pp. 164–166). New York: Longman.

Staples, R. (1995). Health among Afro American males. In D. Sabo & D. F. Gordon (Eds.), *Men's health and illness (gender, power, and the body)* (pp. 121–138). Thousand Oaks California: Sage Publications.

Stavig, G., Igra, A., & Leonard, A. (1984). Hypertension among Asians And Pacific Islanders in California. *Journal of Epidemiology, 119*, 677–691.

Stein, J., & Nyamathi, A. (1999). Gender differences in relationships among stress, coping, and health risk behaviors in impoverished, minority populations. *Personality and Individual Differences, 26*, 141–157.

Steptoe, A., Kimbell, J., & Basford, P. (1998). Exercise and the experience and appraisal of daily stressors: A naturalistic study. *Journal of Behavioral Medicine, 21*, 363–374.

Sternberg, E., & Gold, P. (Spring, 1997). The mind-body interaction in disease. *Scientific American (Special Issue, Mysteries of the Mind)*, 8–16.

Stoney, C., Lentino, L., & Emmons, K. (1998). Environmental tobacco smoke: Association with cardiovascular function at rest and during stress. *International Journal of Behavioral Medicine, 5*, 230–244.

Stratton, V. & Zalanowski, A. (1991). The effects of music and cognition on mood. *Psychology of Music, 19*, 121–127.

Strecher, V. J., Champion, V. L., & Rosenstock, I. M. (1997). The health belief model and health behavior. In D. S. Gochman (Ed.), *Handbook of health behavior research I: Personal and social determinants* (pp. 71–91). New York: Plenum Press.

Sullivan, T., & Farrell, A. (1999). Identification and impact of risk and protective factors for drug use among urban African American adolescents. *Journal of Clinical Child Psychology, 28*(2), 122–136.

Taylor, R., Mattis, J., & Chatters, L. (1999). Subjective religiosity among African Americans: A synthesis of findings from five national samples. *Journal of Black Psychology, 25*, 524–543.

Taylor, S. (1999). *Health Psychology* (4th ed.). New York: McGraw Hill.

Taylor, W., Baranowski, T., & Young, D. (1998). Physical activity interventions in low income, ethnic minority, and populations with disability. *American Journal of Preventive Medicine, 15*, 334–343.

Terwogt, M. & Grinsven, F. (1991). Musical expression of mood states. *Psychology of Music, 19*, 99–109.

Thakore, J., Berti, C., & Dinan, T. (1999). Diurnal variation of nicotine induced ACTH and cortisol secretion in nonsmoking healthy male volunteers. *Human Psychopharmacology, 14*, 179–183.

Thomason, B., Bachanas, P., & Campos, P. (1996). Cognitive behavioral intervention with persons affected by HIV/AIDS. *Cognitive and Behavioral Practice, 3*, 417–442.

Thridandam, M., Louie, L., Fong, W., Forst, M., & Jang, M. (1998). A tobacco and alcohol use profile of San Francisco's Chinese community. *Journal of Drug Education, 28*, 377–393.

Tortora, G. J., Funke, B. R., & Case, C. L. (1998). Disorders associated with the immune system. In *Microbiology: An Introduction* (PP. 520–521). New York: Addison Wesley Longman.

True, R. (1995). Mental health issues of Asian/Pacific Island women. In D. L. Adams (Ed.), *Health issues for women of color* (pp. 89–111). Thousand Oaks, California: Sage Publications.

Tsutsumi, A., Tsutsumi, K., Kayaba, K., & Igarashi, M. (1998). Health related behaviors, social support, and community morale. *International Journal of Behavioral Medicine, 5*, 166–182.

U.S. Department of Health and Human Services (USDHHS). (1987). *Stress management in work settings.* L. R. Murphy, & T. F. Schoenborn, Eds. Public Health Service, Centers for Disease Control, and National Institute for Occupational Safety and Health.

U.S. Department of Health and Human Services (USDHHS). (1994). *Worker deaths in confined spaces: A summary of NIOSH surveillance and investigative findings.* Public Health Service, Centers for Disease Control and Prevention, National Institute for Occupational Safety and Health.

U.S. Department of Health and Human Services (USDHHS). (1997). *National Institute on Drug Abuse: NIH Publication No. 97– 4114. Drug abuse prevention for at risk groups.* Bethesda, MD: National Institutes of Health.

U.S. Department of Health and Human Services (USDHHS). (1998a). No. PHS 98 1232. *Health, United States, 1998.* Washington DC: U.S. Government Printing Office.

U.S. Department of Health and Human Services (USDHHS). (1998b). *National Institute on Drug Abuse: NIH Publication No. 98– 3888. Drug use among racial/ethnic minorities.* Bethesda, MD: National Institutes of Health.

U.S. Department of Health and Human Services (USDHHS). (1999). Study shows how genes can help protect from addiction. *NIDA Notes, 13 (6)*, 5,9

Uetrecht, C., & Greenberg, M. (1999). Factors influencing vegetable and fruit use: Implications for promotion. *American Journal of Health Behavior, 23*, 172–181.

Uvnas Moberg, K. (1999). Physiological and endocrine effects of social contact. In C. S. Carter, I. I. Lederhendler, & B. Kirkpatrick (eds.), *The Integrative Neurobiology of Affiliation* (pp. 246–260). Cambridge, MA: The MIT Press.

Van Tilburg, M., Vingerhoets, J., Van Heck, G., & Kirschbaum, C. (1999). Homesickness, mood, and self reported health. *Stress Medicine, 15*, 189–196.

Vasquez, I., Millen, B., Bissett, L., Levenson, S., & Chipkin, S. (1998). Buena alimentacion, Buena salud: A preventive nutrition intervention in Carribean Latinos with Type 2 diabetes. *American Journal of Health Promotion, 13*, 116–119.

Vassend, O., & Skrondal, A. (1999). The role of negative affectivity in self assessment of health (a structural equation approach). *Journal of Health Psychology, 4*, 465–482.

Vega, W. A., Alderete, E., Bohdan, K., & Aguilar, G. S. (1998). Illicit drug use among Mexicans and Mexican Americans in California: The effects of gender and acculturation. *Addiction, 93*, 1839–1850.

Velletri, P. (1996). Hypertension in African Americans: Basic science initiatives of the National Heart, Lung, and Blood Institute. *Ethnicity and Health, 1*, 115–116.

Villarosa, L. (1994). *Body and soul (the black women's guide to physical health and emotional well being).* New York: Harper Perennial.

Voorhees, C., Stillman, F., Swank, R., Heagerty, P., Levine, D., & Becker, D. (1996). Heart, body, and soul: Impact of church-based smoking cessation interventions on readiness to quit. *Preventive Medicine, 25,* 277–285.

Wade, C., & Tavris, C. (2000). *Psychology,* (6th ed.). Upper Saddle River, NJ: Prentice Hall.

Weidner, G., Boughal, T., Pieper, C., Connor, S., & Mendell, N. (1997). Relationship of job strain to standard coronary risk factors and psychological characteristics in women and men of the family heart study. *Health Psychology, 16,* 239–247.

Wilfley, D. E., & Rodin, J. (1995). Cultural influences of eating disorders. In K. D. Brownell & C. G. Fairburn (Eds.), *Eating disorders and obesity a comprehensive handbook* (pp. 78–82). New York: The Guilford Press.

Williams, D., Spencer, M., Jackson, J., & Ashmore, R. (1999). Race, stress, and physical health: The role of group identity. In R. Contrada & R. Ashmore (Eds.), *Self, social identity, and physical health* (pp. 71–100). New York: Oxford University Press.

Winett, R. (1998). Developing more effective health behavior programs: Analyzing the epidemiological and biological bases for activity and exercise programs. *Applied and Preventive Psychology, 7,* 209–224.

Wolf, D. & Crowe, M. (1992). Postpartum. In The Boston Women's Health Book Collective (Eds.), *The new our bodies, ourselves: Updated and expanded for the 90s* (pp. 477–498). New York: Simon & Schuster.

Wood, M., & Price, P. (1997). Machismo and marianismo: Implications for HIV/AIDS risk reduction. *American Journal of Health Studies, 13,* 44–52.

Wyatt, G. E. (1994). The sociocultural relevance of sex research. *American Psychologist, 49*(8), 748–754.

Yamamoto, J., Silva, J., Justice, L., Chang, C., & Leong, G. (1993). Cross-cultural psychotherapy. In A. Gaw (Ed.), *Culture, ethnicity, and mental illness* (pp. 114–115). Washington DC: American Psychiatric Press.

Younoszai, T., Lohrmann, D., Seefeldt, C., & Greene, R. (1999). Trends from 1987 to 1991 in alcohol, tobacco, and other drug (ATOD) use among adolescents exposed to a school district wide prevention intervention. *Journal of Drug Education, 29,* 77–94.

Zambrana, R., & Ellis, B. (1995). Contemporary research issues in Hispanic/Latino women's health. In D. L. Adams (Ed.), *Health issues for women of color* (pp. 42–65). Thousand Oaks, California: Sage Publications.

Zane, N., Aoki, B., Ho, T., Huang, L., & Jange, M. (1998). Dosage related changes in a culturally repsonsive prevention program for Asian American youth. *Drugs and Society, 12,* 105–125.

Zea, M. C., Quezada, T., & Belgrave, F. (1997). Limitations of an acultural health psychology for Latinos: Reconstructing the African influence on Latino culture and health related behaviors. In M. C. Zea (Ed.), *Psychological interventions with Latino populations* (pp. 255–268). Boston: Allyn & Bacon.

Zerbe, K. (1993). *The body betrayed: Women, eating disorders, and treatment.* Washington DC: American Psychiatric Press.

Zimmerman, J., & Zayas, L. (1995). Suicidal adolescent Latinas: Culture, female development, and restoring the mother-daughter relationship. In S. Canetto & D. Lester (Eds.) *Women and suicidal behavior* (pp. 120–131). New York: Springer.

Zinser, M., Fiore, M., & Davidson, R. (1999). Manipulating smoking motivation: Impact on an electrophysiological index of approach motivation. *Journal of Abnormal Psychology, 108,* 240–254.

INDEX

A

Acculturation, 11
Acetylcholine, 45
Achiron, A., 104
Active and avoidant coping, 143
Acute illnesses, definition of, 1
Adams, T., 168
Adamson, J.E., 11
Addictive behavior, 41
Adolescents
  monitoring of, 68
  smoking and, 48
Aerobic power, 90–91
Affiliation, neurobiology of, 161
African Americans
  active and avoidant coping, 143
  breast cancer mortality rate in
    women, 6
  ethnic identity and substance
    abuse, 62–63
  food habits, 23–26
  HIV/AIDS, 7
  infant mortality rates, 5–6
  lactose intolerance in, 24
  lung cancer and prostate cancer
    rates in men, 6
  obesity in women, 7
  sexual behavior, 68
  smoking, 43–44, 50
  social factors, suicidal behavior,
    and, 123–125
  sociocultural factors, the work-
    place, and, 105–108
  soul food, 25
  spiritual tradition, 170–171
  women and eating disorders, 33
  women and exercise, 83, 84–85
  women and victimization expe-
    riences, 72
African centrality, 63
Afrocentric worldview, 2
Aguilar, G.S., 2, 11
Ahluwalia, I., 30

Ajzen, I., 31
Akan, G., 32
Akser, K., 108
Alaniz, M., 57, 60
Alaska Natives
  diabetes, rate of, 7
  infant mortality rates, 5–6
  smoking, 44
Alcoholics Anonymous, 168
Aldrete, E., 2, 11
Allegrante, J., 112
Alston, M., 124, 125
Altemus, M., 154
Amaro, H., 110
American Institute for Cancer
  Research, 18
American Lung Association, 42,
  43
American Nurses Association, 159,
  160
Ammann, P., 174
Anderson, N., 107
Anderson, S., 124, 125
Andres, P., 47
Anerson, N.B., 107
Anger-in, 138
Anger-out, 138
Annon, K., 74
Anson, C., 139
Ansseau, M., 47
Anthony, J., 121
Antoni, M., 175, 176
Antonuccio, D., 47
Aoki, B., 74
Applied research, 106
Armistead, L., 72
Ashmore, R., 142
Asian Americans
  cardiovascular disease and, 6–7
  food habits, 28–29
  smoking, 44, 50
  social factors, suicidal behavior,
    and, 127–128

  sociocultural factors, the work-
    place, and, 110–111
Atherosclerosis, 21
Atkinson, D.R., 11
Atkinson, M., 177
Audrain, J., 44, 50
Ausman, L., 22
Axinn, W., 153

B

Babakus, E., 103
Bachanas, P., 74
Baker, F., 129
Baligh, M., 30
Balka, E., 60, 61, 63
Balneaves, L., 13
Bandura, A., 143
Barak, Y., 104
Baranowski, T., 82, 83, 89, 92
Barbarin, O., 171
Barber, J., 153
Barret, R., 174
Barringer, H., 108
Barrios, L., 119, 120
Barzan, R., 174
Basford, P., 81, 85
Baum, A., 1, 2, 9, 14
Baxter, J., 103, 111
Bazzarre, T., 82
Beatty, L., 160
Beauvais, F., 66
Becker, A., 32, 33
Becker, D., 49
Beerman, K., 30, 31
Belgrave, F., 74, 171, 172
Bell, R., 59, 63
Bennett, P., 4
Berti, C., 41
Bezner, J., 168
Bhagat, R., 13, 103
Bierman, E., 21
Bindon, J.R., 11
Bing, E., 57, 71, 75, 76

Binge eating disorder, 33
Biomedical model, 9
Biopsychosocial model, 8–10
 and smoking, 43–44
Bishop, G.D., 2
Bisogni, C., 29, 31
Bissett, L., 35
Blair, S., 82
Bliss, R., 47
Bob, S., 2, 12, 13
Bohdan, K., 2, 11
Bolin, L., 47
Boney-McCoy, S., 144
Bottorff, J.L., 13
Boughal, T., 103, 106
Bowman, E., 44, 50
Bragg, M., 160
Brandon, T., 46
Brannon, L., 2, 81, 106
Breastfeeding, health benefits of,
 154
Brener, N., 119, 120
Brennan, L., 84
Brody, C., 45
Brook, D., 60, 61, 63
Brook, J., 60, 61, 63
Brooks, A., 59, 60
Brown, D., 171
Brownell, K., 33
Brownley, K.A., 107
Brownson, R.C., 82, 84
Brunning, S., 136
Brunswick, A., 65
Bucaccio, P., 84, 85, 86
Bucknam, L., 81, 87, 90
Bungam, T., 84, 87, 88, 90
Burton, L., 93
Byravan, A., 141

C

Caetano, R., 57
Campos, P., 74
Cancer, 18–20
Cancer-prone personality, 139
Cancer screening and management,
 6
Canetto, S., 121, 122, 128
Canino, G., 2, 9, 11
Capitano, J., 74

Caporaso, N., 44, 50
Cardiovascular disease, 6–7, 21–22
Carey, M., 140, 141
Cargo, M., 100, 104, 111
Carleton, R., 81, 87, 90
Carlisle, D., 110
Carroll, D., 4, 102
Carroll, J.L., 176
Carter, C.S., 154
Cartwright, S., 112
Case, C.L., 75
Castro, C., 82, 84
Castro, F., 74, 108, 109
Catecholamines, 177
Celentano, D., 70
Centers for Disease Control, 72
Chait, A., 21
Chalmers, K., 158
Chamberlain, K., 9
Champion, V.L., 31
Chang, C., 119, 129
Chape, C., 145
Chapman, G., 29, 35
Chapman, R., 168
Chatters, L., 171
Chavous, T.M., 11
Chen, M., 44, 48, 50, 51
Chen, R., 119
Child and adult immunization
 rates, 7–8
Chipkin, S., 35
Chissell, J., 168
Chokkar, J., 103
Christen, A., 48, 52
Christen, J., 48, 52
Chronic illnesses, definition of, 1
Chun, C., 110, 111
Clance, P., 92, 93
Clark, C., 57
Clark, M., 48
Clarke, H., 13
Classical conditioning, 46
Cody, P., 160, 161, 174
Coe, K., 108, 109
Cognitive restructuring, 129
Cohen, M., 33
Colditz, G., 19
Coleburn, B., 158
Coleman, L., 106

Collective esteem, 102
Collectivism, 108
Collectivism *vs.* individualism, 11
Collectivist culture, 11
Colligan, D., 139
Collins, C., 75
Collins, R., 59, 63
Committed smoker, 41
Community health model, 91–92
Compensatory self-enhancement
 (CSE), 144
Connor, S., 103, 106
Connors, M., 29, 31
Consciousness raising, 90
Construal, 169
Contemplators, 85
Contrada, R., 100, 107
Cook, T., 84, 85, 86, 91
Cooper, C., 112, 139
Core foods, 23
Coronary-prone personality, 139
Corwin, S., 18, 22, 31
Costa, P.T., 135, 136
Crauthers, D., 46, 47, 49
Crosby, H., 74
Crowe, M., 154
Crowe, P., 42
Cuisine, 28
Cultural congruence, 73–74
Cultural sensitivity, 12
Culture, definition of, 1–2
Curandero, 172
Curtis, A., 108
Czarnecki, E., 100, 107

D

Dacosta, K., 26
Daily hassles, 141–142
Dana, 172
Danielson, C., 155
D'Augelli, A., 162
David, J., 138, 142
Davidson, R., 45
Davis, M., 42
Davis, N., 92, 93
Davison, D., 33
Decision latitude, 103
Defensive hostility, 138
DeNeve, K., 136

Depression and self-injurious
      behaviors, 119–133
   gender socialization, 122
   race/ethnicity and suicidal
      behavior, 123–128
   social factors, 121–122
   statement of the problem,
      119–121
   treatment issues, 128–129
DeVita, C., 110
Diabetes, 7, 21
DiClemente, C.C., 31, 83, 85
DiClemente, R., 75
Diet and health, 17–39
   cognitive barriers, 31–32
   diet and disease, 18
      cancer, 18–20
      cardiovascular disease,
         21–22
      diabetes, 21
   dietary trends, 17–18
   disordered eating, 32–34
   food choice, psychology of,
      29–30
   food habits, 22–23
   food habits across ethnic groups,
      23–29
   personal and social barriers,
      30–31
   treatment, cultural sensitivity in,
      34–35
Diller, J., 12
Dinan, T., 41
Disease-specific personality the-
      ory, 139
Disordered eating, 32–34
Distress cycle, diagram of, 100
Dittus, K., 30, 31
Dodds, J., 30
Doljanac, R., 68
Donnermeyer, J., 66
Dopamine, 44
Dorsey, S., 66, 67, 68
Dowda, M., 84, 87, 88, 90
Drabbs, M., 168
Dressler, W.W., 11
Dual minority, 124
Dugan, S., 47
Duncan, C., 49

du Pre, A., 176, 177, 178
Dwyer, E., 125, 126, 129

E
Eating, biology of, 35
Eber, M., 74
Elizur, A., 104
Ellickson, P., 59, 63
Ellis, B., 126
Emic, 2
Emmons, K., 42
Emotion expression, 144–145
Emotion suppression, 138
Employee Assistance Programs
      (EAPs), 113
Enomoto, K., 110, 111
Ensminger, M., 123, 124
Entrainment, 175
   using music, 177
Environmental tobacco smoke
      (ETS), 42
Erfurt, J., 145
Estrada, A., 57, 74
Ethnic affiliation, 61
Ethnic attachment, 61
Ethnic groups, 23
Ethnic identity, 60–61
Ethnoscience methods, 13
Etic, 2
Evans, G., 57, 71, 75, 76
Everett, S., 119, 120
Exercise and health, 81–98
   health benefits of exercise,
      81–82
   interventions, 89–94
      community health model,
         91–92
      culturally based, 92–93
      social networks, 93–94
   personal barriers, 82–85
   social factors as barriers, 85–89
Exercise physiology, 94
Expectancy, 143
Extended family, 155
Eyler, A.A., 82, 84

F
Faith-related coping styles,
      167–168

collaborative, 168
   deferring, 168
   self-directing, 168
Falk, L., 29, 31
Familism, 60
Farrales, L., 29, 35
Farrell, A., 59
Fatalism, 127
Feist, J., 2, 81, 106
Felix-Ortiz, M., 62
Fennell, R., 176
Fernandez, A., 62
Fibrinogen, 42
Fiore, M., 45
Fisher, C., 45
Five-factor theory, 135–138
Flack, J., 110
Flay, B., 42
Follette, W., 47
Fong, W., 50
*Food, Nutrition, and Prevention of
      Cancer: A Global Perspec-
      tive*, 18–19
Food choice, psychology of, 29–30
Food habits, 22–23
Food ideology system, 32
Ford, T., 33
Forehand, R., 66, 67, 68, 72
Forst, M., 50
Forster, J., 103, 111
Fraga, E.D., 11
Frame, M., 175
Frandsen, K., 135, 138, 139, 151,
      152, 153, 157, 158, 169,
      170, 176, 177
Frankowski, J., 140, 141
French, L.A., 61, 62
French, S., 100, 103, 111
Frey, L., 103
Frontier areas, 159
Fuchs, C., 19
Fudge, R., 63, 69, 74, 75
Fujii, J., 129
Fukushima, F., 129
Fukuyama, M., 167, 168, 170, 172,
      173
Funder, D., 108, 140, 143, 145,
      169
Funke, B.R., 75

Furnham, A., 139
Furst, T., 29, 31
Fusilier, M., 141

G
Gailis, A., 92, 93
Gamache, D., 93
Gans, K., 81, 87, 90
Gardner, R., 108
Garvey, A., 47
Gatchel, R.J., 1, 2, 9, 14
Gateway drugs, 59
Gaw, A., 128, 129
Gelernter, J., 65
Geling, O., 119
Gender socialization, 122
General adaptation syndrome,
    141
Generic disease-prone personality
    theory, 138–139
Gerrard, M., 144
Giachello, A., 123, 124, 125, 128
Gibbons, F., 144
Gil, E.F., 2, 12, 13
Gilad, R., 104
Gilbert, D., 46, 47, 49
Gillis, J., 74
Giovannucci, E., 19
Girdler, S.S., 107
Glanz, K., 31
Glunt, E., 74
Gold, P., 141
Gomez, C., 70, 71
Gonzales, M., 124
Gordon, D.F., 122, 129
Gould, M., 119
Green, B., 109
Green, L., 100, 104, 111
Greenberg, M., 30
Greene, G., 20, 32
Greene, R., 66
Gregorich, S., 71
Gregory, A., 175
Griesler, A., 48
Griffith, E., 129
Grills, C., 74
Grilo, C., 32
Grinspoon, S., 32, 33

Grinsven, F., 175
Gross, J., 138, 144
Grossman, G., 162
Guardar, 126
Guarnaccia, P., 2, 9, 11
Guided Imagery and Music (GIM),
    175–176
Gunzerath, L., 45
Gursen, M., 60, 61, 63
Gutierres, S., 108, 109
Gutmann, M.C., 61

H
Hafen, B., 135, 138, 139, 151, 152,
    153, 157, 158, 169, 170,
    176, 177
Halmi, K.A., 33
Halpern, S., 174, 175, 176, 178
Hamel-Bissell, B., 155
Hara laugh, 178
Harburg, E., 145
Hardiness, 140
Harnack, L., 85, 90
Hart, K., 137
Hart, M., 162
Hauenstein, L., 145
Hawkes, C., 84, 85, 86
Head, J., 123
Heagerty, P., 49
Health belief model, 31
Health psychology
    definition of, 1
    and the workplace, 99–117
    diversity in the workforce,
        101–103
    job strain and shift work,
        104–105
    program types, 111–113
    significance of studying,
        99–101
    sociocultural factors and
        African Americans,
        105–108
    sociocultural factors and
        Asian Americans, 110–111
    sociocultural factors and
        Hispanic Americans,
        108–109

    variation in decision latitude
        and job demand, 103–104
Health statistics, cultural group
    differences in, 5–8
    cancer screening and manage-
        ment, 6
    cardiovacular disease, 6–7
    child and adult immunization
        rates, 7–8
    diabetes, 7
    HIV infection/AIDS, 7
    infant mortality rates, 5–6
Healthy People 2000, 4–5
Heaney, C., 44, 48, 50, 51
Heimendinger, J., 31
Helmers, K., 138
Herber, R.F., 113
Herek, G., 74
Herrera, R., 119, 129
Herzog, D., 32, 33
Herzog, T., 46
Hicks, R., 119
High intensity training, 90
Hig-strain job, 103
Hill, J., 168
Hiller, V., 30, 31
Hilton, B., 13
Himmersteib, V., 23, 24
Hinderliter, A.L., 107
Hines, A.M., 2, 11
Hirsch, J., 32
Hispanic Americans
    cervical cancer rate in women, 6
    diabetes, rate of, 7
    food habits, 26–28
    HIV/AIDS, 7
    HIV/AIDS survival rates, 68–69
    infant mortality rates, 5–6
    machismo and *marianismo*,
        70–72
    sexual behavior and familism,
        67–68
    smoking, 43, 50
    social factors, suicidal behavior,
        and, 125–127
    sociocultural factors, the work-
        place, and, 108–109
    spiritual tradition, 171–172

substance abuse, family factor
in, 60
women and eating disorders,
33
women and exercise, 83, 84
HIV/AIDS, 7, 66–67
HIV infection, stages of, 75
Ho, K., 31
Ho, T., 74
Hoffman, J., 74
Hogan, J., 48
Homan, S., 84
Houtsmuller, E., 46
Hovey, J., 125, 127
Huang, L., 74
Huffman, K., 85
Humphries, D., 31
Hunter, D., 19
Hurrell, J., 112, 113
Hydrogenation, 22
Hyman, D., 31
Hypercholesterolemia, 21
Hyperglycemia, 21
Hypothalamus, 154

I
Ibrahim, F., 128
Igarashi, M., 9, 11
Igra, A., 110
Illness behavior, 99
Immersion, 69–70
Impersonal Divine, 170
Individualism, 108
Individualist culture, 11
Infant mortality rates, 5–6
Alaska Natives and, 5–6
American Indians and, 5–6
blacks and, 5–6
Hispanics and, 5–6
whites and, 6
Informational social reference, 85
Ingersoll-Dayton, B., 167
Ingledew, D., 136
Intergenerational discrepancy, 62
Intergenerational families,
156–157
Internal locus of control, 143
Iwanaga, M., 175

J
Jackson, A., 82
Jackson, J., 105, 106, 142
Jacobs, D., 103, 111
Jaffee, L., 51, 84, 85, 86
Jalbert, S., 22
James, B., 167, 169
James, K., 101, 102, 105, 106
James, S., 108
Jang, M., 50
Jange, M., 74
Janson, H., 42, 48
Jeffery, R., 93, 103, 111
Jenkins, W., 110
Jensen, R., 46, 47, 49
Job demand, 103
Job strain, 103
neuroendocrine activation,
immune status, and, 113
John Henryism, 107
Johnson, H., 60
Johnson, J.L., 13
Johnson, P., 60
Jones, K., 49
Jorgensen, R., 140, 141
Juon, H., 123, 124
Justice, L., 119, 129

K
Kalimo, R., 105
Kandel, D., 48
Kanitz, S., 110
Kaplan, M., 119
Karasak, R., 100.103
Kardia, S., 45
Karren, K., 135, 138, 139, 151,
152, 153, 157, 158, 169,
170, 176, 177
Karus, D., 69
Kassel, J., 47
Kato, P.M., 103
Kayaba, K., 9, 11
Keesey, R.E., 34
Kelder, S., 103, 111
Kelley, G., 83, 85, 90, 91
Kelley, K., 83, 85, 90, 91
Khan, Y., 32
Kilbey, M., 44, 50

Kim, L., 110, 128
Kimbell, J., 81, 85
Kimerling, R., 72
Kimh, R., 104
King, A.C., 82, 84
King, C., 125, 127
Kinsey, K., 156, 157
Kiple, K., 23, 24
Kirkcaldy, B., 139
Kirschbaum, C., 137
Kivimaki, M., 105
Klein, B., 50
Klein, H., 74
Klibanski, A., 32, 33
Klonoff, E., 11, 44, 50
Ko, C., 33
Kobasa, S., 141
Koss-Chioino, J., 126, 127
Kotchick, B., 66, 67, 68
Koval, J., 48
Krantz, D.S., 1, 2, 9, 14
Kranzler, H., 65
Krause, N., 167
Kreuter, M., 84
Kristal, A.R., 31
Kristjanson, L., 158
Krogh, D., 45, 47, 49
Krumhansl, C., 174, 175
Krummel, D., 31
Krumpe, P., 47
Kruse, K., 104
Kuiper, S., 113
Kumanyika, S.K., 34
Kumar, M., 175, 176
Kviz, F., 48

L
Lafferty, C., 44, 48, 50, 51
Laforge, R., 20, 32
Lamb, L., 141
Lampl, Y., 104
Lando, H., 103, 111
Landrine, H., 11, 44, 50
Langenfeld, M., 175
Laughter, 176–178
Lauver, D., 173
Laverie, D., 85, 87, 88, 89
Lazev, A., 46

Leake, B., 110
Leclere, F., 159
LeCroy, C., 59, 60
le Grange, D., 33
Leibowitz, S.F., 34, 35
Lentino, L., 42
Leonard, A., 110
Leong, G., 119, 129
Lerman, C., 44, 50
Lester, D., 121, 122, 128
Leukefeld, C., 66
Leukefeld, S., 66
Level I attachment, 152
Level II attachment, 152
Levenson, S., 35
Levin, M., 108
Levin, S., 81, 87, 90
Levine, D., 49
Levy, J., 110
Lewis, B., 175
Lewis, J., 74
Liang, J., 167
Li Chern Pan, R., 100, 107
Lichtenstein, A., 22
Life course, 29
Lifestyle activities, 90
Light, K.C., 107
Linnan, L., 31
Llabre, M., 50
Lloyd, B., 47
Lock, M., 142, 146
Locke, S., 139
Lockshin, B., 44, 50
Lohrmann, D., 66
Longshore, D., 74
Lorist, M., 46
Louie, L., 50
Lowing, L., 83, 85, 90, 91
Lucas, K., 47
Lukaszewski, M., 112
Lutter, J., 84, 85, 86

M
Macario, E., 19, 20, 30
Machismo, 70–72
MacLachlan, M., 4
Main, D., 44, 50
Mancuso, G., 47

Mann, J., 130
Mann, T., 103, 162
Manning, M., 141
Marianismo, 70–72
Marin, B., 70, 71
Marks, D., 41, 49
Marmot, M., 102, 123
Marsella, A., 101
Martin, R., 138, 142
Masculine mystique, 122
Maslow, A., 152
Matheson, L., 172
Mattis, J., 171
Matuszek, P.A., 151, 152, 167
Maximal oxygen uptake, 91
Mays, V., 106
McAuley, E., 84
McCabe, P., 175, 176
McCalla, J., 50
McCarthy, M., 11
McClernon, F., 46, 47, 49
McCrae, R.R., 135, 136
McCraty, R., 177
McDermott, R., 168
McDonald, L., 73
McGovern, P., 103, 111
McGuire, P., 177
McKinney, C., 175, 176
McLerran, D.F., 31
McNair, L.D., 11
McNeilly, M., 107
Meijman, T.F., 113
Mendell, N., 103, 106
Mente, A., 138
Merriam, A., 174
Messe, L.A., 11
Messeri, P., 65
Mexican Americans
    elevated blood pressure and, 7
    obesity in women, 7
    substance abuse and Latina
        adolescents, 62
Michela, J., 112
Millen, B., 35
Miller, B., 57, 71, 75, 76
Miller, K., 66, 67, 68
Milne, D., 82
Minifee, M., 84

Mischel, W., 135
Mixon, M., 110
Montgomery, A., 32
Moon, G., 49
Mooney, D., 46, 47, 49
Morbidity, 4
Moroki, Y., 175
Morrison, T., 75
Morrow, J., 82
Mortality, 4
Moscicki, E., 121
Motivational interviewing, 83
Mott, J., 42
Movement, 92
Multicultural health psychology
    approach of, 2
    definition of, 1
    recurring themes in, 10–12
        acculturation, 11
        collectivism *vs.* individualism,
            11
        cultural sensitivity, 12
        racial identity, 11–12
        research in, 13
Multilevel approach, 156
Munoz, R.F., 11, 129
Murrain, M., 68
Music and health, 174–176
Myers, H., 57, 71, 75, 76, 107

N
Nadelson, C., 122
Nathan, R., 141
National College Health Risk
        Behavior Survey (1995),
        119
Native Americans
    cultural values and substance
        abuse, 61–62
    diabetes, rate of, 7
    health care in rural environments,
        160
    infant mortality rates, 5–6
    smoking, 44, 51
    spiritual tradition, 172–173
    women and exercise, 82–83
Negative reinforcement, 10
Negative withdrawal, 47

Neggers, Y.H., 11
Nelson, D.L., 112, 113, 151, 152, 167
Nelson, M., 45
Neuroticism, 137
Newcomb, M., 62
Nguyen, H.H., 11
Nicotine, 41
Nicotine dependence, 51
Nies, M.A., 84, 85, 86, 91
Nisbet, P., 124
Nketia, J.H., 174
Nonfatal suicide behavior, 125
Norcross, J., 31, 83, 85
Nuclear family, 155
Nucleus accumbens, 44
Nuland, S., 8
Nyamathi, A., 143

O
O'Campo, P., 70
Occupational health psychologists, 106
O'Driscoll, M., 103
Oetting, E., 66
Ogden, J., 34
O'Hanlan, K., 162
Olsen, L., 104
Olson, B., 138, 142
Operant conditioning, 46
Optimal health, 168
Organista, K.C., 11, 125, 126, 129
Organizational culture, 112
Ornstein, R., 176
Ouellette, S., 140, 141
Outlaw, F., 143, 156
Oxytocin, 154

P
Pack-Brown, S., 106, 107
Paradoxical smoking, 46
Parker, W., 106, 107
Parks, S., 152
Pate, R., 84, 87, 88, 90
Patterson, R.E., 31
Pederson, L., 48
Pennebaker, J., 145
Perrin, K., 168

Personality
  biology of, 145
  definition of, 135
Personality and health, 135–149
  disease-specific personality
    theory, 139
  emotion expression, 144–146
  five-factor theory, 135–138
  generic disease-prone personal-
    ity theory, 138–139
  relationship between, 135
  sense of self/identity, 139–141
  sociocultural factors, personal-
    ity, and health, 142–144
  stress, 141–142
Person environment fit (PEF)
  model, 109
Peters, K., 159
Petronis, K., 121
Phinney, J.S., 61
*Physical Activity and Health: A
  Report of the Surgeon
  General*, 82
Pieper, C., 103, 106
Pilisuk, M., 152
Planned behavior, theory of, 31
Polacsek, M., 70
Polednak, A., 27
Pollard, K., 110
Pomerleau, O., 45
Porter, L., 144
Precontemplator, 83
Pressured drive, 107
Prevention, 155
  primary, 155
  secondary, 155
  tertiary, 155
Preventive stress management
    programs, 111–113
  individual focus, 113
  organizational focus, 111–112
Pribut, S., 94
Price, J., 88
Price, P., 70, 71, 73
Primary socialization theory, 66
Problem behavior theory, 68
Prochaska, J., 20, 31, 32, 83, 85
Prohaska, T., 48

Pujol, T., 175
Purging, 33

Q
Quah, S.H., 2
Quezada, T., 74, 171, 172
Quick, J.C., 112, 113, 151, 152, 167
Quick, J.D., 112, 113, 151, 152, 167

R
Racial identity, 11–12
Raghunathan, T., 108
Ramanaiah, N., 141
Ramos Sanchez, L., 11
Rapid smoking, 46
Reinforcement value, 143
Relaxation, 175
Reticular system (RTS), 45
Reuptake, 44
Reutter, L., 155, 156
Rex, J., 84, 85, 86
Rheaume, C., 18, 22, 31
Richards, J., 138, 144
Richardson, J., 42
Robert, S., 159, 160
Roberts, C., 119
Roberts, R., 119
Rodgers, J., 139
Rodin, J., 34
Rogers, A., 11
Rogers, R., 159
Rongen, H., 113
Rosch, P., 141
Rose, J., 17, 18, 22, 28
Rosenstock, I.M., 31
Rotter, J., 143
Rowley, S.A., 11
Rozin, P., 28
Rural, 159

S
Saab, P., 50
Sabo, D., 122, 129
Sabol, S., 45
Saenz, D., 108, 109
Sagan, L., 158

Sallis, J.F., 82, 84
Saltz, R., 57, 60
Samuels, C., 167, 169
Samuels, J., 121
Sanjur, D., 23, 26, 27, 28
Santelli, J., 70
Santeria, 172
Sargent, R., 18, 22, 31
Sarova-Pinhas, I., 104
Satel, S., 65
Satz, P., 57, 71, 75, 76
Saunders, R., 18, 22, 31
Savary, L., 174, 175, 176, 178
Sayger, T., 73
Schaefer, E., 22
Scharff, D., 84
Schechter, J., 104
Schmidt, C., 175
Schneiderman, N., 50, 67, 75
Schork, M., 145
Schull, W., 145
Schwartz, J., 144
Schwarzer, R., 10
Seagal, J., 145
Secondary reinforcer, 46
Seefeldt, C., 66
Self-efficacy, 31
Self/identity, sense of, 139–141
Self-in-relation, 125–126
Sellers, R.M., 11
Sellers, S., 105
Sense of coherence, 140
Serafica, F.C., 1, 11
Set point theory, 34
Sevig, T., 167, 168, 170, 172, 173
Shaffer, D., 119
Shaman, 172
Shapiro, M., 110
Sharpe, J., 141
Sheffield, D., 102
Shelton, N.J., 11
Sherwood, A., 107
Sherwood, N., 85, 90
Shields, P., 44, 50
Shiffman, S., 47
Shift work, job strain and, 104–105
Shin, Y., 91
Shipley, M., 102

Shmidt, J.L. Jr., 176
Shorris, E., 28, 108
Shouyu, L., 93
Shrimshaw, E., 69
Shur, D., 18, 23, 25, 28
Sick role behavior, 99
Siegal, K., 69
Siegrist, J., 105
Silva, J., 119, 129
Simha, A., 174
Simon, T., 119, 120
Singh, A., 172, 173
Sinseh, 2
Skrondal, A., 136
Sloboda, J., 175
Smith, G.D., 4, 102
Smith, M.A., 11
Smith, N., 135, 138, 139, 151, 152,
    153, 157, 158, 169, 170,
    176, 177
Smoking and health, 41–55
    biopsychosocial model and
        smoking, 43–44
    brain activity and smoking,
        45–46
    cognition and smoking, 47–48
    conditioning and smoking,
        46–47
    genetics and smoking, 44–45
    nicotine and the committed
        smoker, 41–42
    smoking and underrepresented
        populations, 49–52
    smoking incidence, 42–43
    social learning, 48
Snel, J., 46
Snowden, L.R., 2, 11
Sobal, J., 29, 31
Sobel, D., 176
Social comparison theory, 87
Social control theory, 63
Social discrimination, 123
Social identity theory, 89
Social interaction theory, 68
Social learning, 48
Social marketing, 88
Social relations and health,
    151–165

relationships, 153–162
    community relations,
        158–162
    family, 154–157
    friendships, 158
    marriage, 157–158
    mother-child, 153–154
    social support, 151–152
Social restraint, 124
Social support, 151–152
Somatization, 111
Sorensen, G., 19, 20, 30
Spencer, M., 142
Spicer, J., 9
Spirituality
    definition of, 167
    Eastern tradition of, 170
    women's health and sexual
        minority health, 173–174
Spirituality, music, and laughter,
    health benefits of, 167–181
    laughter and health, 176–178
    multicultural spiritual traditions
        and health, 170–174
    music and health, 174–176
    spirituality and health, 167–170
Staats, T., 141
Stampfer, M., 19
Stansfield, S., 123
Stanwyck, D., 139
Staple foods, 20
Staples, B., 123
Staples, R., 122, 123, 124
Stavig, G., 110
Stein, J., 143
Steinhardt, M., 168
Steptoe, A., 81, 85
Sternberg, E., 141
Stillman, F., 49
Stitzer, M., 46
Stoddard, A., 19, 20, 30
Stollak, G.E., 11
Stone, A., 33, 144
Stoney, C., 42
Story, M., 85, 90
Stratton, V., 175
Strecher, V.J., 31
Stress, 141–142

Structural strain, 65
Structure, 155–156
Student interviews
    Afghanistan, 77–78
    African American, 131–132,
        163
    Dominican Republic, 36–37
    El Salvador, 114–115
    Greece, 53
    Philippine Islands, 179–180
    Sudan, 95–96
    Sweden, 147–148
Stuewig, J., 59, 60
Subjective well-being, 136
Substance abuse and sexual behav-
        ior, 57–79
    personal factors, 72–73
    prevention/intervention, 73–76
    sexual behavior, 66–72
        ethnicity and HIV/AIDS,
            68–70
        family factors, 67–68
        gender, sexual orientation,
            and, 70–72
    substance abuse, 57–66
        family and ethnic identity,
            60–63
        prevalence of, tables, 58, 59
        primary socialization theory,
            66
        social forces, 63–65
        structural strain, 65
Sue, K., 110, 111
Suicide, 119
    neurobiology of, 130
Sukhdev, G., 13
Sullivan, T., 59
Suttee, 128
Swank, R., 49

T
Tae Bo, 88
Tafoya-Barraza, H., 74
Tailored health communication, 84
Tavris, C., 122
Taylor, R., 171
Taylor, S., 2, 4, 9, 99, 100, 105
Taylor, W., 82, 83, 89, 92

Terwogt, M., 175
Thakore, J., 41
Theorell, T., 100, 103
Thomas, D., 34
Thomason, B., 74
Thornton, A., 153
Thorson, C., 93
Thridandam, M., 50
Thrombi, 42
Tiller, W., 177
Tims, F., 175, 176
Tirelli, E., 47
Tortora, G.J., 75
Traditionalism, 109
Transcendence, 167
Transtheoretical model, 31
Treno, A., 57, 60
Trimble, J., 66
TRIOS model, 92
True, R., 127, 128
Tschann, J., 71
Tsutsumi, A., 9, 11
Tsutsumi, K., 9, 11
Turner, J.R., 107

U
Uetrecht, C., 30
Unwanted childbearing, 153
U.S. Department of Health and
        Human Services (UDHHS),
        6, 7, 8, 45, 59, 73, 100,
        101, 104
Uvnas Moberg, K., 161

V
Value conflict, 102
van Dormolen, M., 113
Van Heck, G., 137
Van Tilburg, M., 137
Vargas, L., 126, 127
Varney, N., 175
Vasopressin, 154
Vasquez, I., 35
Vassend, O., 136
Vega, W.A., 2, 11
Velletri, P., 145
Verbal-autonomic association, 107
Vernoy, J., 85

Vernoy, M., 85
Verve, 92
Victimization experiences, 72
Victim-precipitated homicide, 123
Vietnamese
    cervical cancer rate in women, 6
Villarosa, L., 84
Vincent, M., 84, 87, 88, 90
Vingerhoets, J., 137
Vollman, M., 84, 85, 86, 91
Voorhees, C., 49

W
Wade, C., 122
Wan, C., 138, 142
Ward, K., 47
Watson, D., 138, 142
Wegner, E., 138, 142
Weidner, G., 103, 106
Weigh down diet, 171
Welch, P., 160, 161, 174
Welka, D., 74
Welton, D., 74
Western diseases, 18
Whites
    cardiovascular disease rates,
        6–7
    gay and bisexual males, rate of
        HIV/AIDS, 7
    HIV/AIDS survival rates, 68–69
    infant mortality rates, 6
Whittington, C.L., 106, 107
Whittington, J.L., 151, 152, 167
Wilcox, S., 82, 84
Wilfley, D.E., 34
Williams, C., 175
Williams, D., 142
Wilson, J., 26
Win, P., 60, 61, 63
Winett, R., 88, 90
Wing, R., 93
Wingood, G., 75
Winstead-Fry, P., 155
Wolf, D., 154
Wood, M., 70, 71, 73
Work-site intervention programs,
        99–100
Wyatt, G.E., 67, 72, 73, 142

Y
Yamamoto, J., 119, 129
Young, D., 82, 83, 89, 92
Younoszai, T., 66
Yu, E., 110

Z
Zabarano, R., 168
Zalanowski, A., 175

Zambrana, R., 126
Zane, N., 74
Zayas, L., 119, 125, 126
Zea, M.C., 74, 171, 172
Zerbe, K., 34
Zimmerman, J., 119, 125, 126
Zimmerman, M., 68
Zimmerman, V., 122
Zinser, M., 45